How to *Write* a MASTER'S THESIS

To M. B. with all my love

How to  Write a MASTER'S THESIS

Yvonne N. Bui
University of San Francisco

SAGE

Los Angeles | London | New Delhi
Singapore | Washington DC

For information:

SAGE Publications, Inc.
2455 Teller Road
Thousand Oaks, California 91320
E-mail: order@sagepub.com

SAGE Publications India Pvt. Ltd.
B 1/I 1 Mohan Cooperative
   Industrial Area
Mathura Road, New Delhi 110 044
India

SAGE Publications Ltd.
1 Oliver's Yard
55 City Road
London EC1Y 1SP
United Kingdom

SAGE Publications Asia-Pacific
   Pte. Ltd.
33 Pekin Street #02-01
Far East Square
Singapore 048763

Printed in the United States of America.

Library of Congress Cataloging-in-Publication Data

Bui, Yvonne N.
How to write a master's thesis/Yvonne Bui.
    p. cm.
Includes bibliographical references and index.
ISBN 978-1-4129-5710-6 (pbk.)
    1. Dissertations, Academic—Handbooks, manuals, etc. I. Title.

LB2369.B75 2009
808'.02—dc22   2008049627

This book is printed on acid-free paper.

09   10   11   12   13   10   9   8   7   6   5   4   3   2   1

Acquisitions Editor:	Vicki Knight
Associate Editor:	Sean Connelly
Editorial Assistant:	Lauren Habib
Production Editor:	Astrid Virding
Copy Editor:	Taryn Bigelow
Typesetter:	C&M Digitals (P) Ltd.
Proofreader:	Ellen Brink
Indexer:	Will Ragsdale
Cover Designer:	Bryan Fishman
Marketing Manager:	Stephanie Adams

Brief Contents

List of Students' Master's Theses   xi

Preface   xv

About the Author   xviii

Chapter 1   Overview of the Master's Degree and Thesis   1

Chapter 2   Selecting a Research Topic   21

Chapter 3   Using the Literature to Research Your Problem   45

Chapter 4   Conducting Ethical Research   77

Chapter 5   How to Write Chapter One, Introduction   96

Chapter 6   How to Write Chapter Two, Review of the Literature   120

Chapter 7   How to Write Chapter Three, Methods   137

Chapter 8   How to Write Chapter Four, Results   160

Chapter 9   How to Write Chapter Five, Discussion   191

Chapter 10   Final Formatting, APA Style   208

Appendixes   247

Glossary   276

References   287

Author Index   291

Subject Index   293

Detailed Contents

List of Students' Master's Theses	xi
Preface	xv
About the Author	xviii
Chapter 1 Overview of the Master's Degree and Thesis	**1**
The Master's Degree	2
Benefits of Obtaining a Master's Degree	4
Master's Degree Program	5
Master's Thesis Committee and Chairperson	5
What Is a Master's Thesis?	6
The Difference Between a Master's Thesis and a Term Paper	7
The Difference Between a Master's Thesis and a Doctoral Dissertation	7
Components of a Master's Thesis	8
Chapter One, Introduction	9
Chapter Two, Review of the Literature	10
Chapter Three, Methods	11
Chapter Four, Results	11
Chapter Five, Discussion	12
Quantitative Versus Qualitative Studies	12
Quantitative Methods	12
Qualitative Methods	13
Style Form	14
Summary	15
Resources	16
Common Obstacles and Practical Solutions	16
Reflection/Discussion Questions	17
Try It Exercises	17
Key Terms	19
Suggested Readings	19
Web Links	19

Chapter 2   Selecting a Research Topic   **21**

Important Factors to Consider When Selecting a Topic   22

    Personal Significance   23

    Critical Issues in the Field   24

    Existing Research Literature   24

       Search Engines   25

       Electronic Databases   26

    Ethical Considerations   28

How to Narrow and Refocus Your Topic   29

    Feasibility   29

    Accessibility   31

    Time and Resources   32

Developing Answerable Research Questions   33

    Answerable Questions   33

    Defining Terms   34

Creating a Realistic Timeline   35

Time Management   38

    Reserving Time   38

    Chunking Method   39

Summary   40

Resources   41

    Common Obstacles and Practical Solutions   41

    Reflection/Discussion Questions   42

    Try It Exercises   42

    Key Terms   43

    Suggested Readings   43

    Web Links   44

Chapter 3   Using the Literature to Research Your Problem   **45**

Benefits of Conducting a Literature Review   46

Sources of Data: Primary Versus Secondary   48

    Primary Sources   48

    Secondary Sources   48

Selecting Key Terms   50

Conducting Searches in Electronic Databases   52

    Basic Search   55

       Limiters   56

       Expanders   57

    Advanced Search   58

       Boolean Operators   58

       Symbols   59

    Using the Thesaurus   61

       Search Terms   62

       Relevant Subject Headings   64

Conducting Searches on the Internet   68
Different Types of Articles   69
    Refereed Versus Non-Refereed   69
Staying Organized   70
Summary   73
Resources   74
    Common Obstacles and Practical Solutions   74
    Reflection/Discussion Questions   74
    Try It Exercises   75
    Key Terms   76
    Suggested Readings   76
    Web Links   76

Chapter 4   Conducting Ethical Research   77
Background and History   79
    Nuremberg Code   79
    Thalidomide   80
    Tuskegee Syphilis Study   80
Legal and Ethical Principles   81
    Belmont Report   81
        Respect for Persons   81
        Beneficence   82
        Justice   83
Federal Regulations   84
    Common Rule   84
Institutional Review Board (IRB)   85
    IRB Application Process   85
    Preparing the IRB Research Plan   86
Ethical Behavior   90
    Plagiarism   90
Summary   91
Resources   92
    Common Obstacles and Practical Solutions   92
    Reflection/Discussion Questions   93
    Try It Exercises   93
    Key Terms   94
    Suggested Readings   95
    Web Links   95

Chapter 5   How to Write Chapter One, Introduction   96
Writing Style   97
Chapter One Sections   98
    Introduction   99
    Statement of the Problem   103
        Three Parallel Ladders Strategy   104

Background and Need 107
    Three Parallel Ladders Strategy 107
Purpose of the Study 109
Research Questions 112
Significance to the Field 113
Definitions 113
Limitations 114
Ethical Considerations 115
Summary 115
Resources 116
    Common Obstacles and Practical Solutions 116
    Reflection/Discussion Questions 117
    Try It Exercises 117
    Key Terms 119
    Suggested Readings 119
    Web Links 119

Chapter 6   How to Write Chapter Two, Review of the Literature 120
Preparation and Organization 122
Chapter Two Sections 123
    Introduction 123
        Advance Organizer 124
    Body of the Review 124
        Research Synthesis 125
        Section Summary 131
    Chapter Summary 131
Summary 132
Resources 133
    Common Obstacles and Practical Solutions 133
    Reflection/Discussion Questions 134
    Try It Exercises 134
    Key Terms 135
    Suggested Readings 136
    Web Links 136

Chapter 7   How to Write Chapter Three, Methods 137
Preparation and Organization 138
Chapter Three Sections 139
    Introduction 140
    Setting 142
    Sample/Participants 142
    Intervention and Materials 144
    Measurement Instruments 146
        Validity and Reliability 149

Data Collection/Procedures 150
Data Analysis 153
Summary 155
Resources 156
Common Obstacles and Practical Solutions 156
Reflection/Discussion Questions 157
Try It Exercises 157
Key Terms 158
Suggested Readings 158
Web Links 159

Chapter 8 How to Write Chapter Four, Results 160
Preparation and Organization 162
Chapter Four Sections 162
Quantitative Data 163
Descriptive Statistics 164
Measures of Central Tendency 164
Measures of Variability 167
Additional Ways to Report Data Descriptively 169
Inferential Statistics 171
Tests of Significance 172
Independent-Samples t Test 172
Independent-Samples t Test SPSS Output 174
Paired-Samples t Test 176
Paired-Samples t Test SPSS Output 177
Qualitative Data 180
Major Themes and Patterns 180
Research Questions 183
Validity of Findings 185
Summary 186
Resources 187
Common Obstacles and Practical Solutions 187
Reflection/Discussion Questions 187
Try It Exercises 188
Key Terms 189
Suggested Readings 189
Web Links 190

Chapter 9 How to Write Chapter Five, Discussion 191
Preparation and Organization 192
Chapter Five Sections 193
Introduction 193
Discussion 194
Limitations 197
Recommendations for Future Research 199
Conclusion 200

Summary	204
Resources	205
Common Obstacles and Practical Solutions	205
Reflection/Discussion Questions	205
Try It Exercises	206
Suggested Readings	207
Web Links	207
Chapter 10 Final Formatting, APA Style	**208**
Preparation and Organization	211
APA Style	211
Levels of Heading	212
Citations in Text	216
Direct Quotes and Paraphrasing	216
One Work, One Author	216
One Work, Multiple Authors	217
One Work, Group Author	218
Two or More Works	218
Web Sites and Web Pages	219
Personal Communications	219
Secondary Sources	219
Reference List	220
Order and Format	220
Periodicals	222
Books and Book Chapters	222
Electronic Sources	223
Online Journals and Electronic Versions	225
Online Documents	226
Web Sites and Web Pages	227
Tables	228
Tables in Text	230
Placement and Spacing	230
Title	230
Headings and Body	230
Notes	232
Figures	233
Figures in Text	233
Placement, Size, and Font	234
Captions and Labels	234
Graphs	235
Appendixes	235
Appendixes in Text	236
Placement and Cover Pages	236
Front Pages	237
Title Page	237

Signature Page   237
Acknowledgments   239
Abstract   239
Table of Contents   239
Lists of Tables and Figures   240
Copying and Binding   240
Final Tips and Checklist   242
Summary   242
Resources   243
Common Obstacles and Practical Solutions   243
Reflection/Discussion Questions   244
Try It Exercises   244
Key Terms   245
Suggested Readings   245
Web Links   246

Appendixes   247

Glossary   276

References   287

Author Index   291

Subject Index   293

List of Students' Master's Theses

By Student

Cheryl Gomes: Chapters 7, 9

Lindsey Henderson: Chapter 8

Lori Hess: Chapter 9

Amelyn Ho: Chapter 6

Diana Iniguez: Chapter 8, Appendix G

Robin Irey: Chapters 7, 8, 9

David Kendall: Chapters 7, 8, 9, Appendix G

Michelle Kornhauser: Chapter 7

Sara Mireles: Chapter 8

Barbara Nixon: Chapter 7

Shain Rau: Chapters 8, 9

David Stephens: Chapter 7

Aprille Williams: Chapters 7, 8, Appendix G

By Chapter

Chapter 6:

- Ho

Chapter 7:

- Williams
- Kendall
- Irey
- Kornhauser
- Gomes
- Nixon
- Stephens

Chapter 8:

- Henderson
- Irey
- Iniguez
- Rau
- Williams
- Mireles
- Kendall

Chapter 9:

- Gomes
- Hess
- Kendall
- Rau
- Irey

Appendix G:

- Williams
- Kendall
- Iniguez

Preface

The purpose of this book is to teach and model how to write a master's thesis. The book is intended for graduate students who will write a thesis as part of the requirements for a master's degree as well as for university faculty who are teaching and advising students pursuing this goal. As a faculty member at the University of San Francisco, a major part of my role has involved teaching and advising graduate students pursuing their master's degree. This has been an enjoyable, fulfilling, and educational experience. Most of my students are employed professionals working and going to school full-time, caring for families, or assuming other responsibilities that require their attention. As the culminating experience of their graduate program, some see the master's thesis as an opportunity to research new solutions to problems they have encountered in their course work or in their professional work. Behind their enthusiasm, however, there is often fear and uncertainty about how to conduct the research and write the thesis.

Based on my experiences in advising and teaching master's students, I have undertaken the task of demystifying the process of how to write a master's thesis. In writing the book, I assumed that you are familiar with the content in your field or discipline. However, I did not take for granted that you know the *process* of writing a master's thesis because the only way to know how to write a master's thesis is to have already written one! Thus, my goal was to provide a useful, straightforward, and practical book that goes beyond informing what "should" be done. In addition to the "should-do's," the organization and structure of the book is designed to offer guidelines on how to research and write the master's thesis, step-by-step.

There are 10 chapters in the book, and each one begins with a detailed outline of the content in the chapter. Chapter 1 provides an overview of the master's thesis. Chapters 2 and 3 focus on how to select a research topic and search the existing research literature in electronic databases and Internet search engines. Chapter 4 discusses the ethical issues when conducting research and the process of applying for approval from the Institutional Review Board for the Protection of Human Subjects (IRBPHS). Chapters 5, 6, 7, 8, and 9 introduce how to write the main components of each of the five chapters in a traditional master's thesis: Introduction, Review of the Literature, Methods, Results, and Discussion. Chapter 10 focuses on editing and formatting citations, references, tables, and so on using the writing style from the American Psychological Association (APA). Within each chapter, I describe and explain what is expected within a specific section in the thesis, give tips and strategies on how to prepare and write the section, and provide sample excerpts adapted from students' completed master's theses to illustrate my suggestions. There are also numerous figures and captured "screen shots" from relevant Web sites to enhance the text.

At the end of each chapter, there are *Resources* that can be used to deepen your understanding or to tailor information in the text to your particular thesis. The *Resources* are suitable for use by individual students or in group/class settings. The *Resources* include Common Obstacles and Practical Solutions, Reflection/Discussion Questions, Try It Exercises, Key Terms, Suggested Readings, and Web Links. In the Common Obstacles and Practical Solutions section, I discuss problems that students typically face and make suggestions that may help prevent or alleviate these frustrations. In the Reflection/Discussion Questions, I offer broad questions that may help synthesize the information in the chapter. The Try It Exercises are opportunities to practice what was discussed in the chapter to prepare for or write sections of your particular thesis. The Key Terms are critical concepts that were defined in the chapter and are included in the glossary. In the Suggested Readings and Web Links, I offer recommendations for additional readings (many of which are in PDFs that are linked to the Sage Publications Web site at http://www.sagepub.com) and Web sites on the Internet to supplement your understanding of the information in the chapter. Taken as a whole, the book is full of detailed explanations, examples, and supplemental materials that I have successfully used to advise students to complete their master's theses.

Writing a master's thesis is a complex task, and I would be less than honest if I suggested that all you need to do is read this book, and the task will be easy. You will work hard in doing your research, and you will spend long hours writing the thesis. I have great respect for you as you undertake this important and admirable task to fulfill a worthy goal, both personally and professionally. Your master's research will cause you to think and write differently, give you confidence in your professional role, and open new doors for you. In the absence of not having the opportunity to work with you personally, I hope this book serves your needs during your journey, and you benefit from it as much as I have from working with students like you.

Acknowledgments

I would like to acknowledge and express my appreciation for the individuals who helped to make this book a possibility. I would like to thank the following reviewers for their comments and suggestions on how to strengthen the book:

- Johanna Filp-Hanke, Sonoma State University
- Harrison Yang, State University of New York at Oswego
- Mark C. Griffin, San Francisco State University
- Stephanie W. Hartwell, University of Massachusetts at Boston
- Theodore N. Greenstein, North Carolina State University
- Juanita N. Baker, Florida Institute of Technology
- James P. Donnelly, University at Buffalo, State University of New York
- Todd Migliaccio, Sacramento State University
- Charles D. Palmer, Mississippi State University
- Hugh D. Spitler, Clemson University

To Vicki Knight, my amazing editor at SAGE Publications, I cannot thank you enough for your wisdom, guidance, understanding, and friendship. To the editorial, production, and support staff at SAGE Publications, thank you for your assistance and patience throughout the entire process. To my students, thank you for all that you taught me and for sharing your master's theses with others. To my confidant and mentor, Edward Meyen, thank you for all your help, encouragement, and insight. To my loving parents and family, thank you for believing in me and supporting all my endeavors. To my devoted friends and colleagues, thank you for providing sustenance and comfort. I am grateful to you all.

About the Author

Yvonne N. Bui (PhD, Special Education, Learning Disabilities, University of Kansas) is an Associate Professor in the Department of Learning and Instruction, School of Education at the University of San Francisco. She teaches master's and doctoral level courses in Special Education, Research Methods, Master's Thesis, Statistics, Grant Writing, and Dissertation Proposal Development. She serves as the chairperson and committee member for students' theses and dissertations within the School of Education. She is the coeditor of *Exceptional Children in Today's Schools: What Teachers Need to Know*.

1

Overview of the Master's Degree and Thesis

The Master's Degree	2
Benefits of Obtaining a Master's Degree	4
Master's Degree Program	5
Master's Thesis Committee and Chairperson	5
What Is a Master's Thesis?	6
The Difference Between a Master's Thesis and a Term Paper	7
The Difference Between a Master's Thesis and a Doctoral Dissertation	7
Components of a Master's Thesis	8
Chapter One, Introduction	9
Chapter Two, Review of the Literature	10
Chapter Three, Methods	11
Chapter Four, Results	11
Chapter Five, Discussion	12
Quantitative Versus Qualitative Studies	12
Quantitative Methods	12
Qualitative Methods	13
Style Form	14
Summary	15

(Continued)

(Continued)

Resources   **16**
    Common Obstacles and Practical Solutions   **16**
    Reflection/Discussion Questions   **17**
    Try It Exercises   **17**
    Key Terms   **19**
    Suggested Readings   **19**
    Web Links   **19**

> Always bear in mind that your own resolution to succeed is more important than any one thing.
>
> —Abraham Lincoln

If you are reading this page, congratulations! This signifies that you have already successfully completed a bachelor's degree in your field, a major accomplishment. Now you are ready to embark on the next phase of your educational journey, completing a thesis for a master's degree. The **master's degree** is a postbaccalaureate degree conferred by a college or university upon candidates who complete one to two years of graduate study (Glazer, 1988). Why congratulations and not condolences? Because whether or not the master's degree is the highest professional degree in your field or a gateway to doctoral studies, completing the thesis will open many doors for you, both personally and professionally. The intent of this book is to give you a blueprint of the research process as well as provide you with step-by-step guidance on how to write the actual thesis, one chapter at a time.

The Master's Degree

There is a vast number of types of master's degrees in a variety of disciplines and specialty areas. The two main types of academic degrees at the master's level are the Master of Arts and the Master of Science. The **Master of Arts (MA)** degree is typically awarded in the disciplines of arts, sciences, social sciences (e.g., education, psychology), and humanities (e.g., history, philosophy, religion). The **Master of Science (MS)** degree is typically awarded to students in technical fields such as engineering, nursing, mathematics, and health care management but can also be in the social sciences ("About Graduate Education," n.d.). Table 1.1 lists a variety of master's degrees in the humanities and social sciences.

Table 1.1   List of Master's Degrees in the Humanities and Social Sciences

Master of Applied Anthropology (MAA)

Master of Arts in Liberal Studies (MALS)

Master of Arts in Teaching (MAT)

Master of Criminal Justice

Master of Counseling

Master of Education

Master of Fine Arts (MFA)

Master of Liberal Arts (MLA, ALM)

Master of Liberal Studies (MLS)

Master of Mass Communications

Master of Occupational Therapy

Master of Science in Nursing

Master of Social Work (MSW)

Master of Special Education

In some fields, the master's degree is referred to as a professional degree or terminal degree (not the same as terminal illness). A **terminal degree** is the generally accepted highest academic degree in a field of study. Some examples of terminal master's degrees are the Master of Business Administration (MBA), Master of Social Work (MSW), Master of Fine Arts (MFA), and Master of Public Administration (MPA). For the purposes of this book, no distinction will be made between the MA, MS, or professional degrees, as all will be referred to as the "master's degree."

Depending on the discipline and the institution, there may be several pathways to obtain the master's degree. In some cases, students may take a certain number of units through coursework and complete a fieldwork project at the end of their studies. For example, graduate students may submit a project related to a particular topic such as a curriculum unit, a handbook or manual, or even a visual arts performance. In other cases, students may take courses and pass a comprehensive oral or written exam at the end of their studies. In still other cases, the degree may require coursework and a thesis or research study. There may be a combination of the options mentioned involving coursework, an exam, and a final project or study. Although each discipline has its own specific requirements for the master's degree, they all share a commonality of having a cumulative or final activity to show that students have "mastered" the necessary content. Thus, before you proceed in your studies, it is best to find out the requirements for the master's degree within your own discipline, field, and institution of higher education. For the purposes of this book, I will only address the master's thesis option.

Benefits of Obtaining a Master's Degree

There are many benefits of obtaining a master's degree. Again, this depends on your particular discipline or specialty area. As mentioned, the master's degree is sometimes the terminal degree for the field. Thus, if you hold a master's degree, you would be considered an "expert" in the field and highly regarded. This would also allow you to obtain a high-ranking position such as curriculum director, program manager, or faculty member. For example, if you hold a master's degree in education, you would be able to teach full-time at a community college or teach as a part-time adjunct instructor at a four-year college or university. If you are a K–12 classroom teacher with a master's degree, some school districts will increase your salary because of the number of postbaccalaureate units that were completed.

A master's degree may also increase your value in the job market. For example, in 2000 in the field of journalism and mass communications, 90% of master's degree recipients had at least one job offer at the time of their graduation (with a mean of 2.3 job offers per recipient) compared to 82.4% of bachelor's degree recipients (Becker, Vlad, Huh, & Prine, 2001). Imagine you are applying for a job in marketing at a cutting-edge firm. If the human resources manager receives 300 applications, he or she may separate applicants into two piles—those who have advanced degrees and those who have bachelor's degrees. In order to save time, the manager may look only at the pile of applicants with master's degrees or consider these applicants first (O'Donovan, 1997). In other words, having a master's degree may give you an advantage during the screening process (it is up to you to wow them at the job interview!). Further, depending on the discipline, the master's degree may also be the minimal degree requirement for certain jobs or positions (such as managerial positions) and may also increase your starting salary.

In addition to the tangible benefits, another major benefit of obtaining the master's degree is the amount of personal satisfaction that it brings. I always tell my students (especially when they are on the verge of giving up), "Yes, it is a tremendous amount of work; yes, I know that you have not seen your children in a week, and yes, I understand that the dog is angry at you. However, when you are done and you have completed your master's degree, no one can take that away from you." This usually keeps them going for about a week. The point is that although it will seem like a long (and virtually endless) journey, and it will not always be easy to see the finish line, once you bring your final draft to have it bound and copied, a unique sensation will overcome you (unrelated to the fatigue). This sensation comes from knowing that despite the adversity and hurdles, you have accomplished your own personal goal, acquired by only a small proportion of the general population. Thus, the master's degree will open many personal and professional doors for you; it is up to you to find them and walk through.

Master's Degree Program

If you are thinking about or preparing to write your master's thesis, most likely you are at the end or toward the end of your master's degree program. A **master's degree program** is a graduate-level, postbaccalaureate program in a specific field or discipline that typically involves a culminating activity, project, or thesis. Although master's degree programs are not typically designed to teach students how to write a thesis, the course of study and experiences from the program benefit you greatly as you go through the research and writing process for the thesis. First, the master's degree program provides you with multiple opportunities to learn the critical and core content in your field or discipline. This content knowledge will help you as you select an appropriate topic to study, one that is both relevant and significant to your field, and frame your research interests. Next, most master's degree programs require students to take course(s) in research methods. This experience will help you research the literature, analyze and synthesize research articles, develop answerable research questions, and create a rigorous, yet feasible, design for your study. Thus, throughout the thesis-writing process, you will be constantly relying on the content knowledge and experiences that you gained from the master's degree program to demonstrate that you have "mastered" the content and associated research skills in your field or discipline.

Master's Thesis Committee and Chairperson

Another critical benefit of almost completing your master's degree program is getting to know the different faculty in your program! By this time, you will have a better sense of which faculty would be the most compatible in terms of working style and research interests to select as your chairperson. The **chairperson** is the faculty member who is assigned or selected by the graduate student to advise him or her throughout the master's thesis process. Keep in mind that your chairperson may be different from your faculty adviser or department chairperson. At some institutions, the program selects the chairperson for you while in others you select your chairperson as well as the other members of your committee. Typically, there are three faculty members on your master's thesis committee: the chairperson and two committee members (i.e., readers). However, it is best to check with your institution because this number can vary from two to five members. Most commonly, it is required that the chairperson be a faculty member within the degree program while the committee members could be faculty from within or outside the program and department. Again, it is a good idea to check with your institution as to the specific criteria for the selection process.

If you are allowed to pick your own chairperson, there are a few things to keep in mind. First, your chairperson is not the coauthor of the master's thesis. In other words, he or she will not be writing the thesis *with* you (or for you). Rather, the role of your chairperson is to guide and direct your study. This does not include writing, editing, conducting research, or collecting or analyzing data. In other words, your chairperson will assume that you have all the necessary skill sets to complete the thesis—he or she will be there to facilitate the process. Another thing to consider when selecting a chairperson is his or her area of *expertise.* Having a chairperson who is familiar with the topic of your thesis is helpful as he or she can offer suggestions on critical research literature. The chairperson that you select may also have expertise in a particular research design that you want to utilize in the study. Another factor to consider when selecting a chairperson is *fit.* Here, you should consider whether or not you could have a positive working relationship with the faculty member. Keep in mind that you are not trying to make a new friend, but you do want someone who will offer insight and constructive feedback on your work. Finally, make sure to consider whether or not the faculty member is *accessible.* The role of the chairperson can be time-consuming (especially when it comes to the writing part); so do not pick a person who is already overwhelmed with his or her other responsibilities.

Once you have selected a chairperson, set up an initial meeting to discuss how you will work together. Each chairperson will vary on how he or she will want to work with graduate students, so it is critical for you to know and follow his or her expectations. See the *Resources* section at the end of this chapter for a list of possible questions to ask at your initial meeting. These questions will help you and your chairperson get off to a great start with a mutual understanding of your working relationship.

What Is a Master's Thesis?

For the purposes of this book, the master's thesis is an empirically based research study that is an original piece of work by the graduate student. An **empirically based** research study is based on data that are produced by experiment or observation (rather than opinion). The thesis must be an original piece of work because it represents the student's culminating research and writing abilities. Thus, this book focuses on the research process and a traditional five-chapter thesis rather than an artistic performance or production. Completing a thesis demonstrates your ability to conduct original research, review the existing literature, collect data, analyze the results, and discuss conclusions and draw implications from your research. Moreover, the completion of a thesis represents your perseverance, discipline, and scholarly writing.

The Difference Between a Master's Thesis and a Term Paper

One of the biggest hurdles for students when writing the master's thesis is adjusting from the writing style of a term or research paper format, a common expectation at the undergraduate level. There is a qualitative difference between the master's thesis and a term paper. As mentioned, the master's thesis is based on original research on a particular topic conducted by the student. In comparison, the term paper is typically a summary of research or other sources about a particular topic. In the term paper, there may be a subject or question that will be answered using examples from books, journals, articles from newspapers, and so on to support the findings (Raygor, n.d.). However, the student is not conducting a research study in order to answer the question. For example, a term paper may consist of presenting the argument that the use of technology via e-mail and cell phone has actually decreased rather than increased the quality of relationships within society. The student would then cite research and other sources to persuade the reader and support his or her argument. For a master's thesis, on the other hand, the student would develop a research question and conduct a full literature review on the topic. Then she would collect data, perhaps administering a survey to 200 people at random to find out their perspectives about cell phone and e-mail use and the quality of their social relationships. Finally, she would analyze the data and discuss the conclusions and implications of her findings (based on the data that were collected).

The Difference Between a Master's Thesis and a Doctoral Dissertation

In some cases, you will hear the word "thesis" used to refer to both master's and doctoral degrees. More commonly, universities use the term thesis to refer to the requirement for a master's and a dissertation for the doctorate. A **dissertation** is typically the culminating requirement for a doctoral degree. The difference between the thesis and the dissertation depends on your particular discipline, specialty area, and institution. In many instances, there are more similarities than differences between the two, especially when considering the "traditional" research form of a master's thesis. For example, both the thesis and dissertation studies should follow a *systematic* process where there is a researchable problem, literature to support and contextualize the problem, data collection methods (e.g., sampling, measurement instruments), analysis of the data, and discussions and conclusions based on the results of the study.

However, at every step of the process, the dissertation may require the student researcher to go into more depth and/or breadth. For example, at some institutions, the dissertation must include a theoretical rationale or conceptual model that relates to the problem. Sometimes the purpose of the dissertation could be to develop or to refine an existing theory. This is not commonly required for a master's thesis. The dissertation may also require a larger sample size or complicated sampling plan, more measurement instruments, and complex statistical or rich qualitative analysis of the data. Thus, the length of the dissertation study (both in time spent collecting data and page numbers) may be significantly longer than the master's thesis.

Another distinction between the dissertation and the master's thesis is the number of people involved in the process. For the dissertation, most institutions require that the doctoral student form a committee with a chairperson, and two, three, or sometimes four other faculty members who serve as readers. Students have to "defend" their dissertation proposal to the committee members before they are allowed to proceed with the study and a final defense after they have completed the study. For the master's thesis, it is more common for the student to work with his or her assigned faculty chairperson and one other faculty member throughout the process.

Finally, another important distinction between the two is the focus or purpose of the study. For the master's thesis, the focus of the study can be referred to as *applied research,* which is "conducted for the purpose of applying, or testing, a theory to determine its usefulness in solving practical problems" (Gay, Mills, & Airasian, 2006, p. 6). For example, a graduate student who is getting a master's degree in education might conduct a study around a particular issue in his or her classroom, such as using a new reading comprehension strategy. The results of the study would have direct application to his or her teaching and students. For a dissertation in this area, the focus may be broader, such as exploring differences across subgroups of students (e.g., by ethnicity, ability, age, socioeconomic status) on national or statewide reading assessments. The results of the study may have application to teacher training at the university level, policy implications, or serve as an initial study for a line of research. In other words, the master's thesis may have a narrow practical focus whereas the dissertation may have a broader and theoretical focus. Although both have practical implications, the master's thesis may be more directly related to a present or immediate problem. Thus, one way to differentiate between the two is to think of the dissertation as a more complex and sophisticated master's thesis. In fact, when I advise students on their master's theses, I am constantly reminding them that this is to prepare them for their dissertation!

Components of a Master's Thesis

For the purposes of this book, the master's thesis will consist of five distinct chapters. Each chapter has a specific focus and objective. The titles of the five chapters are: (1) Introduction, (2) Review of the Literature, (3) Methods,

(4) Results, and (5) Discussion. The structure of the five chapters is the same whether you are conducting a qualitative or quantitative study. A **qualitative research study** delves into a particular situation in order to better understand a phenomenon within its natural context and the perspectives of the participants involved (Gay et al., 2006). A **quantitative research study** includes but is not limited to research using descriptive, correlation, prediction, and control (cause-effect) methods. Depending on your research questions, selecting a qualitative or quantitative research design affects how you conduct the study (methods) and analyze and interpret the data (results). Each chapter will be described briefly here. There will be a more comprehensive discussion of how to write each chapter of the thesis in Chapters 5–9. To avoid confusion, I will refer to chapters of this book with numbers (e.g., Chapter 1, Chapter 2) and chapters of the master's thesis with their word forms (e.g., Chapter One, Chapter Two). Keep in mind that your school or program may use other terms, such as "sections," to refer to the different components of the master's thesis.

Chapter One, Introduction

Chapter One introduces the topic of the thesis to the reader. The critical part of writing Chapter One is to establish the statement of the problem and research questions. Basically, you are justifying to the reader *why* it is necessary to study this topic and *what* research question(s) your study will answer. Usually, the topic is based around a particular problem area that you want to focus on (I will discuss how to select an appropriate topic in Chapter 2). For example, if your master's degree is in social work, your topic of interest may be homeless single women with children, and the specific problem may be that these mothers are not able to find appropriate child care or educational services for their children because they are always in transition. However, before you introduce the reader to the specific topic and problem, you have to first provide the reader with the broader context (the general problem) and consequences related to the topic. In other words, before you discuss the specific problem, you need to contextualize your topic within the larger problem. For example, you would first discuss the problems related to homeless women with children in general and use national or state data and statistics to support your claims. This part would include the consequences related to the social and emotional effects on the mothers and their children.

Chapter One of the thesis includes a section on the *Statement of the Problem* (information about the specific problem), *Background and Need* (the background literature related to the problem), the *Purpose of the Study* (the focus and goal of the study), *Research Questions* (what questions the study proposes to answer), and other significant sections. In this chapter, you need to support all of your claims and positions using citations from empirical research studies, government reports and data, Web sites, and theory and opinion papers. How to write Chapter One and its major sections will be discussed in great detail in Chapter 5.

Chapter Two, Review of the Literature

Chapter Two introduces the reader to the research literature related to the topic. The critical part of writing Chapter Two is to identify the most relevant and significant research related to your topic rather than conduct an exhaustive search. Basically, you are informing the reader of the *critical* studies that have been conducted related to this topic. This provides the reader with the background information that he or she needs to understand the problem(s) related to your topic. The literature review also provides the justification for your study as you indicate the gaps and weaknesses in the existing research. Chapter Two provides credibility to your study as it shows you have done your "homework" in reading the research for this topic, and your study is "grounded" in the research. In other words, your thesis did not simply appear from thin air; instead, it was developed because there was a need to conduct the study, and it will contribute to the body of research related to this problem.

In order to organize Chapter Two, you will first start with an introduction about the general problem and your topic. Then you will provide an advance organizer, which indicates what will be covered in the literature review. For the purposes of this book, you will cover three areas that are related to your problem. The **advance organizer** explicitly states the three areas of research that will be addressed and the order of the discussions. This will help to structure the literature review and manage the research articles that you find. For example, in the social work example, three areas related to the problem could be: (1) homelessness and its effect on children's development, (2) quality of parental interactions between homeless mothers and their children, and (3) collaboration of school and social agencies. Where did these areas come from? Do not worry; the three related areas will emerge as you read the existing literature and develop the *Statement of the Problem* and the *Background and Need* sections in Chapter One and the literature review in Chapter Two.

After you have introduced the three related areas, you will locate and synthesize three to four research articles (with empirical data) for each of the three areas related to the topic. Each section should start with a brief introduction about the area and end with a summary paragraph to recap the main points and limitations within the area. At the end of the literature review, there should also be a summary that ties together all of the literature related to the topic. How to write Chapter Two and the three major sections will be discussed in great detail in Chapter 6.

Chapter Three, Methods

Chapter Three explains the research methods and design that were used to conduct the study. The critical part of writing Chapter Three is to describe the actual procedures that were used to conduct the study. Basically, you are informing the reader of *how* the study was conducted. Thus, you need to include detailed descriptions about every aspect of your study. Chapter Three will include the following components: (1) *Setting* (where the study took place), (2) *Participants* (the individuals who participated in the study and how they were selected), (3) *Instructional* or *Intervention Materials* (any materials or instructional strategies that were used to conduct the study), (4) *Measurement Instruments* (the tools you used to collect data), (5) *Procedures* (how you collected the data and/or implemented the study), and (6) *Data Analysis* (the statistical or qualitative techniques that were used to analyze the data). Enough detail should be included so that another researcher could replicate your study. How to write Chapter Three and the major sections will be discussed in great detail in Chapter 7.

Chapter Four, Results

Chapter Four reports the results of the study. The critical part of writing Chapter Four is to present the findings from the data collection process in Chapter Three. Basically, you are informing the reader of *what* was discovered. This chapter integrates a narrative, numerical, and/or tabular presentation of the outcomes of the study, depending on whether you have conducted a qualitative or quantitative study. In Chapter Four, you will report the results of the data analysis for each variable and measurement instrument that was discussed in Chapter Three. For example, if you conducted a qualitative study, you would provide a narrative description of the findings in relation to the research questions. If you conducted a quantitative study, you could include descriptive statistics for each participant or for the entire group (or both). **Descriptive statistics** are the basic level of statistical analysis for a data set from a sample group. Typically, reported statistics include the mean, median, mode, variance, and standard deviation. If you conducted an intervention for a large group or more than one group of participants in the study who received different treatments, you could apply inferential statistics to indicate any differences observed in performance before and after the intervention or between the two groups (if appropriate). **Inferential statistics** are the higher level of statistical analysis where inferences are made from a sample to a population. Inferential statistics may also include hypothesis testing and set probability levels to test for statistically significant differences between groups (or treatments). How to write Chapter Four and the major sections will be discussed in great detail in Chapter 8.

Chapter Five, Discussion

The last chapter in the thesis, Chapter Five, discusses the results from Chapter Four and draws conclusions about the study's findings. The critical part of writing Chapter Five is to discuss the findings in relation to the statement of the problem and the research questions that were identified in Chapter One. The discussion section includes the significant findings and the researcher's interpretation based on the results. You may also discuss the relationship of your findings to previous research conducted in the literature. Chapter Five also includes a section on *Limitations*. The limitations section discusses the limitations or weaknesses of the study's design or findings. Another section in Chapter Five is the *Recommendations for Future Research*. In this section, you make recommendations for future areas of research that should be conducted related to your study (e.g., follow-up). Additional recommendations could include those for actions, policies, or procedures related to the study's findings. Finally, the last section of Chapter Five is the *Conclusions*. In this section, you will identify the critical conclusions about the results (e.g., lessons learned) and their implications. How to write Chapter Five and the major sections will be discussed in great detail in Chapter 9.

Quantitative Versus Qualitative Studies

Thus far, I have briefly mentioned quantitative versus qualitative studies, assuming you know the difference between the two types. Because you are reading this book, it is likely that you have taken or are currently taking a course in research methods, so I will not go into too much detail about the different research designs. However, since the type of study you conduct, whether quantitative or qualitative, informs the writing of the five-chapter thesis, I will briefly distinguish the two broad methods and give examples of possible topics from different disciplines. Note that what drives a researcher to conduct either a quantitative or qualitative study is not so much a match to the personality of the researcher (although this is important), but the research question(s) that needs to be answered.

Quantitative Methods

Studies that use quantitative approaches collect numerical data to answer the research question(s). **Numerical data** are mathematical data (i.e., numbers). Quantitative methods include but are not limited to research using descriptive, correlation, prediction, and control methods (Gay et al., 2006). The researcher can measure the outcome of cause-effect scenarios with single or multiple independent variables. The **independent variable** is the variable that is deliberately manipulated (e.g., cause) by the researcher to produce a change in the dependent variable. The **dependent variable** is the variable that is observed to see if there is a change (e.g., effect) in response to the independent variable. The researcher cannot manipulate the dependent variable. In quantitative research, typically, **deductive reasoning** is used, which is moving from the general to the specific. Typically, a quantitative researcher has a set **hypothesis** (prior to conducting the study) based on a theory that he or she tests in order to support or not support the given hypothesis. In quantitative studies, a hypothesis involves making assumptions or predictions based on probability distributions or likelihoods of events.

Data are often collected with one or several measurement instruments. **Measurement instruments** are data collection tools (e.g., surveys, observations, tests) that are used to measure changes in dependent variables or variables of interest. The data are recorded in numerical format such as a percentage score, grade point average, mean score, or rating. After the data are analyzed, the hypothesis is either confirmed or unsupported. Quantitative studies typically have large sample sizes and can also have multiple groups within the sample. In addition, the researcher may have limited direct interactions with the participants in the study. Once the data are collected, descriptive or inferential statistics are applied to inform the results. Some of the strengths of quantitative methods are that the researcher has control over many aspects of the study and given a large sample size, the results of the study can be generalized to a broad population.

Quantitative studies can be conducted in many different disciplines and topics, again depending on the research question(s). For example, in counseling, a study could be conducted on the effects of parents' divorce on children's social and emotional behavior for 4-year-olds at one preschool. In criminology, a study could be conducted surveying adolescents whose parents are incarcerated to assess their attitudes and perceptions toward law enforcement. In organization/business management, a study could be conducted on the relationship between employees' use of self-care strategies to mediate stress (e.g., exercise, yoga, meditation, acupuncture) and their level of productivity. In social work, a study could be conducted on the effects of having aging parents on sibling relations within Asian American families. Finally, in education, a study could be conducted on differences in math scores between female and male high school students in coed or same-sex classrooms. As you can see from the examples mentioned, there is no limit to the topics and studies across the disciplines that can be conducted using quantitative methods. Notice that all of the mentioned potential studies would require numerical data collection using surveys, tests, and/or observation checklists.

Qualitative Methods

Studies that use qualitative approaches collect nonnumerical data to answer the research question(s). **Nonnumerical data** are narrative data (i.e., words). There are many different kinds of qualitative research designs. Some commonly found approaches in the social and health sciences literature are narrative research, phenomenology, grounded theory, ethnography, case study, and participatory action research (Creswell, 2007; Kemmis & Wilkinson, 1998). Unlike quantitative researchers, qualitative researchers do not start their study with a hypothesis that they set out to find support for or to test. In qualitative research, typically, **inductive reasoning** is used, which is moving from the specific to the general. A qualitative researcher starts with specific situations, finds patterns or themes in the data, establishes a tentative hypothesis, and then develops theories or conclusions. Data are often collected through extensive and detailed field notes, observations, interviews, and focus groups with the participants in a natural setting (i.e., the researcher does not control or manipulate the environment). Qualitative studies typically have small sample sizes, which allow the researcher the time and opportunity to have extensive interactions with the participants. Once the data are gathered, they are coded, analyzed, and organized or categorized according to the themes and patterns that emerge. This provides the researcher with results in a narrative format. Some of the strengths of qualitative methods are that the researcher has investigated a topic in depth, interpreted the outcomes based on the participants', not the researcher's, perspectives, and created a holistic picture of the situation.

Qualitative studies are becoming more popular and can be conducted in many different disciplines and topics. For example, in counseling, a study could be conducted on the perceptions of single parent Latinas on utilizing mental health services. In criminology, a study could be conducted on how incarcerated teenage mothers cope with raising their children in juvenile detention centers. In organization/business management, a researcher might be interested in how volunteerism affects employee motivation and satisfaction at a nonprofit organization. In social work, a study could be conducted on the factors that promote resiliency within domestic violence victims. Finally, in education, a researcher could conduct an ethnographic study on the experience of first generation African American college students. As you can see from the examples mentioned, there are certain topics that require using qualitative methods such as interviews and observations to answer the research question(s).

Although quantitative and qualitative approaches have been described separately, it is important to keep in mind that these approaches fall on a continuum rather than on polar opposites. Neither method is considered to be better or more important than the other. In fact, studies with mixed methods, where both quantitative and qualitative methods are used, are possible, and may even strengthen the results. For the purposes of this book, however, quantitative and qualitative methods will be discussed separately in Chapter 7 (methods) and Chapters 8 (results) since these are the main areas where the distinction between the two methods is the greatest.

Style Form

All scholarly writing such as books, journal articles, reference materials, dissertations, and theses must comply with a style form. Style form refers to both writing style and editorial style. The **editorial style** is a set of rules or guidelines that writers must adhere to for publishing manuscripts, books, and so on. Some of the critical elements include how to format headings, citations, references, tables, figures, and so forth. The style form developed by the **American Psychological Association** (referred to as APA style) was selected for this book and the master's thesis because it is commonly used in various social science disciplines such as education, psychology, sociology, business, economics, nursing, and social work. Specifically, I follow the fifth edition of the *Publication Manual of the American Psychological Association* (APA, 2001). The APA manual is a reference book that has the rules and guidelines for the APA writing and editorial style. As new issues arise, the manuals are revised or updated on the APA Web site (http://www.apastyle.org), so make sure that you are following the most current edition. The APA style is widely accepted in the behavioral and social sciences, but the particular style form varies by discipline or academic departments. Other common form styles include the Chicago style from the University of Chicago Press and the Modern Language Association (MLA) style, which is widely used in the humanities. Check with your chairperson for the one that applies to your thesis.

The thesis must be written in a format that complies with a style form, so it is always helpful to be familiar with the style form as you begin to write. However, the style form is not a research method. Rather, it is a tool to use in communicating your thesis. In this book, Chapter 10 is devoted to helping you comply with the APA style. The placement of the chapter late in the book does not diminish its importance. If you have used the APA style for previous papers or are familiar with the style form, this chapter will be a review for you. If you have not used the APA style before, I recommend referring to Chapter 10 as you proceed through the data collection and writing process for each chapter.

Summary

Congratulations on getting through the first chapter of the book (only nine more to go)! You should now have a sense of the overall thesis and feel energized, empowered, and ready to embark on this educational adventure. Thank you for allowing me to be your tour guide. In the next chapter, I will discuss how to select a research topic and questions. I wish you all the best of luck and will lead you to the finish line (and pull you through if I have to)! Here is a summary of the most critical points from Chapter 1:

- The master's degree is a postbaccalaureate degree conferred by a college or university upon candidates who complete one to two years of graduate study.

- In some fields, the master's degree is referred to as a professional degree or terminal degree, meaning that the program or degree is the highest academic level for that profession rather than a gateway to the doctoral degree.

- The master's program provides you with multiple opportunities to learn the critical and core content in your field or discipline and research methods.

- For the purposes of this book, the master's thesis is an empirically based research study written in five distinct chapters.

- Chapter One introduces the topic of the thesis to the reader and establishes the statement of the problem and research questions.

- Chapter Two introduces the reader to the research literature related to the topic and identifies the most relevant and significant research.

- Chapter Three explains the research methods and design that were used to conduct the study and describes the actual procedures.

- Chapter Four reports the results of the study and presents the findings from the data collection process in Chapter Three.

- Chapter Five discusses the results from Chapter Four in relation to the statement of the problem and the research questions that were addressed in Chapter One and draws conclusions about the study's findings.

- What drives a researcher to conduct either a quantitative or qualitative study is not a match to the personality of the researcher (although this is important), but the research question that needs to be answered.

Resources

 ### Common Obstacles and Practical Solutions

1. A common problem that students face at this stage is feeling overwhelmed with the magnitude of the thesis. Words that come to mind are, "What did I get into?" If you are feeling anxious because you have never conducted research or written something like a master's thesis, do not panic! This book (and your chairperson) will help divide the parts into manageable and feasible chunks and guide you through the entire process. However, it might be helpful for you to review the text and notes from any research methods course that you took.

2. Another common obstacle that students face at this stage is trying to decide between conducting a quantitative or qualitative study. Instead of

putting pressure on yourself to make that decision now, it is better to let the design emerge as you read the existing research and develop your research questions.

 ## Reflection/Discussion Questions

Before you delve into the thesis, it is a good idea to take some time to make the "mental shift" from the type of conceptualizing and writing that was required in your undergraduate years and the type of conceptualizing and writing that will be required for the master's thesis. In addition, now is a good time to think broadly about the issues and problems in your discipline and whether they would be amenable to quantitative or qualitative methods. The following reflection/discussion questions will help to guide this process.

1. What constitutes a master's thesis? What are the similarities and differences between a master's thesis and a term paper? What are the similarities and differences between a master's thesis and a doctoral dissertation?

2. What are the similarities and differences between quantitative and qualitative research methods? Brainstorm and discuss critical research problems in your specific field or discipline. What would be the best method(s) to address these research questions? Provide the pros and cons of selecting each method.

 ## Try It Exercises

The following exercises (Activities One and Two) will help you to identify potential faculty to serve as your chairperson and committee members as well as prepare for that first critical meeting with your chairperson. Activity Three is designed for you to research the professional and personal benefits of receiving a master's degree in your field or discipline. This knowledge will help keep you motivated as you progress through the thesis knowing that when it is all done, you can reap the rewards!

1. Activity One: For this activity, focus on the faculty within and outside of your master's degree program.

> • Make a list of all the professors/instructors from whom you have taken a course.
> • Make a list of all the professors/instructors with whom you have worked on projects outside of coursework.

- Review the professors/instructors' curriculum vitae (usually available on the university Web site), and list the professors/instructors with whom you have common (research) interests.
- Make a list of potential professors/instructors who could serve as your faculty chairperson and additional committee members.
- Create an e-mail message that gives a general overview of your research interest(s) and ask one of these professors/instructors if he or she would be willing to serve as your master's thesis chairperson or committee member. Set up an initial meeting.

2. Activity Two: The first meeting with your chairperson is very critical. This meeting sets the tone for future meetings and also clarifies the expectations for the relationship between you and your chairperson.

- Make a list of questions that you would ask at the initial meeting with your chairperson. Keep in mind that you may only have 30 minutes with your chairperson, so the questions should be succinct and related to your thesis. You should also be prepared to answer questions that your chairperson might have related to his or her expectations of you. The following is a list of possible questions that may be included in your list:

1. How often should we meet—weekly, biweekly, as needed?
2. What are the best times to meet—mornings, afternoons, evenings—and where?
3. What is the best way to contact you if I have to schedule/cancel an appointment?
4. In which format should I present drafts—electronically by e-mail or with hard copy?
5. What is the typical turn-around time to receive feedback for my drafts?
6. What is the typical turn-around time you will want me to return the next draft?
7. What are some tasks I should be doing while waiting for feedback?
8. What resources are available on or off campus to help with writing, editing, and data analysis?

3. Activity Three: For this activity, focus on personal and professional benefits of receiving a master's degree in your field or discipline.

- Imagine that you have completed your master's degree and have been asked to give the keynote address at your graduation. The department chair has asked you to conduct research in your field/ discipline related to how the degree will enhance/further your career goals. You have to write a five-minute speech that addresses the professional and personal benefits of receiving your master's degree (as well as thanking everyone who supported you along the way).

Key Terms

- advance organizer
- APA style
- chairperson
- dependent variable
- descriptive statistics
- dissertation
- editorial style
- empirically based
- hypothesis
- independent variable
- inferential statistics

- master's degree
- Master of Arts (MA)
- Master of Science (MS)
- master's degree program
- master's thesis
- measurement instruments
- nonnumerical data
- numerical data
- qualitative research
- quantitative research
- terminal degree

 ## Suggested Readings

- Ercikan, K., & Roth, W. M. (2006). What good is polarizing research into qualitative and quantitative? *Educational Researcher, 35*(5), 14–23.
- Fletcher, K. M. (2005). The impact of receiving a master's degree in nonprofit management on graduates' professional lives. *Nonprofit and Voluntary Sector Quarterly, 34*(4), 433–447.
- Labaree, D. F. (2003). The peculiar problems of preparing educational researchers. *Educational Researcher, 32*(4), 13–22.
- Little, S. G., Akin-Little, A., & Lee, H. B. (2003). Education in statistics and research design in school psychology. *School Psychology International, 24*(4), 437–448.
- Morrow, S. L. (2007). Qualitative research in counseling psychology: Conceptual foundations. *The Counseling Psychologist, 35*(2), 209–235.
- Patenaude, A. L. (2004). No promises, but I'm willing to listen and tell what I hear: Conducting qualitative research among prison inmates and staff. *The Prison Journal, 84*(4), 69S–91S.
- Sternberg, E. (1994). What is a master's thesis in planning? *Journal of Planning Education and Research, 7*(13), 284–289.
- Yauch, C. A., & Steudel, H. J. (2003). Complementary use of qualitative and quantitative cultural assessment methods. *Organizational Research Methods, 6*(4), 465–481.

Web Links

- APA Style

  http://apastyle.apa.org/

- The Chicago Manual of Style Online

  http://www.chicagomanualofstyle.org/home.html

- Education Portal: Glossary of Master's Degree Programs
  http://education-portal.com/article_directory/Glossary_of_Master's_Degree
  _Programs.html
- Modern Language Association (MLA)
  http://www.mla.org/
- The Princeton Review: Grad Program Search
  http://www.princetonreview.com/grad/research/programProfiles/search.asp

2

Selecting a Research Topic

Important Factors to Consider When Selecting a Topic	22
Personal Significance	23
Critical Issues in the Field	24
Existing Research Literature	24
Search Engines	25
Electronic Databases	26
Ethical Considerations	28
How to Narrow and Refocus Your Topic	29
Feasibility	29
Accessibility	31
Time and Resources	32
Developing Answerable Research Questions	33
Answerable Questions	33
Defining Terms	34
Creating a Realistic Timeline	35
Time Management	38
Reserving Time	38
Chunking Method	39
Summary	40
Resources	41

(Continued)

(Continued)

Common Obstacles and Practical Solutions	41
Reflection/Discussion Questions	42
Try It Exercises	42
Key Terms	43
Suggested Readings	43
Web Links	44

> Writing is making sense of life. You work your whole life and perhaps you've made sense of one small area.
>
> —Nadine Gordimer

Now that I have covered the basic overview of the master's thesis, it is time to start the work! As in most writing projects, the first step is to select a topic. This is often a difficult task because there are many interesting unanswered research questions to study. Obviously, the topic that you choose for your thesis should be related to your field or discipline. However, keep in mind that your study should address a *research problem* and *questions* that you want answered because they are important to you and you have been unable to find meaningful and validated solutions. Your research problem and question could address original research (a new question) or be a replication of a previous study. For example, if I am earning my master's degree in counseling, then I would want to study some aspect of counseling that is important to the process of counseling, the issues and problems related to counseling, or the people involved in counseling. However, I also have to focus on a research question or a few that my study will attempt to answer. For the counseling process, perhaps I want to find out the differences in client participation and satisfaction during group or individual therapy. For the issues or problems related to counseling, my research question could examine the differences in treatment by the therapist for men and women. Finally, for the people involved in counseling, I could research the impact of grief counseling for young children after losing a parent. Framing research questions is an important part of planning your thesis. Later, I will discuss research questions in depth.

Important Factors to Consider When Selecting a Topic

A common question asked by graduate students is, "Where do I start?" Often, students feel anxious about selecting a research problem because it is like making a long-term commitment to someone you have not met! However, selecting a research problem should not be like going on a blind date or a random act. Instead, it is a systematic process that requires time, reflective thinking, discussion, and of course, research. You want to select a problem that has significance and is in need of a solution. You should also select a problem that you can research within the time that is available to you for your thesis. I will discuss four important factors to consider when selecting a research problem: (1) personal significance, (2) critical issues in the field, (3) the existing research literature, and (4) ethical considerations.

Personal Significance

The first place to look for a research topic is within. The research problem that you select should be first and foremost meaningful to you! There was a reason why you chose to enter your particular field or discipline, and most likely you have an affinity or passion for what you are studying. This is where all the course work and experiences that you have had in your master's degree program should come in handy. Through your course work, you reviewed research and are familiar with several studies. Some of these studies may have caused you to think about additional research problems. Perhaps there was a topic or problem from a course, reading, something an instructor said, or fieldwork experience that intrigued you. Keep in mind that your research study and thesis may take one to two years to complete, so the topic should be something that you care about or are passionate about since you will be devoting a lot of time and energy.

When I pursued my master's degree, I was having problems selecting a topic because there were so many educational problems that I was interested in or that I cared about. All of them that concerned me were broad, societal issues related to students with disabilities, but none were within my reach. When I finally sat down with my chairperson and rattled off 10 ideas, he said, "What is important to you? Where do you come from? Who can you give a voice to that so few others can?" I was stunned. Important to me? Why would anyone want to hear about what is important to me? I replied, "Well, there are a lot of recent Vietnamese refugees who have children with disabilities who emigrate to the United States, and I wonder if they know much about special education services since they do not speak the language and there are few special education services in Vietnam." Thirty minutes later, I walked out of his office with a research problem and questions in hand and excitement in my heart! I had just been given permission to conduct a research study that was personal and meaningful to me. Conducting a study on a topic that was personally significant changed my entire perspective about the process. Instead of viewing the data collection process as a burden, I was excited to meet different families and was truly interested in their perspectives and experiences related to obtaining special education services for their children with disabilities. When I completed my study and presented the findings at a national conference, I was absolutely amazed by the roomful of people who wanted to hear about the perspectives and stories of refugee Vietnamese families with children with disabilities—I guess I was not the only one who thought this was important after all. Thus, the lessons learned here are to select a topic that you are passionate about and get guidance from your chairperson who will help you focus on the critical issues. After all, you cannot go wrong if you follow your heart (well, most of the time).

Critical Issues in the Field

The second place to look for a research topic is right in your own backyard. In other words, what problems or issues are you or your colleagues currently facing in the immediate environment whether it is at a school, classroom, clinic, juvenile detention center, foster home, business, or non profit organization? Often, the research opportunity "calls" to you because it is an issue or problem that you and your colleagues have been grappling with and need some help to find solutions. For example, maybe you are interested in finding out why so few people promoted to the manager or director level at your nonprofit organization are female or people of color. At a school setting, maybe you are concerned that the level of fighting among the children during recess time has increased over the past few years. Perhaps you are interested in the transition process for young adults who "age out" of the foster care system at 18.

If you are not sure about the problematic issues in your field, a good idea is to talk to your colleagues, administrators, and your chairperson. They will have a plethora of ideas, and it is always helpful to bounce your ideas off another person, especially someone who is familiar with the issues in the field. The research problem could be something that has a direct relationship and implication to what you do or see at your professional setting. However, keep in mind that the goal is to focus on one problem, not all the problems in your field (or obtain world peace).

Existing Research Literature

A third way to find a research topic is by doing good, old-fashioned research of the literature. Conducting research through the Internet or at the library is often a good method of finding a topic because it gives you a sense of the broad and critical issues in your field. This is very important because your study should make a contribution to the research literature. As is the case with most research studies, you want to be able to add to the existing knowledge base in your field. Conducting research gives you a general sense of what studies have already been conducted, the "best practices," and the gaps that still remain. Based on your findings, you may choose to replicate an existing study, implement a previously validated practice with a new population, or conduct a study that fills one of the gaps in your field.

An often overlooked resource for existing research is national and government reports. These reports are typically based on research studies that were funded by grants and are published in many different fields and disciplines. National and government reports are a good place to start your research because they are indicators of the major issues and problems in a particular area. For example, the National Institute of Justice within the U.S. Department of Justice (USDJ, 2005) published a report based on two studies of co-offenses (crimes involving more than one offender) among juveniles. The report has implications for further research and intervention related to the patterns of co-offenders in terms of: (1) age of the offenders, (2) recidivism, and (3) violence. This report points to many research problems that could have a significant impact on the field. Advantages of looking at national and government reports is that they are usually readily available, free to the public, and provide a broad overview of the issues and problems in a particular area.

The process of conducting research of the literature has changed dramatically over the past 15 years. When I conducted research for my master's thesis, I had to actually walk into the library (yes, in the snow), first locate the books and periodicals through the card catalog, then find and take books and periodicals off the shelves, and finally bring rolls of nickels and dimes to feed the copy machine. Sometimes I had to figure out how to use and make a copy from the microfiche! Now, with modern technology, conducting research of the literature involves sitting comfortably in front of your home or library's computer in a plush chair with a cup of coffee and a half-dozen donuts.

Search engines. Through the Internet, there are many available search engines to help you with your research of the literature. A **search engine** is a computer system where information is stored and organized for easy retrieval. The most common search engines search for information on the World Wide Web through the Internet. However, when searching the Internet, you want to make sure that your research is *guided* rather than general. **Guided research** is setting specific parameters (e.g., date, author, and subject) around your search in order to narrow the pool of resources and results. This helps you avoid reading thousands of article abstracts. One place to start your research is Google Scholar (http://scholar.google.com). This search engine will locate thousands of research articles in many discipline areas in less than a few seconds. In order to narrow your search, start with a general search and then use an Advanced Scholar Search (see Figure 2.1 for Google Scholar search screen). In the Advanced Scholar Search, you can find articles about a topic using specific words, by author, publication, date, or by subject area in the search field. For example, pretend I want to conduct a study on dyslexia. When I typed "dyslexia" into Google Scholar, I retrieved over 79,000 articles (see Figure 2.2 for Advanced Scholar Search screen)! Then, when I used the Advanced Scholar Search and asked for articles where "dyslexia" is in the title, I retrieved 6,900 articles (see Figure 2.3 for Advanced Scholar Search screen using title of the article). I further narrowed my search and put a five-year limit on the dates and retrieved 1,320 articles. Finally, I looked only at studies where "phonology" is the focus and guess what—I only have to read 10 articles (see Figure 2.4 for Advanced Scholar Search screen using exact phrase and date limits). That is quite a big difference from the 79,000 that I started with! Narrowing your search fields and conducting a guided search will help you sort through the information and cull out the research that is important, but not specific enough to your research problem. Your chairperson is a good resource if you need help shaping your search terms to conduct the guided search. A 15-minute meeting with your chairperson could save you hours and hours of being lost in cyberspace.

Electronic databases. Searching through electronic databases is another method to find a potential research topic. An **electronic database** is an electronic collection of information (e.g., books, journal articles, reference materials) where an individual can research and retrieve resources.

Figure 2.1   Search engine Google Scholar search screen.

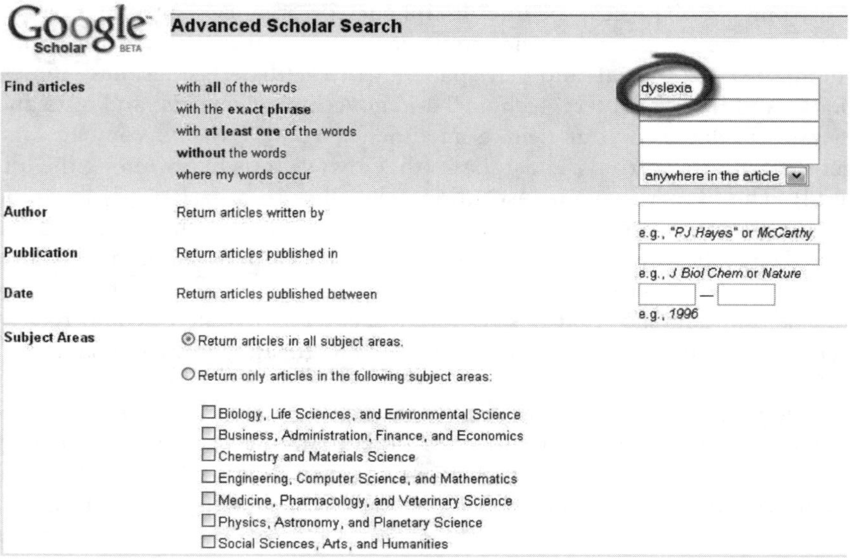

Figure 2.2   Advanced Scholar Search screen in Google Scholar.

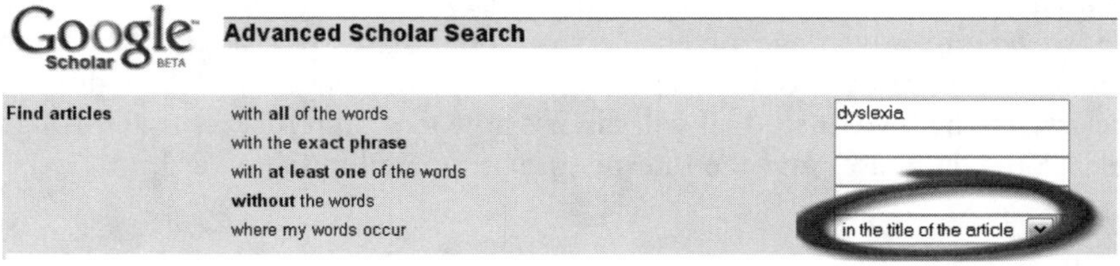

Figure 2.3   Advanced Scholar Search screen using the title of the article.

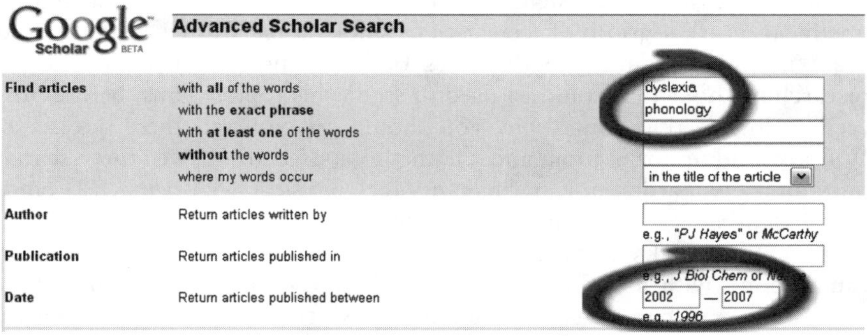

Figure 2.4   Advanced Scholar Search screen with exact phrase and date limits.

Electronic databases can be interdisciplinary or organized around a particular subject area or field. In electronic databases, you can find citations and summaries to journal and newspaper articles, dissertations and theses, books and book chapters, technical and government reports, and tests and measures related to your field. Sometimes, if you are lucky, you can even get the full article from the database (that always feels like winning the lottery!). The library at your institution subscribes to a variety of electronic databases, and as an enrolled student, you may access the databases for free. Typically, you can search these databases by subject or alphabetically. For example, PsycINFO (http://www.apa.org/psycinfo) is a very popular and helpful database that has resources related to psychology and related fields such as nursing, sociology, education, linguistics, anthropology, business, and law.

If you do not have access to your institution's library, there are other electronic databases that are free to the public although some of them may charge a small fee for their articles. For example, ERIC (Education Resources Information Center) is a huge database related to education that contains over 1.2 million citations, abstracts, digests, and full-text articles from 1966 to the present. ERIC is sponsored by the U.S. Department of Education, Institute of Education Sciences (http://www.eric.ed.gov) and updated regularly. Once you enter the electronic database, the process is very similar to a typical search engine. Again, you will want to conduct a guided search with set parameters in terms of topic, author, dates, and so on. However, an advantage of an electronic database over a general search engine is that most of the resources in the electronic database will be directly related to the field of study. I will discuss how to search for research through electronic databases and the Internet in more detail in Chapter 3.

Ethical Considerations

Finally, another important factor to consider when selecting a research topic is ethics. For example, a topic such as the effects of teenage smoking on heart disease may be significant to the medical field, but it would be unethical to ask a group of teenagers to smoke a pack of cigarettes for 20 years in order to measure the rates of heart disease (there are actual research methods that could be used to study this topic). Thus, before proceeding in selecting your topic, you should ask yourself these questions: Will my study on this topic and the methods used to answer the research question(s) jeopardize the participants' (1) physical well-being, (2) emotional well-being, (3) academic well-being, (4) economic or financial well-being, (5) spiritual well-being, (6) social well-being, or (7) privacy? If you can respond with a definitive "No" to these questions, then most likely your study will pass muster on ethical considerations. If you are unsure

whether or not your study will violate an ethical consideration, do not
worry; every institution of higher education requires that graduate students
submit their master's thesis study proposals through the **Institutional
Review Board for the Protection of Human Subjects (IRBPHS)** for approval
prior to conducting the study. The IRBPHS is a group that has been formally designated by the institution to review and monitor research applications involving human subjects. I will discuss ethical considerations, the
IRBPHS process, and how to write an IRBPHS proposal in more detail in
Chapter 4.

How to Narrow and Refocus Your Topic

Once you have selected a potential research topic, you will probably need to
narrow it down. Often, students select topics that have met the four criteria
above—personally significant, critical issue in the field, contributes to the
existing research, and meets ethical standards—only to discover that the topic
is way too broad and outside the scope of their immediate surroundings. This
can be somewhat frustrating, but fortunately there are ways to make your
research study more concrete and manageable. Sometimes students will select
significant problems to study, but because they did not narrow and refocus the
study prior to starting, they eventually feel overwhelmed, helpless, unmotivated,
and finally quit altogether. In order to avoid these pitfalls, schedule an appointment with your chairperson early in the process to discuss ways to narrow
your study but still keep the essence of what interests you. Investing this time
at the beginning will save you time and frustration later and could make the
difference between completing or not completing the thesis within the allocated
time. As I often remind my students, "The 'best' master's thesis is the one that
is completed!" In addition to getting advice from your chairperson, you will
also have to draw on your own personal research skills and knowledge about
research methods and designs. Throughout this process, it will help you to
have access to research methods textbooks and academic journals in
your field to use as references. In this section, I will discuss three factors to
consider when focusing and narrowing the scope of your study: (1) feasibility,
(2) accessibility, and (3) time and resources.

Feasibility

Often, students will be so excited when they find a topic of personal and
professional interest that they may choose a problem that is not feasible to
study. **Feasibility** refers to how realistic it will be to access data or participants and the time needed to complete the study. For example, the topic of
study may be the "Perceptions of high school students on their high school

exit exam for graduation in a school district," and I want to measure students' perceptions using a survey and some follow-up interviews. However, because the problem is so broad, it would require a team of experienced researchers with sizable resources to make this a feasible study to complete.

One method to increase feasibility is to limit the sample group. The **sample group** is the group of participants in a study. They are the group that the researcher collects data from or about. How to reduce or shape your sample group will depend heavily on your research question(s), but this is one of the best ways to make your study more feasible and manageable. For example, in the study above, rather than measure the perceptions of *all* high school students in the school district, I could study the perceptions of high school students at *one* high school within the school district. However, if it is like the public high school I went to, the sample group would be 2,400 students! That is still too large for one person to manage. One method to further reduce the sample size would be to randomly select a certain number (50) of students from each of the grade levels. This would still give me a "representative" sample of the entire school, but I would only have to manage 200 surveys rather than 2,400. Another method to reduce my sample size would be to measure the perceptions of students from *one grade level,* such as the juniors. This shows only one slice of the high school, but perhaps this is the group most affected by the exit exam. Again, this could be 600 students, so taking a random sample from one grade level would also be another possibility to narrow the study. By limiting my sample size, I have made the study more feasible, which increases my chances of successfully collecting the data (and completing my thesis).

Another method of narrowing the study and increasing feasibility is by reducing the number of research questions. (I will discuss how to develop research questions in more depth later in the chapter.) Keep in mind that the more research questions you have, the more data you will have to collect and analyze (and possibly include more participants). Remember that the intent of the thesis is not to study everything with regard to your topic; often, it is better to study one or two things in depth. By limiting the amount of data you collect, you gain more control over the process. In many ways, conducting a study is like cooking (something I have never been able to master). If you select a recipe with 10 ingredients (some of which you have to buy in specialty stores), the cooking process becomes more complicated than if you had a recipe with five ingredients because there are more factors outside of your control. If done correctly, you could end up with a mouth-watering dish and get rave reviews from friends and family. However, with so many ingredients to mix, blend, blanch, or puree, there is an increased chance of making mistakes, burning something, cutting yourself, over- and undercooking items, and basically losing your sanity in the process.

Accessibility

Another related factor to consider when narrowing your study is accessibility. **Accessibility** refers to the ability to gain access or entry to the research site and participants. This is related to feasibility because without access to the research site or participants, it will be almost impossible to conduct and complete the study. Keep in mind that some places of business, schools, detention centers, hospitals, and clinics do not allow individuals outside of the organization to conduct research at their sites. If they do allow outside researchers, the application/approval process may take months to complete, so you need to plan accordingly. Thus, before you finalize your research plan, it is best to get a letter of permission to access participants from the administrator at the research site (some IRBPHS applications require this for the proposal). This will ensure that you can at least get through the front door.

If you do gain access to the research site, another factor to consider is ease of access and proximity. Basically, you need to determine how easy it will be for you to collect the data for your study. For example, I want to conduct a study on the "Parenting skills of teenage mothers in juvenile detention centers," and I will measure their parenting skills by conducting observations while they are interacting with their children. The administrators at the detention center have given me permission to access the participants for my study. The center is 15 miles away from my house, and the visiting hours for mothers and their children are Monday through Friday from 12:00 P.M. to 2:00 P.M. In the morning from 8:00 A.M. to 12:00 P.M. and in the afternoon from 2:00 P.M. to 6:00 P.M., the children are at the on-site child care center. However, my normal work hours are from 8:00 A.M. to 1:30 P.M., which means by the time I get to the center, I will be able to observe the mothers and children for only 15 minutes! This is not enough time to collect rich observation data for the study. Even though I had access to the research site and participants, because of other external factors outside of my control, I did not have access to conduct the study in terms of ease and proximity. Thus, when considering your study, make sure that you will have true access to collect data for your study. One way to increase true access is by conducting the study at a setting where you already spend a good deal of time such as at your place of employment, volunteer site, or training/school site. For the example study above, since I could not quit my job but was able to access the children at their child care center in the afternoon, I could refocus my topic to study the effects of incarcerated teenage mothers on children's social and emotional development. By refocusing the topic, I was still within the broader area of teenage mothers in juvenile detention centers, but I made the study's participants truly accessible by observing the children rather than the mothers.

Time and Resources

In addition to feasibility and accessibility, you must consider available time and resources before starting a study. **Time** refers to the researcher's time that is available to devote to the study as well as the duration (length of study) and frequency (how often the researcher will interact with participants). **Resources** are tangibles such as materials and finances necessary to conduct a study but also include nontangibles such as personal health and energy. For example, make sure you have the time and resources to complete the tasks required by the study such as traveling to the research site, implementing an intervention if required, purchasing or developing materials, collecting data, analyzing the data, and reporting the data. Remember that most likely your "team" of researchers will consist of yourself, a computer, and a supportive spouse, partner, friend, pet, or family member if you are lucky. Thus, before you start, it is critical to narrow and refocus your study so that you are not overcommitting and stretching yourself too thinly.

For example, your school district has required all teachers to receive in-service training on research-based practices to improve students' statewide reading test scores. Since you are in a master's degree program for education, your principal has asked you to conduct your thesis on this topic. She wants you to lead 20 hours of professional development sessions at the school site with 15 kindergarten through fifth-grade teachers, collect data on the teachers' implementation of the research-based practices, and report on the students' outcomes. The in-services would start in January after the winter break, the state assessments start in April, and, because of budget cuts, you would have to find and provide all the training materials. To be fair, the principal has given you two 50-minute periods of release time per week from your third-grade class. Should you do it? You have access to willing participants, some release time, and the support of the principal, so it should be feasible, right? WRONG! Clearly this study is above and beyond what you have available in terms of time and resources. First, the allocated time is much too short. Three months is not enough time to research and locate materials, conduct 20 hours of in-service trainings, conduct observations for 15 teachers, and collect student data—all of this on top of your normal teaching responsibilities. Second, there are no curriculum resources available, which means you would probably have to borrow or buy materials (out of pocket) or develop your own materials (in your spare time) for the trainings. Thus, even though it may have seemed like a good study to conduct because of the accessibility, this is an unrealistic study because of the demand on your time and resources. Some suggestions I would make to narrow the focus of the study would be to reduce the training from 20 to 10 hours, limit the responsibilities so that you would only provide training and observation to the third-grade-level team, and ask the principal to provide a small budget for materials and more release time. By making the parameters more realistic (both in length of the study and time to devote to the study) and having resources available, you have increased the feasibility and quality of the study.

Developing Answerable Research Questions

Once you have selected and narrowed your problem, it is time to develop the research question. A **research question** is related to the problem in a study and is the question that the researcher attempts to answer. The research question guides the type of data that will be collected and/or how the data should be collected. For example, I want to conduct research around the problem(s) related to violent neighborhoods and children's development. The broad problem is "violent neighborhoods" and the research problem within this topic is "How violent neighborhoods affect children's cognitive development." Once I know my research problem, I need to generate a research question(s) that will guide my research study. Some programs or disciplines may use different terms to refer to the research questions, such as research hypothesis or null hypothesis. Always check with your chairperson to make sure you are using the appropriate terms.

Answerable Questions

The most important consideration when developing a research question is whether or not you can *answer* the question (i.e., the question is research-able). That may seem a bit strange because are not all questions answerable? Not necessarily. An **answerable research question** is one where the researcher is able to collect data or information (using a measurement instrument) to answer the question related to the problem. There has to be some measurement instrument or tool that can used (e.g., survey, observation, test, interview) to collect data or information from the participants in the study. In other words, if you cannot *measure* the research problem in some way, then you cannot answer the research question. For example, for my research problem of "violent neighborhoods and children's cognitive development," the research question is about the effects that a violent neighborhood has on children's cognitive development. Thus, one possible research question is, "What are the effects that a violent neighborhood has on young children's academic achievement?" This is a possible research question because I can collect data to measure the effect or outcome of the problem on my participants. However, the research question is not very clear because there are several ambiguous terms. These ambiguous or subjective terms must be *defined* before I can determine what exactly is being studied. For example, what constitutes a *violent neighborhood*? Who are considered *young children*? What is meant by *academic achievement* and which indicators will be used? When considering whether or not a term is ambiguous, ask yourself if you and a complete stranger would have a different definition of the term or if the term would be unfamiliar to a person outside of your field; if so, it is best to define the term.

Defining Terms

There are three ways you can define terms related to your research question and study: by dictionary, example, or operationally (Fraenkel & Wallen, 2006). A **dictionary definition** is a definition that is offered in a dictionary to define ambiguous terms related to the study or research question. This may not always be applicable to your study, especially when it is a compound word such as *violent neighborhood* or if the terms represent a concept or idea. For example, when I look up *neighborhood* in the dictionary the closest definition is, "the people living near one another" ("Neighborhood," n.d.). Then, when I look up *violence*, the closest definition is, "exertion of physical force so as to injure or abuse." When I put the two together my definition of a *violent neighborhood* would be, "exertion of physical force so as to injure or abuse by people living near one another." This is close to what I am thinking of but does not really capture what I want to research because it is vague in terms of the parameters of the neighborhood.

Another way to define terms is by giving an example definition. An **example definition** is a definition that uses examples to define ambiguous terms related to the study or research question. For instance, for *violent neighborhood,* an example definition would be an area where violent crimes such as shootings or stabbings, home and auto theft, gang-related activity such as fighting, muggings, and so on occur regularly. This gives the reader a better idea of what I want to study, but there is still ambiguity as to the size of the area and how regularly the violent crime must occur in the neighborhood to label it as a *violent neighborhood.*

Perhaps the best way to define terms is to give an operational definition. An **operational definition** is a definition that describes attributes or characteristics of the term that need to be present in order to measure it. For example, a *neighborhood* could be determined by the area within a given zip code, and a *violent neighborhood* could be one where the monthly average rate of violent crimes exceeds the average rate of violent crime for the area for six consecutive months. In this study, a *young child* could be a child between the ages of six and nine and *academic achievement* could be the child's performance on a standardized achievement test. By operationally defining the ambiguous terms in my research question, it is now clear to me and to the reader the exact phenomenon I am studying. I have also defined the terms in such a way that I can now collect measurable data to answer the research question.

There are at least three types of questions that would *not* be good research questions: philosophical/rhetorical, value/moral, and hypothetical (Fraenkel & Wallen, 2006). The first kind is philosophical or rhetorical in nature and resembles questions asked by four-year-olds that leave you scrambling for an answer. For example, "Why was I born? Why did our dog have to die? What is the meaning of life?" are all nonresearchable questions. A **nonresearchable question** is a type of question where the researcher cannot collect measurable data to answer the question, or the "answers" are based on philosophical, spiritual, or personal beliefs. The second kind of nonresearchable question involves making a value or moral judgment. For example, "Should plastic bags be eliminated at grocery stores? Should all children be tested annually? Does counseling help or hurt clients?" are not researchable questions because again you cannot collect data to answer the question. Additionally, the "answers" to the questions are based upon personal values and biases. The third type of nonanswerable research question is based on hypothetical situations. For example, "What if there was no war? What if everyone grew their own food? How long would humans live if disease were eliminated?" are all nonresearchable questions because you cannot collect data in a setting that exists only hypothetically. Additionally, there would not be any measurable outcomes.

Look at these questions from my example study and decide which type of nonresearchable question they are:

- Why are neighborhoods plagued with violence?

- What is the best way to save children from neighborhood violence?

- Should handguns be banned to reduce neighborhood violence?

- What would happen to children's development if they did not witness regular violence in their neighborhoods?

In summary, it is critical that the research questions for your study are answerable and any ambiguous terms are clearly defined. This is a necessary first step because the research questions will guide the rest of your study and the methodology (e.g., research design, setting, participants, measurement instruments, data analysis) that you use to answer the questions.

Creating a Realistic Timeline

Now that you have narrowed your topic and developed answerable research questions, it is time to create a timeline. A **timeline** is a schedule that is created by the researcher that outlines all the necessary steps and phases to complete the study within the allocated time. This is necessary because often students will be so excited about finding a research problem that interests them that they plan a study that does not have a realistic timeline. For example, imagine that you have one academic year to complete your study, and it is due by the end of the spring semester (typically in May). Your intervention is going to take 3 months, and you cannot start the intervention until the beginning of January. This will leave you one month to score all the data, complete the data analysis, report the data, and write up the results (not to mention the multiple revisions you will have to make). This "narrow" timeline will not only put unnecessary stress on you (and your chairperson), but it may also deter you from completing the study. A better timeline would be to start the intervention earlier and if that is not possible, then shorten the intervention.

A realistic schedule or timeline is one that gives you some cushion and a reasonable amount of time to complete each section or chapter. Keep in mind that when developing a timeline, every part of the process will probably take longer than you expect, and there are sure to be "surprises" along the way. You should also expect to write multiple revisions of every chapter. In addition, there may be events or situations (personal or professional) that cause interruptions that you cannot predict or control. Thus, putting "buffers" into your timeline will give you the flexibility to stay on track (and not feel guilty about always being behind schedule).

Here are some possible tasks to include in your timeline and a sample schedule for one academic school year. As every institution is different, it is best to check what the expected procedures are at your institution.

August-September

- ✓ Conduct preliminary research to find possible research topics
- ✓ Speak to colleagues about possible research topics
- ✓ Meet with chairperson to discuss how to narrow topic and refocus study
- ✓ Develop answerable research questions
- ✓ Obtain permission from research site to conduct study and access participants

September-October

- ✓ Meet with chairperson to discuss Chapter One
- ✓ Locate and finalize sample group of participants
- ✓ Submit application to university's Institutional Review Board for the Protection of Human Subjects
- ✓ Submit application to organization, school district, or other entity for permission to conduct research
- ✓ Submit first draft of Chapter One

October-November

- ✓ Make revisions and submit final draft of Chapter One
- ✓ Locate and finalize measurement instruments
- ✓ After receiving permission from all parties involved, start the pretest phase (if appropriate)
- ✓ Begin conducting interviews and/or classroom observations (if appropriate)

✓ Meet with chairperson to discuss Chapter Two
✓ Conduct review of the literature
✓ Submit first draft of Chapter Two

November-December

✓ Make revisions and finalize Chapter Two
✓ Begin the intervention phase of your study (if appropriate)
✓ Continue with the interviews and field observations (if appropriate)
✓ Meet with chairperson to discuss Chapter Three
✓ Gather information and demographic data of participants and research site
✓ Submit first draft of Chapter Three

December-January

✓ Meet with chairperson to discuss ongoing progress
✓ Begin the intervention phase of your study (if appropriate)
✓ Continue with the interviews and field observations (if appropriate)
✓ Make revisions and finalize Chapter Three

January-February

✓ Complete intervention and/or data collection
✓ Begin the posttest phase (if appropriate)
✓ Meet with chairperson to discuss data analysis

February-March

✓ Score measurement instructions and complete data analysis (if appropriate)
✓ Transcribe field notes and complete data analysis (if appropriate)
✓ Meet with chairperson to discuss Chapter Four
✓ Submit draft of Chapter Four

March-April

✓ Make revisions and finalize Chapter Four
✓ Meet with chairperson to discuss Chapter Five
✓ Submit draft of Chapter Five

April-May

✓ Make revisions and finalize Chapter Five
✓ Double-check all citations and references for appropriate format (e.g., APA)
✓ Create necessary tables and figures
✓ Locate all documents for appendices

✓ Create abstract and table of contents
✓ Conduct final formatting
✓ Meet with chairperson for final printout and review
✓ Bind and copy final thesis

May

✓ Submit final revisions and copies of the thesis to committee members for signatures
✓ Graduation celebrations

June

✓ Take a much-deserved vacation

Time Management

Realizing all the tasks that need to be done for the entire thesis can be a bit daunting. However, if you manage your time well, meet regularly with your chairperson, and try to stick as closely as possible to your timeline, it is very possible to complete the study in a reasonable amount of time and do a high-quality job. Because the thesis is different from traditional course assignments where there are hard and fast deadlines, it is easy to let the months go by without any real progress. Unfortunately, the thesis is not like those term papers that you wrote in college the night before (and got an A!). You will need to make consistent progress on the research and data collection aspects as well as the writing process. There are two strategies that will help you be successful in this process.

Reserving Time

The first strategy is to *reserve time* for the thesis. In this day and age, we are all busy, all the time. There never seems to be enough time to finish everything that needs to be done—who can possibly eat healthy food, exercise, and get enough sleep? Like other big projects (e.g., cleaning the garage), the thesis will fall to the bottom of the to-do pile unless you allocate and reserve time to work on it on a consistent basis. The reserved time can be one day a week, one hour every morning, or even 20 minutes every evening. You can pick whatever works best for you and your schedule; however, once you have made that reservation with yourself and the computer, you must treat it as sacred time. This means there are no excuses for not keeping the "appointment" or putting it off and saying, "I'll do double time tomorrow or next week." Let's face it, if you could not find 20 free minutes today, why would you be able to have 40 free minutes tomorrow? Of course there will be emergencies and surprises that come up now and then, but it is really critical that you devote a consistent and regularly-scheduled amount of time to work on the thesis and be self-disciplined. This means turning off the cell phone, e-mail, television, or anything that will disrupt you. You should also find a place to work where you will be most productive whether it is in a home office, library, or cafe. Meeting with a "writing partner" on a regular basis might also keep you from canceling appointments although make sure it does not become a social event!

Chunking Method

Another strategy that will help you be successful in the process is the chunking method. The **chunking method** refers to breaking up large tasks into smaller, more manageable chunks such as writing one section of a chapter rather than the entire chapter. If the task is to write an entire chapter or transcribe all the interviews, this will seem very intimidating and the natural response is to do anything (e.g., clean out your desk, household chores) to avoid the required task. Believe me, I am the master of procrastination and have a very clean desk. However, if you set a goal to work on only one small chunk of the larger task (e.g., one section of the chapter, transcribe one interview), this will feel less daunting, and you will be more likely to start the task. Writing the thesis is similar to sticking to an exercise plan (something I had to do after an ankle injury). When I set my goal to ride the exercise bike for 40 minutes every other day, it was almost impossible to find 40 minutes of "free time," and I just kept putting it off until the next day. Since my riding time was supposed to be every other day, this meant I never rode the bike! Meanwhile the bike was a constant reminder of my "failure" and was being used as a very expensive clothes hanger. However, when I set the goal to ride the bike 15 to 20 minutes at the end of my day, I was able to stick to this schedule more regularly, and sometimes I even stayed on the bike for another 20 minutes! Once I got into the "habit" of getting on the bike, it became part of my daily routine. I can now proudly say that I ride the bike for 30 minutes almost every day and even look forward to it (that is a bit of an exaggeration)! The point is that one of the hardest parts of writing the thesis will be to motivate yourself to sit down and just turn on the computer. However, once you start and begin to build momentum and form a routine, you will find that not only will it be easier to continue, but you might actually enjoy yourself in the process. Building in small rewards (eating a bag of chips as I did after the bike ride is not recommended) after each chunk is another way to reinforce your productive behavior. The next time that you are feeling overwhelmed and ready to quit, take some deep breaths and remember the adage of how to eat an elephant (also not recommended) ("You Can Eat," n.d.).

You can eat an elephant.

Oh, yes you can it's true.

They may be huge but not to worry,

they aren't too big for you.

"Just how can I eat such a thing

that's so immense in size?"

"Just look at it in pieces

and make them all bite size."

You see to look from head to tail

can be a daunting task.

Many would just give up now

and let the elephant pass.

Look at it as if you can

eat it piece by piece,

It may take you a while,

but your goal you will reach.

So, next time you have a task

that is difficult to do,

Remember, you can eat an elephant

so take a piece and chew!

Summary

Selecting your research topic/problem is perhaps the most important (and difficult) phase of the thesis process, so I hope this chapter has given you ideas on where to start and how to narrow the focus. In the next chapter, I will discuss in detail how to research the existing literature related to your research topic/problem. Here is a summary of the most critical points from Chapter 2:

• The topic that you choose for your thesis should be related to your field or discipline and address a *research problem* and *questions*.

• The research problem that you select should have personal significance, could be a problem or issue that you or your colleagues are currently facing in the immediate environment, and should make a contribution to the research literature.

- In electronic databases such as ERIC, you can find citations and summaries to journal and newspaper articles, dissertations and theses, books and book chapters, technical and government reports, and tests and measures related to your field.

- An important factor to consider when selecting a research topic is ethics, as you should not jeopardize the participants' well-being in any way.

- Every institution of higher education requires that graduate students submit their master's thesis study proposals through the Institutional Review Board for the Protection of Human Subjects (IRBPHS) for approval *prior* to conducting the study.

- Three important factors to consider when narrowing your study are feasibility, accessibility, and available time and resources.

- The most important consideration when developing a research question is whether or not you can *answer* the question (i.e., the question is researchable).

- There are three ways you can define terms related to your research question and study: by dictionary, example, or operationally.

- There are at least three types of questions that would *not* be good research questions: philosophical/rhetorical, value/moral, and hypothetical.

- Once you have narrowed your topic and developed research questions, create a schedule and timeline so that you can complete the study within the allocated time period.

Resources

 ### Common Obstacles and Practical Solutions

1. A common problem that students face at this stage is feeling anxious about selecting a research topic. Words that come to mind are, "Everything sounds interesting—how do I choose just one topic?" At this point, do not put so much pressure on yourself to find the "perfect" research topic. Instead, select a few, do some scanning of the research, and then see which one seems the most interesting, feasible, and accessible. Remember that you can always change topics, and sometimes in doing the research, the topic will "find" you.

2. Another common obstacle that students face at this stage is thinking about the time issue. Words that come to mind are, "How will I ever have enough time to write?" If you are like me and your days are packed from the moment you open your eyes in the morning until you close them again in the

wee hours of the morning, finding "free time" is like winning the lottery without buying a ticket—chances are pretty slim. That is why it is critical for you to *schedule* time to write—schedule writing time in your daily planner just as you would a doctor's appointment. Think of it as an appointment to benefit you (without copayments)!

 ## Reflection/Discussion Questions

As you begin to think about possible research topics, it is important to frame them in the context of research questions. Having answerable research questions related to problems in your field or discipline will help narrow the focus of your study (and ensure that you have a feasible study!). The following reflection/discussion questions will help to guide the process of developing answerable research questions and defining the appropriate terms.

1. What makes a research question answerable versus nonanswerable? What are the different types of nonanswerable questions? Brainstorm critical problems in your field and develop three answerable questions and three nonanswerable questions related to the problem. Discuss why the questions are answerable or not answerable.

2. What are the differences in the three methods for defining terms? Discuss the pros and cons of each type of method. Based on the answerable research questions you developed earlier, identify and define ambiguous terms using the most appropriate method.

 ## Try It Exercises

The following exercises (Activities One and Two) will help you to identify a potential topic for the thesis and ways to narrow the topic so that it is feasible to study. Activity Three is designed for you to create a timeline with the help of your chairperson. This timeline and personal writing schedule will help you to stay on track and finish the thesis in a timely manner (remember the rewards from Chapter 1!).

1. Activity One: For this activity, focus on the knowledge and experience you have gained from your master's degree program that will help you throughout the thesis process.

DREAM TOPIC: In the perfect world where I had limitless time, money, and energy, I would conduct a study with this topic:
Now that you have that out of your system, follow the steps below to choose a topic for your master's thesis. Remember that you're saving the dream topic for your doctoral dissertation.

- Make a list of the topics/problems (based on course work) that would be interesting to research further.
- Make a list of the topics/problems (based on community, field-work, or clinical experience) that would be interesting for you to research further.
- Based on the information above, finish the statements below:

   (1) A topic that has personal significance:
   (2) A topic that is a critical issue in my field:
   (3) A topic that I found in existing research:
   (4) A topic that is ethical to research:

- Now choose the BEST topic for *you* from 1–4 and write a one-paragraph description of the research topic/problem that you are interested in pursuing for your master's thesis study.

2. Activity Two: Based on the research problem that you selected for Activity One, discuss with a colleague or your chairperson how to narrow the focus of your study considering feasibility, accessibility, and time/resources.

3. Activity Three: Meet with your chairperson to create a realistic time-line for completion of the thesis. Use the sample list of tasks from Chapter 2 and modify the tasks and timeline to match the chairperson's and university's expectations for submitting written work and the final thesis. Then create a personal contract where you schedule when and where you will focus on the writing tasks. Sign both the timeline and contract, give one copy to your chairperson, and tape one copy by your work space.

Key Terms

- accessibility
- answerable research question
- chunking method
- dictionary definition
- electronic database
- example definition
- feasibility
- guided research
- Institutional Review Board for the Protection of Human Subjects (IRBPHS)
- nonresearchable question
- operational definition
- research question
- resources
- sample group
- search engine
- time
- timeline

Suggested Readings

- Alter, S., & Dennis, A. R. (2002). Selecting research topics: Personal experiences and speculations for the future. *Communications of the Association for Information Systems, 8*, 314–329.

- Thomas, C. (1995). Helping students complete master's theses through active supervision. *Journal of Management Education, 5*(19), 240–249.

 Web Link

- So what is a (Diploma) Thesis? A few thoughts for first-timers. http://www.ifi.uzh.ch/ddis/theses/what-is-thesis/

3

Using the Literature to Research Your Problem

Benefits of Conducting a Literature Review	46
Sources of Data: Primary Versus Secondary	48
Primary Sources	48
Secondary Sources	48
Selecting Key Terms	50
Conducting Searches in Electronic Databases	52
Basic Search	55
Limiters	56
Expanders	57
Advanced Search	58
Boolean Operators	58
Symbols	59
Using the Thesaurus	61
Search Terms	62
Relevant Subject Headings	64
Conducting Searches on the Internet	68
Different Types of Articles	69
Refereed Versus Non-Refereed	69
Staying Organized	70
Summary	73

(Continued)

(Continued)

Resources 74

    Common Obstacles and Practical Solutions 74

    Reflection/Discussion Questions 74

    Try It Exercises 75

    Key Terms 76

    Suggested Readings 76

    Web Links 76

> The greatest part of a writer's time is spent in reading, in order to write; a man will turn over half a library to make one book.
>
> —Samuel Johnson

Now that you have finished selecting and refining your research problem, it is time to determine how important your research problem is to others and what is already known about the problem. The way that researchers do this is to search the literature to identify prior research about the problem. One of the questions that might occur to you is, "Why do I need to know about what others think of the problem when I already know what I want to do with my study? Isn't that just going backwards?" You need to keep in mind that your master's thesis is a research study, and your goal is to do research that yields answers to problems that have not been fully answered. If you can find an answer to your research problem in the literature, then it is not necessary to do all of the work that is involved in researching a problem. Through the literature review, you will read what is known about your research problem and also learn who else shares your interest. Later, you may find it helpful to correspond with them as you progress in your research.

Although the literature review can be a time-consuming and arduous process, it is also one of the most important aspects of completing the master's thesis. Once you become familiar with the tools and strategies available to you in conducting literature reviews, you will be knowledgeable and up-to-date with historical and current studies, learn new ideas, and have a better feeling about how your study fits into the existing research (Fraenkel & Wallen, 2006).

Benefits of Conducting a Literature Review

There are several benefits of conducting a literature review. One major benefit is to know the research that has already been done related to your proposed study. This includes being familiar with the historical and seminal theories and research studies as well as the most recent cutting-edge studies. Once you are able to bridge the existing literature with your research topic, you enhance the credibility of your study and yourself as the researcher. The literature review shows that you are knowledgeable of the content related to your topic and can now apply it to new situations (McMillan, 2008). The knowledge base in disciplines such as social sciences and the humanities moves very quickly as researchers develop new theories or confirm or repudiate existing theories. Additionally, new interventions and processes are continually tested and supported through research studies. Thus, it is important for you to keep up with the research by subscribing to and reading professional journals and attending research conferences in your field so that your knowledge is not outdated.

Another benefit of conducting a literature review is to get new ideas for your research study. By reviewing the existing research related to your problem, you can learn from other researchers' successes and mistakes (and try not to repeat them). This may also help you to narrow further your research problem and focus or restate your research hypothesis (McMillan, 2008). For example, by examining a previous study's research questions, methodology, and results you can determine what has worked and not worked with a particular sample group. If a particular intervention or process was successful with a sample group (e.g., adolescents) that is similar to yours, you may want to replicate part of or the entire study. Similarly, if a particular intervention or process was successful with a sample group (e.g., children) that is very different from yours, you may want to study whether or not the same results would be obtained with your sample group (e.g., adults). Sometimes you can find a validated measurement instrument or data analysis process in the "Methods" section that would be relevant to include in your study. A great place to look for the researcher's advice is in the "Limitations" section. In this section, the researcher usually discusses some of the problems that were encountered, mistakes that were made, and suggestions for how to improve the study. Conducting a literature review prior to starting your research study prevents you from reinventing the wheel. Reading and analyzing other researchers' studies gives you new perspectives or ideas that you can incorporate into your study. Further, you learn how important your research problem is and what is already known. This will make your task of refining the research questions and methods much easier and should strengthen your study.

Finally, conducting a literature review allows you to see how your study fits into the existing literature. Remember that one of the goals of your research will be to move the field forward and add to the current knowledge base. This means either adding to, extending, or building upon previous research (McMillan, 2008). By reviewing the literature, you will be able to determine whether or not your study will fill a gap or need in the literature and/or extend what is known about a specific topic. A great place to see how your study fits into the existing literature is to read the "Recommendations for Future Research" section in the studies. This section usually offers suggestions for how future studies can extend the current research and indicates the unanswered questions related to the topic. Pay close attention to this section from the studies you find through your literature review.

Sources of Data: Primary Versus Secondary

Before you begin your literature review of the research, it is important to distinguish between the different sources of data available in the literature. The two main sources of data are primary and secondary. Each serves a different purpose, but both are important to consider in your literature review. I will discuss each type of data source briefly and how you might want to use each in your search.

Primary Sources

Primary sources are the actual or the original results of studies reported by researchers (i.e., firsthand information). These research articles are usually very detailed and include all the information about the study: research questions, sample, methodology and research design, data analysis and results, and discussion. Primary sources are typically published in professional journals in the form of articles or monographs but can also be papers presented at conferences. Basically, in order to identify a primary source, ask yourself whether the information comes directly from the person(s) who developed and conducted the research, similar to someone writing an autobiography about his or her life.

Secondary Sources

Secondary sources describe or summarize the work of others (i.e., secondhand information). These sources are typically not as descriptive or comprehensive as primary sources. Secondary sources are typically published in research journals in the form of meta-analyses, literature syntheses, research reviews, or textbooks. You can also find secondary sources in reference materials. **Reference materials** are collections of information such as encyclopedias, handbooks, indexes, and dictionaries. Listed below are sample reference materials found in most academic libraries (make sure you check to see what reference materials are available through your library).

- Multidisciplinary:
  o *Encyclopaedia Britannica Online*
  o *Oxford Reference Online*
  o *SAGE eReference*

- Business and Management:
  - *Encyclopedia of Business*
  - *The New Palgrave Dictionary of Money and Finance*
- Communications:
  - *Communication Yearbook*
  - *Language and Communication: A Cross-Cultural Encyclopedia*
- Education:
  - *Handbook of Research on Curriculum*
  - *Handbook of Research on Teacher Education*
  - *Encyclopedia of Education*
- Philosophy:
  - *Concise Routledge Encyclopedia of Philosophy*
  - *World Philosophers and Their Works*
- Sociology:
  - *Encyclopedia of Sociology*
  - *Encyclopedia of Crime and Justice*
  - *International Encyclopedia of the Social and Behavioral Sciences*

In addition, secondary sources may appear in articles published in newspapers and magazines. When identifying secondary sources, ask yourself whether the information comes from a source other than the work of the original researcher. If it comes from someone who is describing the research of others, then it is a secondary source (like a biography). Secondary sources are helpful in that they help you identify primary sources, and they illustrate the value placed on the primary sources.

There are advantages of reviewing both types of data sources. Secondary sources are actually probably the best place to start your research because they give you a broad overview of the information related to your topic, and they offer a wide range of materials to explore. Searching through secondary sources may also help you refine your research problem and questions (Fraenkel & Wallen, 2006). Starting with secondary sources is also a good way to immerse yourself in the literature (without drowning) because the articles or summaries are typically short and easy to read, so you will not be bogged down with too much specific information. For example, pretend my research topic involves immigration, particularly families who emigrate from other countries. I start my search in the secondary source *Encyclopedia of Sociology* (Borgatta & Montgomery, 2001), and type "immigration" in the quick search (see Figure 3.1 for a quick search for immigration articles).

With this search I retrieve eight articles. I select the article on "international migration," which is eight pages and provides an overview of issues and consequences related to migration, major trends and statistical patterns

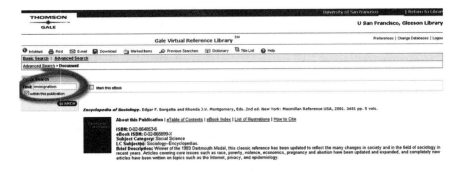

Figure 3.1   Quick search for immigration articles in the *Encyclopedia of Sociology*.

of migration, a historical perspective of immigration, and legislation related to international immigration (see Figure 3.2 for retrieval of immigration articles). Just from reading these eight pages, I now have a general context and gist of my research topic and some background information that I will need to write Chapter One, Introduction of the thesis.

However, you will need to locate primary sources to write Chapter Two, Literature Review of the thesis. The primary sources give you a full depiction of the research study, and you can synthesize the data as they relate to your specific research topic and questions. In addition, by making your own analysis, you can avoid the possibility of relying on someone else's erroneous interpretations of the results. Thus, you should use the secondary sources to help you identify critical primary sources related to the research topic. For example, at the end of the article on international immigration, there is a full page of citations for primary sources and other secondary sources. I now have leads on some specific research articles related to my topic.

Selecting Key Terms

A comprehensive review of secondary sources will also help you find primary sources through the use of key terms. **Key terms** are typically two to three words or short phrases that are fundamental to the research topic, problem, or questions and are used to refine the search process. Selecting appropriate key terms early in the search process will save you a lot of time and frustration later on. A good strategy is to use the words or phrases that are commonly used in the current literature related to the specific topic (Creswell, 2008). For example, some of the key concepts mentioned in the article on international immigration were migration stream, free migration, impelled migration, forced migration, return migration, chain migration,

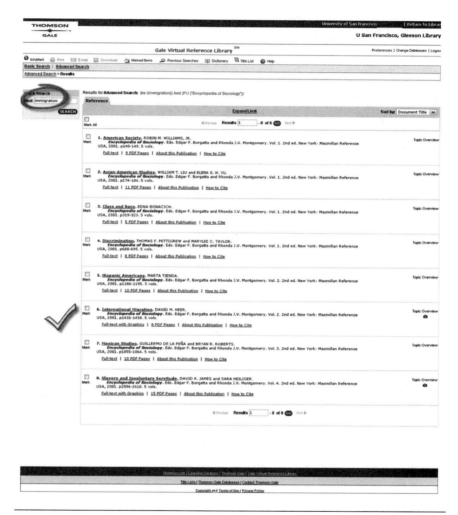

Figure 3.2   Retrieval of immigration articles in the *Encyclopedia of Sociology.*

labor migration, brain drain, illegal immigration, and undocumented immigration. However, not all these would be key terms for my search because they are not all centrally related to the research topic. Since I am particularly interested in migration related to families, I select "chain migration" as a key term and do another quick search in the *Encyclopedia of Sociology* (Borgatta & Montgomery, 2001). The results of this search provide five new articles (see Figure 3.3 for retrieval of chain migration articles), one of which is entitled "Immigration" from the *International*

Figure 3.3   Retrieval of chain migration articles in the *Encyclopedia of Sociology.*

Encyclopedia of Marriage and Family (Johnson, 2003). This article is more closely related to my research topic because of the specific focus on the consequences for families who migrate. In this six-page article, I found more key terms related to family immigration: push/pull factors, target earner, assimilation, and acculturation. At the end of the article, I also have a list of primary sources from sociology journals as well as marriage and family journals that I can use for my literature review.

Conducting Searches in Electronic Databases

One of the best places to research the literature is in electronic databases. Electronic databases are storage banks of thousands of books, articles, reports, presentations, and so on. The major benefits of an electronic database are that you can set limits on your search such as dates, language, and type of resource, and search using different descriptors. **Descriptors** are used in electronic databases to give every record a subject indexing term (i.e., controlled vocabulary or subject headings). These allow you to find resources that are very specific to your research problem. Most databases also allow you to keep a record of your search, save resources to your computer, or e-mail searches and resources to another computer; this keeps you from researching with the same key terms or losing precious findings. The database can be related to a specific field or discipline or multidisciplinary.

There are many multidisciplinary databases. A **multidisciplinary database** is an electronic database that covers different subjects rather than just one specific field or discipline. These are important databases to search through if your particular field or discipline does not have a specific database or if your research problem is related to several different fields. Some of the multidisciplinary databases, Academic OneFile, ProQuest, and Wilson OmniFile Full Text, include articles, citations, and abstracts across subjects. One advantage of these multidisciplinary databases is that they frequently offer the articles in full-text format. **Full-text** is when the entire resource is available either in a printable Web page format or a PDF format. The **PDF** format is a full-text electronic "picture" of a document and resembles how a research article actually looks in the journal. This often saves you time from searching other databases for the resource or taking a trip to the library to locate the "hard" copy. Here is a tip for searching in full-text databases—if you have a choice between selecting the printable Web page format or PDF format, always select the PDF format because with the PDF format, you have the journal's page numbers (e.g., 534–552) from the table of contents. You will also be able to provide specific page numbers for APA style citations if you are selecting quotations from the article (see Chapter 10 for APA style). Another multidisciplinary database is the Dissertation Abstracts International database. This will give you access to doctoral dissertations and master's theses across disciplines from various universities and colleges. Although you can view the citations and abstracts for free, there is often a nominal fee to obtain a full copy of a dissertation or thesis.

There are also more than 50 electronic databases available for specific fields or disciplines. Two very popular databases mentioned in Chapter Two were PsycINFO for psychology and ERIC for education. Keep in mind that there are many other electronic databases that may be specific to your field. For example, ABI/Inform is a collection of articles, abstracts, and citations related to business, management, and economics. Other examples are Sociological Abstracts and Social Science Citation Index, which are collections of citations and abstracts in sociology and other related disciplines. Listed below are sample subject databases found in most academic libraries (make sure you check to see what databases are available through your library).

- Business and Management:
  - o ABI/Inform
  - o Business and Company Resource Center
- Communication/Media Studies:
  - o Communication and Mass Media Complete
  - o Communication Abstracts
- Education:
  - o ERIC
  - o Education Full Text
- Ethnic Studies:
  - o Ethnic NewsWatch
- History:
  - o America: History and Life
  - o Historical Abstracts
- Law:
  - o LegalTrac
  - o Legal Periodicals Full Text
- Literature and Language:
  - o Literature Resource Center
  - o MLA International Bibliography
- Nursing and Health Science:
  - o CINAHL Plus With Full Text
  - o Nursing and Health Professions Premier Collection
  - o PubMed
- Politics:
  - o Worldwide Political Science Abstracts
  - o CQ Researcher
- Psychology:
  - o PsycINFO
  - o PsycARTICLES
  - o Psychology and Behavioral Sciences Collection
- Sociology:
  - o Sociological Abstracts

Although each database's search formats are slightly different, they all share common search tools and features that make it easy to navigate and switch from one database to another. In some cases, your institution's library may have a database license through a commercial vendor (e.g., EBSCOhost, Gale, and Cambridge Scientific) that allows you to search through multiple databases at the same time.

In order to show you how to conduct a basic and advanced search on an electronic database, I will use ERIC as an example since it is one of the largest databases in education and is free to the public through the U.S. Department of Education. If you use the ERIC database through the U.S. Department of Education Web site (http://www.eric.ed.gov), the interface may be different from the one you will find at your institution's library because of the different commercial vendors that license databases to libraries (see Figure 3.4 for ERIC Web site home page). For ERIC, my institution's library has a contract with EBSCOhost. However, despite the different interfaces, the underlying database and resources within it will be the same across libraries and the U.S. Department of Education Web site.

Basic Search

Since electronic databases such as ERIC are so large and may hold over a million records, the key to having a successful search is being able to narrow it so that you find the resources most relevant to your research problem. With that in mind, it is critical for you to start with at least 10 to 15 key terms that are related to your research question or problem (other key terms will be generated during your search). For example, if the research question is, "What are the most effective reading strategies

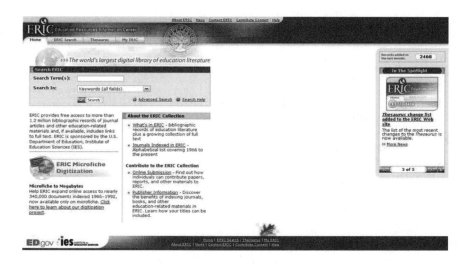

Figure 3.4   ERIC Web site search screen from the U.S. Department of Education.

for elementary students who are English learners with learning disabilities," some of the key terms could include English learners, English language learners, second language, learning disability, reading difficulty, reading disability, dyslexia, literacy, reading, reading instruction, reading strategy, reading method, and elementary. These are the key terms that you would type into the "find" field and then click the "search" button (see Figure 3.5 for the basic search screen). If you want to remove the search terms and start again, click the "clear" button. The basic search option also allows you to search for literature using two key features: limiters and expanders. I will briefly explain each of these features.

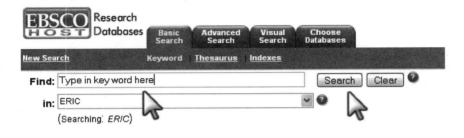

Figure 3.5   Basic search screen in ERIC (via EBSCOhost).

Limiters. If I want to narrow my search, I would use the limiters feature. The **limiters feature** narrows an electronic search by allowing the user to set specific limits, so the search results will only contain research with the chosen specific criteria. For example, you can set the following limits:

- full-text: only retrieves records that have a link to the full-text copy of the article or document (be careful with this limit because you may miss important references that require a little more searching to find)
- journal: can specify the name of the journal
- date published from: can specify the time period with beginning month/year to ending month/year
- ERIC number: can search by the number of the record (issued by ERIC)
- journal or document: can limit search to only articles published in academic journals (EJ) or ERIC documents (ED), which includes government reports, presentations at conferences, books, and so on
- intended audience: can specify who the record would be written/targeted for, such as teachers, parents, or researchers
- language: can specify the language that the record is written in, such as English, Spanish, and so forth

Because of the huge quantity of records, setting limits is a very critical step in narrowing your search. However, you have to be careful not to set too many limits at the beginning of the search because you may not get enough records or you may miss some critical records. A good strategy is to start with a few critical limits and then set more limits as needed. For example, in my search I am going to set the limits for full-text only, records from 2000 to 2008 since I want to find recent information, journal articles since I want research-based strategies, and English (see Figure 3.6 for limiters feature in basic search). However, if setting these limits means I get no or too few results, I would remove some or all of the limits.

Expanders. If I wanted to expand or broaden my search, I would use the expanders feature. The **expanders feature** is the opposite of the limiters feature and broadens an electronic search by allowing the user to combine or add key terms (see Figure 3.7 for expanders feature in basic search). If you need to reset the limiters or expanders, just click the reset button.

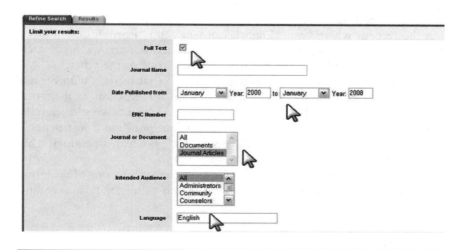

Figure 3.6   Limiters feature in ERIC basic search.

Figure 3.7   Expanders feature in ERIC basic search.

Advanced Search

Although a basic search is a good starting point, conducting an advanced search offers several additional features. The advanced search allows you to refine your research by combining multiple "find" fields using Boolean operators. **Boolean operators** are used in electronic databases and other search engines to define the relationships between words or groups of words. The advanced search also allows you to select "search fields" and find appropriate descriptors through the thesaurus. The **thesaurus** contains alphabetized descriptors that are used in the electronic database and can be browsed online or from a printed copy. I will discuss each briefly.

Boolean operators. In the advanced search, I can combine and search with multiple keywords by using Boolean operators. Three Boolean operators will be critical for your search: "and," "not," and "or." The **"and"** Boolean operator combines two or more terms so that each record contains all of the terms. For example in the study on reading strategies, I could search for the terms English learners "and" learning disabilities (see Figure 3.8 for advanced search using "and" Boolean operator). This would provide me with the records where both "English learners" and "learning disabilities" are present. In essence, using "and" between terms narrows my search because it does not include records that have only one or the other.

The **"not"** Boolean operator searches terms so that records with certain terms are excluded from the results. For example, if I search using the terms reading instruction "not" math instruction, my results would contain records where "reading instruction" is present but not "math instruction" (see Figure 3.9 for advanced search using "not" Boolean operator). This would be another way to narrow the search.

The **"or"** Boolean operator searches terms so that at least one of the terms is present in the record. For example, if I search using the terms reading

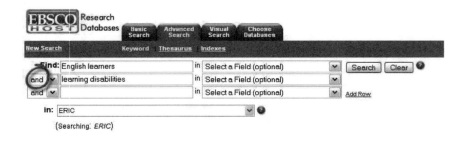

Figure 3.8   Advanced search in ERIC using "and" Boolean operator.

disabilities "or" learning disabilities, my results would contain records where either "reading disabilities" or "learning disabilities" are present (see Figure 3.10 for advanced search using "or" Boolean operator). In essence, using "or" between terms broadens my search because it retrieves records containing any of the terms included.

Symbols. In addition to Boolean operators, many electronic databases also recognize and use symbols in the search field. The two most common are the truncation and wildcard symbols. The **truncation symbol** is represented by an asterisk (*) and when used at the end of a term, it allows the user to expand the search term to include all forms of the root word. For example, if I want to search for all the forms of the word instruction, I can type "instruct*" and the search retrieves all records with instruction, instructional, instructor, and so on. The **wildcard symbol** is represented by a question mark (?) and can be used to find the correct spelling or alternative spellings of a word (each question mark placed in the word represents

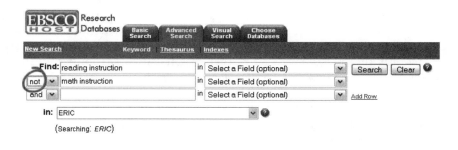

Figure 3.9   Advanced search in ERIC using "not" Boolean operator.

Figure 3.10   Advanced search in ERIC using "or" Boolean operator.

a single character, but you can have multiple question marks). For example, I can insert a question mark in the word "wom?n" and the search will include records with wom<u>a</u>n and wom<u>e</u>n. If there is a multiple spelling for an ending such as in "theat??" the records will include theat<u>re</u> and theat<u>er</u>. In both cases, the symbols have allowed me to expand my search (with relevant records)(see Figure 3.11 for advanced search using truncation and wildcard symbols).

The advanced search also gives me the option to choose the "search field" from a drop-down list. This will help to narrow the search. Some of the options are by title, author, abstract, and so forth. Unless I know the specific resource that I am looking for, I tend not to use this feature and prefer to set my limits within the limiters section or refine my keywords.

Now that I am ready to conduct an advanced search, I will use the following search terms: English "and" reading instruction "and" disab*. Then I click "search" (and cross my fingers for good luck). YIPPEE! My search gave me 93 results (see Figure 3.12 for advanced search using three search terms and Boolean operators). That is still quite a few records to review, so I could go back and revise my search terms.

Another option to narrow my findings is to review the results by subject. On the left side of the results screen in Figure 3.12, the 93 studies have been divided into subcategories (e.g., elementary education, learning disabilities). If I select one of these subcategories, I would be able to review only those results related to that specific subject from within the 93 results. For example, if I select learning disabilities, there are now 43 records to review instead of 93 (see Figure 3.13 for advanced search results by subject and search record folder). Remember that when doing searches, it is very easy to get "lost" in the process. I highly recommend that you add relevant results to your folder as you find them. This way you can have a record of your results and will be able to print, e-mail, or retrieve them later.

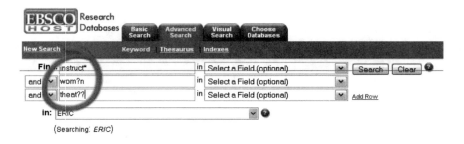

Figure 3.11   Advanced search in ERIC using truncation and wildcard symbols.

Figure 3.12   Advanced search in ERIC using three search terms and Boolean operators.

Figure 3.13   Advanced search results in ERIC by subject and search record folder.

Using the Thesaurus

Unfortunately, you can search ERIC for hours using terms that you think are most appropriate to the research question and come up with "no results were found." That is when you want to pull out your hair or change your research questions! However, there is still hope by browsing through the database's thesaurus of descriptors. The thesaurus lists the descriptors alphabetically, which can be browsed online while you are searching, or your library should have a printed copy available. By finding out the exact descriptors used by the database to describe your research problem, you can save a lot of time and also focus your review on the records most relevant to your research problem. For example, in the sample study, I am using the key term "English learners" to describe students whose native language is not English. However, ERIC may use a different descriptor such as "limited English speaking" or "English as a second language" to refer to the same population or concept. By using the ERIC descriptors in the thesaurus, I have less of a chance of missing relevant articles for my search.

Search terms. Once you select the thesaurus feature, you can enter a search term in the "browse for" field. Then you have three choices of how you want to search for the term in the thesaurus: term begins with, term contains, and relevancy ranked. I will discuss each briefly.

The **term begins with** option searches and lists the subject headings (i.e., descriptors) in alphabetical order. For example, if I type "reading strategy" in the "browse for" field, the results will indicate whether that exact term is used in the database and the order in which it appears. If "reading strategy" is not included, it will tell you where it should have been on the list (see Figure 3.14 for thesaurus search using "term begins with"). This is very

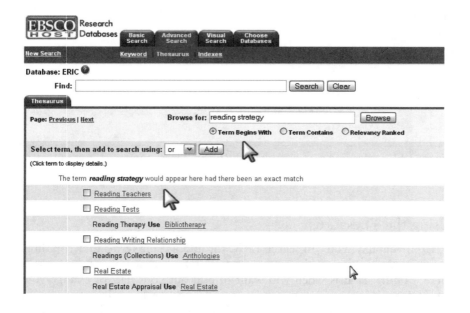

Figure 3.14   Thesaurus search in ERIC using "term begins with."

important for my search because now I know the term "reading strategy" is not an exact match with the descriptors used in the database, and I should search using a new term.

The **term contains** option shows the search term first followed by an alphabetized list of subject headings (i.e., descriptors) that contain or include it. For example, if I type "reading instruction" in the "browse for" field, the results indicate other subject headings that contain "reading instruction" (see Figure 3.15 for thesaurus search using "term contains"). This is important for my search because now I have some alternate terms to conduct my search.

The **"relevancy ranked"** option shows the search term first and then lists subject headings (i.e., descriptors) that are related to the search term displayed in order of relevance. For example, if I type "reading instruction" in the "browse for" field, the results indicate other subject headings that are related to reading instruction in a hierarchical order from most to least relevant (see Figure 3.16 for thesaurus search using "relevancy ranked"). This is important for my search because now I have the descriptors that are most relevant (or closely related) to my search term, which helps prioritize my search process.

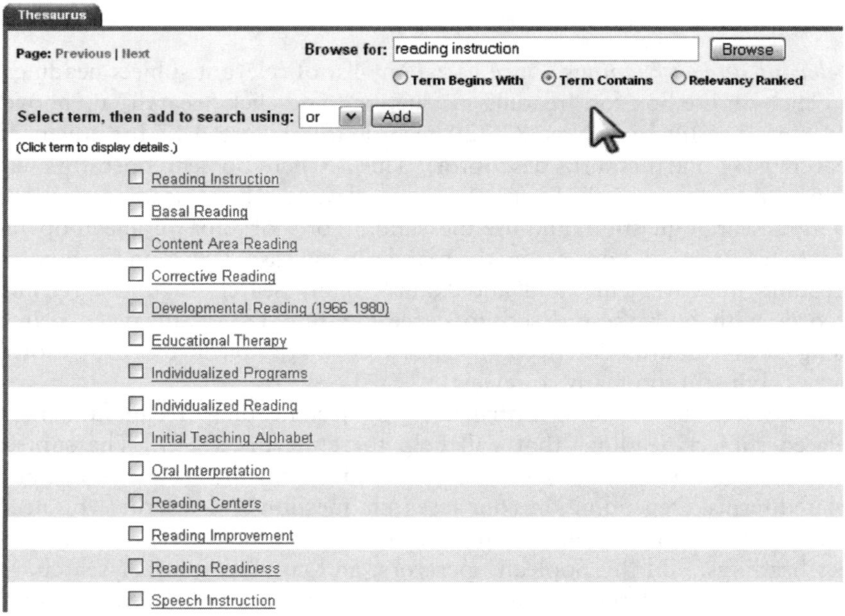

Figure 3.15   Thesaurus search in ERIC using "term contains."

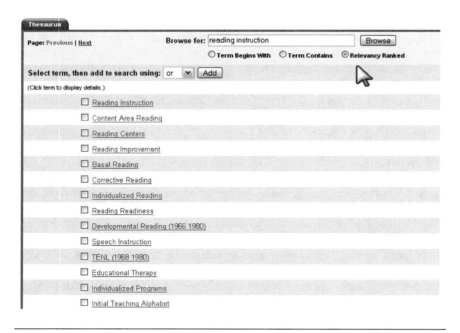

Figure 3.16   Thesaurus search in ERIC using "relevancy ranked."

Relevant subject headings. Once I have my list of relevant subject headings, if I click on the box for "reading instruction" and click "search" up above, my search results will have 22,720 records (see Figure 3.17 for advanced search using one thesaurus descriptor)! This is where Boolean operators will help to refine the search. I can select any relevant subject headings (related to my research question) and use the "and," "or," or "not" Boolean operators to either expand or narrow the search. In my case, I click on the box for "reading improvement" and add "and" to my search so that I retrieve records with both these descriptors (see Figure 3.18 for advanced search using two thesaurus descriptors). Once I do that, I retrieve 2,240 records (better, but still too many to review).

If I select the "reading instruction" subject heading, I can find more related subject headings that will help to refine my search. The subject headings are listed and categorized by broader terms, narrower terms, and related terms. Depending on your research question and whether you need to expand or narrow your search, you can click on the boxes for these subject headings, add the Boolean operators, and conduct another search. In the sample case, I need to narrow the search, so I will select "reading instruction," "remedial reading" (if I click on this subject it gives me a definition and more subject terms), and "reading strategies" and add "and" to my search (see Figure 3.19 for advanced search using three thesaurus

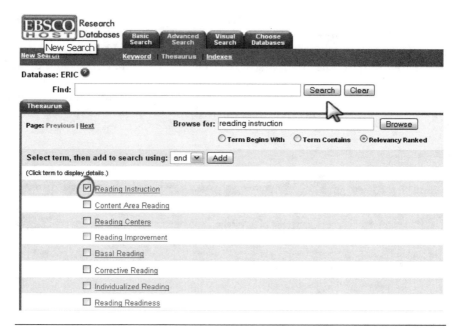

Figure 3.17   Advanced search screen in ERIC using one descriptor from the thesaurus.

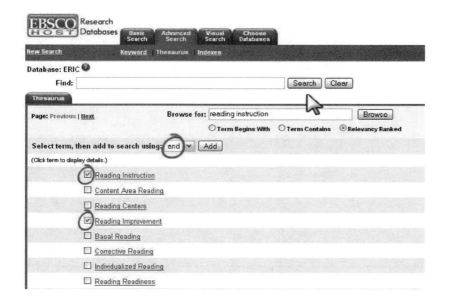

Figure 3.18   Advanced search screen in ERIC using two descriptors from the thesaurus.

descriptors). Once I do that, I retrieve 88 records, which is a manageable number of records to review. More important, the results should be related to my research problem (see Figure 3.20 for search results screen).

In order to select the articles most relevant to my research problem, I do a cursory review of the titles and authors, and note whether the record is a research article from an educational journal (EJ) or an educational document (ED). Based on these three characteristics, I would either add them to my

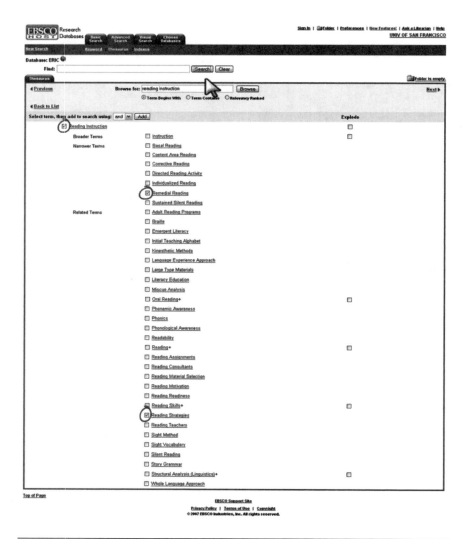

Figure 3.19   Advanced search screen in ERIC using three descriptors from the thesaurus.

folder for a more detailed review later or click on the title to get more information about the record. The record screen gives me very critical information about the study: the title, authors, name of the journal (including the volume, issue, and page numbers), the ERIC descriptors, the abstract, and the accession number (identification number assigned by ERIC) (see Figure 3.21 for

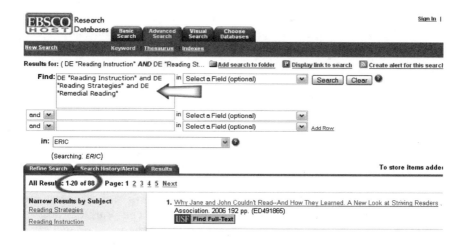

Figure 3.20   Search results screen in ERIC using three descriptors from the thesaurus.

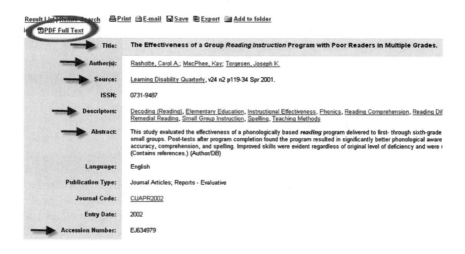

Figure 3.21   Sample record screen for ERIC journal article.

sample record screen for a journal article). In addition, the record tells me whether or not the full-text article (PDF) is available. With the PDF full-text choice, I can view/print the article, save, or e-mail the article to another computer. If the full-text article is not available, I will have to search in another database or the library's collection for the article. As you are researching, it might be a good idea to keep a notebook handy to keep track of articles that you do not have immediate access to in full-text. You should also note authors who have written a few articles related to your research problem (in case you want to contact them for more information), or articles that you may need to search for in other databases, on the Internet, or order through interlibrary loan. **Interlibrary loan** is a service provided by libraries whereby a user of one library can borrow books, acquire photocopies of articles in journals, and so on that are owned by another library (sometimes there is a fee involved).

Conducting Searches on the Internet

Conducting searches on the Internet offers advantages and disadvantages over conducting searches on electronic databases. The search process is similar to the electronic database in that once you type in a key word, the search engine will find Web sites and Web pages that are related to your key word. Some advantages of the Internet search are that it is fast, easy, and accessible anytime. In addition, the information is relatively current, and you will get a wide variety of resources. One disadvantage of the Internet search is that since you have so much information and it is not well-organized, it may be more time-consuming and difficult to find relevant information. To be both effective and efficient in searching the Internet, you must develop rather sophisticated search techniques. An additional disadvantage is that the information may not be of high quality or reliable (Creswell, 2008; Fraenkel & Wallen, 2006; Mertler & Charles, 2008). For example, often there is no author listed on the Web site, so it is unclear whether or not the article was written by an "expert" in the field. Additionally, there is no way to check whether or not the article was externally reviewed.

However, sometimes the Internet is the easiest or the only way to retrieve articles that are listed in the electronic database but not available through the library. If you want to use the Internet for research, some of the best search engines are Google (http://www.google.com), Yahoo!Search (http://search.yahoo.com), and Ask.com. (http://www.ask.com) ("Recommended Search Engines," n.d.). Typically, I use the Internet search engines only when I am looking for a specific reference.

There are also several Web sites that are easy to use, have a large collection of research documents (some charge a fee to access the articles), and are organized by subject areas. Some popular Web sites for research are IngentaConnect (http://www.ingentaconnect.com), the Librarians' Internet Index (http://lii.org), and The Internet Public Library (http://www.ipl.org). These would be particularly helpful at the beginning of a search or if you do not have access to electronic databases. If you do retrieve information or documents from the Internet, keep a record of the Web site or Web page address and the date that you retrieved the information. You will need these for APA style citations and references (see Chapter 10 for APA style).

Different Types of Articles

As you continue your search in electronic databases or through the Internet, you will encounter different types of articles. This includes theoretical articles, empirical research studies, position papers, literature syntheses, and meta-analyses. A **literature synthesis** (also referred to as a research synthesis) is a type of article in which the results of several related studies are compared and summarized. A **meta-analysis** research study is one in which the results of several related studies are analyzed and reported with statistical measures (e.g., effect sizes). Each of the different types of articles serves a different purpose. For example, if I were looking for a theoretical rationale or basis for my research study, then I would want to search for articles that discuss an existing theory or suggest a new theory (Galvan, 2006). If I want to review research that is based on systematic observation, I would search for empirical research studies (very critical for writing Chapter Two in your thesis). If I want an article that gives a broad overview or synthesis in a particular area such as "reading strategies," I would search for a meta-analysis or literature synthesis on that specific subject. Finally, if I want support for a particular position or to quote an expert's opinion on a particular topic, I would search for position/opinion papers.

Refereed Versus Non-Refereed

As a consumer (in this case of research), you always want to make sure that you get the best quality. Thus, when deciding on which research articles to include in your thesis and particularly the literature review, it is important to keep in mind that like most consumer products, there is a hierarchy of quality involved. A natural tendency is to assume that if something has been printed in a journal or published on a Web site, the article is of high quality. Unfortunately, this is not always the case. In research, the main stamp of quality is refereed. A **refereed** (also referred to as peer-reviewed) article has been submitted for external review by a panel of reviewers before being published. This means that when author(s) send in their manuscripts, the manuscripts are reviewed by the journal's editor as well as other "experts" in the field. Often, the reviewers are "blind" to the identity of the author(s) of the manuscript, which reduces the chance of bias. This panel then decides whether the manuscript should be accepted or revised for publication, or rejected for publication in the journal (Creswell, 2008; McMillan, 2008). As the acceptance rate for most refereed journals is typically below 50 percent, this process ensures that only the most rigorous and high-quality research is accepted for publication. A **non-refereed** article is one that did not go through an external review process before being published. With that in mind, it is best for you to search in research journals that use a refereed review process (most databases will allow you to set this as a limit).

Staying Organized

One of the most important strategies during the search process is to stay organized. After all, you may end up with 40 or 50 articles, books, and documents by the time you are done searching. This means keeping track of your search records, saving, printing, and/or e-mailing relevant records, and also creating an organizational system. The first step in creating an organizational system is to develop a physical organizational system. First, designate a file cabinet drawer or buy a large portable plastic file box with dividers. Then, print out a copy of each article (you may do this electronically on your computer if you prefer). Next, decide how you want to file the articles. If you file alphabetically by the author's last name, this will be an easy way to retrieve the articles (as long as you can remember who wrote which article). You can also file the articles by date of publication if you are interested in a chronological or historical analysis. Finally, you can group the articles by themes/categories based on specific common attributes (e.g., topic, sample, intervention, methods). I prefer this method because it helps me to conceptually organize the body of literature and will help facilitate the writing process later on. Remember that if the article or information comes from an electronic source (i.e., Web site) you will need to record the Web site address and the date that you retrieved the information from the Internet (keep a log). After you have selected your method for physical organization, it is time to organize the information within the articles.

Rarely will you find an article that is completely relevant to your research problem or study. More often, you will find that you will use specific parts from different articles to support your ideas. Pulling together the studies in a literature review is very much like putting together a complex puzzle (with some missing pieces). Thus, how you organize the information within the studies is very important. You need to have a system that is efficient in terms of recording critical information but also easy to access for retrieval purposes. One method that I find helpful is using different color highlighters as I read to code different types of information (e.g., yellow = problems, green = possible solutions, orange = background information, pink = definitions).

One popular method of organizing the information within the articles is abstracting. **Abstracting** is a method of organizing information about an article that includes a brief summary and selected critical information about the study (Creswell, 2008). This is different from copying and pasting the author's abstract, which does not always include the most critical information about the study (from your perspective). The summary should be brief and does not have to be in complete narrative form. However, the abstract should contain the following components: "research problem, research questions or hypotheses, data collection procedure, results of the study" (Creswell, 2008, p. 105). Once you have abstracted the studies in your collection, it will be much easier to see the *relationships* between them. This is a critical step in the organization process because ultimately in writing the literature review, you will need to make the explicit connections between the studies that you select and how they relate to your proposed study.

To help you find the relationships and connections between the studies, the next step is to create a literature matrix. A **literature matrix** is an organizational tool such as a table, chart, or flow chart to display the relationship or common attributes among multiples studies. The purpose is to show the relationships between the studies, so use the format that is best for you. For example, for my "reading instruction" study, I may want to group all the studies related to reading instruction for English learners together. Then, another group would be the studies of reading instruction for students with learning disabilities. Next, a third group would be studies of reading instruction for students who are English learners and have learning difficulties, and so on (see Figure 3.22 for a sample literature matrix). By grouping the studies together into subgroups, this will allow you to see if you have overlaps or gaps in your pool of studies (which may require you to conduct another search). I realize that this may seem like a lot of hard work (and it is), but believe me, it will save you time later. This process will also make it easier for you to organize your thoughts about the research problem, conceptualize your research questions and study, and write the literature review in the thesis.

Reading Intervention Categories	Direct Instruction Approaches	Graphic Organizers (Mapping)	Strategic Instruction Model	Collaborative Strategic Reading	Story Grammar Instruction	Reciprocal Teaching	Peer-Assisted Learning Strategies (PALS)
Authors, Year	1. Carr & Thompson, 1998 2. Malone & Mastropieri, 2001 3. Gajria & Salvia, 2000	1. Boyle, 1999 2. Gardill & Jitendra, 2001 3. Idol & Croll, 1987	1. Clark, Deshler, Schumaker, Alley, & Warner, 1982 2. Schumaker, Deshler, Alley, Warner, & Denton, 1982 3. Schumaker & Deshler, 1988	1. Klingner, Vaughn, & Schumm, 1998 2. Klinger & Vaughn, 1998 3. Vaughn, Chard, Bryant, Coleman, Tyler, Thompson, & Kouzekanan, 2000	1. Gurney, Gersten, Dimino, & Carnine, 1990 2. Carnine & Kinder, 1985	1. Palinscar & Brown, 1984	1. Fuchs, Fuchs, & Kazdan, 1999 2. Fuchs, Fuchs, Mathes, & Simmons, 1997
Type of Intervention	1. Activate prior knowledge 2. Paragraph summary & self-monitoring 3. Brown & Day's five summarization rules	1. Cognitive mapping (main idea and details) 2. Story maps 3. Story maps	1. Visual imagery & self-questioning 2. Multipass (textbooks) 3. Paraphrasing	1. CSR: Preview, click & clunk, gist, wrap-up 2. Reciprocal teaching + CL and cross-age tutoring 3. CL vs. partner reading	1. Story grammar instruction 2. Story grammar vs. visual imagery	1. Reciprocal teaching: question, summarize, clarify, prediction	1. PALS: Partner reading, paragraph shrinking, prediction relay

Figure 3.22 Sample literature matrix for reading interventions.

Summary

Researching the literature related to your research problem is a giant step in the thesis process. As you immerse yourself in the literature, you will be inundated with resources, so remember to be very critical and selective keeping only those directly related to your research problem. In the next chapter, I will discuss the ethics of conducting research and how to prepare a research study application for review by the Institutional Review Board for the Protection of Human Subjects (IRBPHS). Here is a summary of the most critical points from Chapter 3:

- The major benefits of conducting a literature review are to know the research that has already been done that relates to your proposed study, learn from other researchers' successes and mistakes, and determine whether or not your study will fill a gap or need in the literature and/or extend what is known about a specific topic.

- Primary sources are the actual or the original results of studies reported by the researcher(s) (i.e., firsthand information).

- Secondary sources describe or summarize the work of others (i.e., secondhand information).

- Key terms are typically two to three words or short phrases that are fundamental to the research topic, problem, or questions.

- The major benefits of an electronic database are that you can search using different descriptors (e.g., author, title, subject) and set limits on your search such as dates, language, and type of resource.

- Electronic databases and other search engines often use Boolean operators "and," "not," and "or" to define the relationships between words or groups of words.

- The thesaurus contains alphabetized descriptors that can be browsed online while you are searching, or may be obtained in "hard" copy from your library.

- Disadvantages of an Internet search include that it may be more time-consuming and difficult to find relevant information or the information may not be of high quality or reliable.

- The term refereed refers to a "quality control" process that includes an external review of the research manuscript.

- One popular method of organizing the information within the articles is abstracting, that is, writing a brief summary about the article (usually a research study) that includes selected critical information.

Resources

 ### Common Obstacles and Practical Solutions

1. Since we live in a world of information overload, a common problem that students face at this stage is feeling overwhelmed and not knowing where to start looking for research. Words that come to mind are, "Lost in cyberspace." If you have a general sense of your topic and are familiar with the Internet, search engines would be a good place to start. If you have a good sense of your research topic, I recommend searching within electronic databases that are specific to your field or discipline (as this may save you some time). If you feel completely "lost in cyberspace," I recommend setting up an appointment with the reference librarian at your institution to help you get started. Remember that the search for research articles is like a treasure hunt; it is time-consuming and continual (finding one source usually leads to another).

2. Once you find the research articles, a common obstacle that students face is organizing all of them. Words that come to mind are, "My floor is covered in research articles!" From the very beginning, it is really important to set up an organization system and stick to it (everything should have a home). Set up a filing system that you are comfortable with (not piles on the floor) and start categorizing your research articles. This will cut down the time later when you need to refer to a specific article or find missing references.

 ### Reflection/Discussion Questions

As you begin to find research articles, it is important to consider how and why you are conducting the literature review and the types of sources that you will rely on. For example, the research literature can help to identify existing gaps and weaknesses around a specific topic. In other cases, the research literature can be used to rationalize or justify using different components in an intervention. The following reflection/discussion questions will help you determine how you want to approach the literature review and the advantages and disadvantages of different types of sources.

1. What is a literature review and why is it an important part of the research process?

2. What are the major benefits of conducting a literature review before planning and implementing the study?

3. What are the differences between primary and secondary sources? What are the advantages and disadvantages of using each type of source?

When is it appropriate to use one or the other during the search process? Brainstorm and list critical primary and secondary sources in your field or discipline.

 ## Try It Exercises

The intent of the following exercises is to help you get started with your literature search. In Activity One, you will identify potential databases and Web sites where you can find research and/or information related to your field or discipline area. In Activity Two, you will use key terms and an advanced search to find empirically based research articles. In Activity Three, you will write a short abstract based on one of the research articles.

1. Activity One: For this activity, focus on the resources specific to your field or discipline area.

- Through your institution's library, locate at least five electronic databases that have information related to your field or discipline area.
- Through an Internet search engine, locate at least five organization-sponsored Web sites that have information related to your field or discipline area.
- Through an Internet search engine, locate at least three national or state-sponsored (e.g., U.S. Department of Education) Web sites that have information related to your field or discipline area.

2. Activity Two: For this activity, focus on your chosen research problem as you conduct a literature search.

- List 15 key terms that can be used for your literature search.
- Conduct an advanced search (using limits and Boolean operators) in one of the electronic databases from Activity One. You may use the thesaurus to help you find the descriptors if necessary. Remember to keep track of the key terms that you use and your search record.
- Select five empirically based research articles related to your research problem (make sure at least two come from refereed journals).

3. Activity Three: For this activity, focus on one of the selected research articles selected in Activity Two.

- Write an abstract for one of the research articles that includes the following information about the study: (1) research problem/question, (2) research design, (3) methods (e.g., sample group, intervention, measurement instruments, data collection, data analysis), and (4) results/findings.

Key Terms

- abstracting
- and (Boolean operator)
- Boolean operators
- descriptors
- expanders feature
- full-text
- interlibrary loan
- key terms
- limiters feature
- literature matrix
- literature synthesis
- meta-analysis
- multidisciplinary
- non-refereed

- not (Boolean operator)
- or (Boolean operator)
- PDF
- primary sources
- refereed
- reference materials
- relevancy ranked
- secondary sources
- term begins with
- term contains
- thesaurus
- truncation symbol
- wildcard symbol

 ## Suggested Readings

- Granello, D. H. (2001). Promoting cognitive complexity in graduate written work: Using Bloom's taxonomy as a pedagogical tool to improve literature reviews. *Counselor Education and Supervision, 40*(4), 292–307.
- Lomand, T. C. (2007). *Social science research* (5th ed.). Glendale, CA: Pyrczak.

Web Links

- Ask.com Search Engine
  http://www.ask.com/

- Education Resources Information Center (ERIC)
  http://www.eric.ed.gov/

- Google Search
  http://www.google.com

- IngentaConnect
  www.ingentaconnect.com

- The Internet Public Library
  http://www.ipl.org/

- Librarians' Internet Index
  http://lii.org/

- Yahoo!Search
  http://search.yahoo.com

4

Conducting Ethical Research

Background and History	79
Nuremberg Code	79
Thalidomide	80
Tuskegee Syphilis Study	80
Legal and Ethical Principles	81
Belmont Report	81
Respect for Persons	81
Beneficence	82
Justice	83
Federal Regulations	84
Common Rule	84
Institutional Review Board (IRB)	85
IRB Application Process	85
Preparing the IRB Research Plan	86
Ethical Behavior	90
Plagiarism	90
Summary	91
Resources	92
Common Obstacles and Practical Solutions	92
Reflection/Discussion Questions	93
Try It Exercises	93
	(Continued)

(Continued)

Key Terms   94

Suggested Readings   95

Web Links   95

I have learned two lessons in my life: first, there are no sufficient literary, psychological, or historical answers to human tragedy, only moral ones. Second, just as despair can come to one another only from other human beings, hope, too, can be given to one only by other human beings.

—Elie Wiesel

You might be wondering why it is necessary to include a chapter on ethical practices in research in a book on writing a master's thesis. Is it not obvious that when conducting a study involving human subjects, the researcher would have to disclose the purpose and procedures of the study to the participants and get their permission? Doesn't the researcher know that he or she must treat the participants with respect, minimize their risk of harm, and protect their rights for confidentiality? Unfortunately, history tells us that this has not always been the case. At times, mistakes are made due to lack of experience or failing to think about the unintentional consequences of involving human subjects in research. The inexperienced researcher may not have received instruction on the ethical practices of conducting research, been insensitive to the circumstances that arise in conducting research, or their research may have been a noninvasive intervention. Unfortunately, past situations have indicated that researchers have also intentionally deceived participants (at great personal cost) without their knowledge or consent. When conducting research of any kind, there is always the possibility that you will encounter ethical issues. Thus, it is especially important early in your research career that you understand the policies governing research with human subjects and develop an ethical perspective that will guide your research. Central to doing research is ensuring that you take the necessary steps to protect the rights of the human subjects who consent to participate in your study. This chapter will provide you with an overview of the history of experiments with human subjects, legal and ethical standards related to the treatment of human subjects, and prevailing policies that govern the research you will be conducting for your master's thesis.

Background and History

Although the answers to the questions presented above were meant to be evident, it is important to recognize that until 1974, there were no regulations or standards with regard to the treatment of human subjects in research studies. This meant that physicians could conduct harmful and inhumane medical experiments on patients without the patients' knowledge or consent. Drug companies could manufacture and market unsafe drugs to the public that had not been approved by the Food and Drug Administration (FDA). Information about a life-threatening illness and medical treatment could be denied to patients even when a cure was available. Sadly, these are not hypothetical situations but actual events that took place in the history of research. You might question the relevance of these practices to your field of study or your proposed research. However, sometimes it is hard to distinguish between research that clearly places subjects at risk and those that might. Pharmaceutical and medical research may be more risky than social science research, but there is an element of risk in all research. Unfortunately, it was not until history revealed research practices that placed subjects in very serious harm did the public and in turn policymakers address the need for laws and polices to govern all research conducted with human subjects. Three of the most well-known abuses of human experimentation were in the Nazi concentration camps during World War II, the use of the thalidomide drug by pregnant women, and the Tuskegee Syphilis Study on African American males. Each one will be discussed briefly, highlighting their implications for conducting ethical research today.

Nuremberg Code

One of the most atrocious abuses of human experimentation occurred during World War II by the German Nazi regime. During this time, inhumane medical experiments were imposed on thousands of prisoners in concentration camps without their consent or knowledge. As a result of these experiments, all of the human subjects suffered tremendous physical and psychological harm, and most either died or were permanently crippled ("History of Research Ethics," n.d.). At the end of the war, the U.S. military courts held the Doctors Trial, the first of the Subsequent Nuremberg Trials, against 23 defendants (20 were doctors). In 1947, 16 of the defendants were found guilty and either received death sentences or prison sentences ranging from 10 years to life imprisonment ("The Nuremberg Trials," n.d.).

As a result of the trials, the Nuremberg Code was established. The **Nuremberg Code** is a set of standards of ethical medical behavior that all physicians should adhere to when involving human subjects in medical experiments (see *Resources* for a Web link to the text of the Nuremberg

Code). One of the main standards of the Nuremberg Code is voluntary informed consent. **Voluntary informed consent** exists when a person has the capacity to give consent and receives sufficient and accurate information about the study (e.g., purpose, methods, risks, benefits) to make an informed decision to participate. The second main standard is avoiding all unnecessary physical and mental suffering and pain. This is to ensure that subjects are protected against injury, disability, or death. The third standard is to weigh the risks against the expected benefits. This is to ensure that the study will result in benefits to society but not at the expense of causing harm to the subjects. Although the Nuremberg Code was not a legal mandate, it was the first international document that supported voluntary participation and informed consent.

Thalidomide

The use of the thalidomide drug was another horrific abuse of human experimentation. In the late 1950s and early 1960s, thalidomide was sold and prescribed to pregnant women to abate symptoms of nausea and sleeplessness in over 40 countries, especially in Europe. The drug was not approved by the FDA in the United States since the side effects on humans were still unknown. Tragically, over 10,000 babies were born with severe birth defects (stunted limbs or no limbs at all) due to the effects of thalidomide (U.S. Department of Health and Human Services [USDHHS], 2005b). This disaster changed how drugs are tested, manufactured, and sold in the United States. In 1962, Congress passed the Kefauver-Harris Drug Amendments Act. The **Kefauver-Harris Drug Amendments** increased the regulatory powers of the FDA so that drug manufacturers had to prove that their drugs were safe and effective before marketing and selling them to the public. The act also required that subjects from medical studies give their informed consent (USDHHS, 2005a).

Tuskegee Syphilis Study

The Tuskegee Syphilis Study was another tragic example of the abuse of experimentation with human subjects. In 1932, the U.S. Public Health Service and the Tuskegee Institute in Alabama began a study to monitor the effects of untreated syphilis on 600 low-income and mostly illiterate African American males (399 had syphilis and 201 did not). The men did not give informed consent to participate in the study and were not told that they had syphilis. Instead, they were told that they were being treated for "bad blood," and in exchange for their participation, the men received free medical exams, meals, and burial insurance (USDHHS, n.d.). Although the study was supposed to last for only six months, it continued for 40 years, even after a cure for syphilis (penicillin) was made available in 1947. The men in the study were not offered the penicillin by the researchers and were even prevented from receiving treatment elsewhere. As a result, many of the men unnecessarily died of syphilis during the study. The study was finally stopped in 1972 because of a leak to the press, and reparations for the subjects (and eventually their families) were started in 1974.

Legal and Ethical Principles

Ultimately, the abuses in research from the Tuskegee Syphilis Study attracted the attention of the media, which led Congress to pass the **National Research Act of 1974 (Public Law 93-348).** The National Research Act created the **National Commission for the Protection of Human Subjects of Biomedical and Behavioral Research,** the first national public group whose responsibility it was to identify a set of basic ethical principles and guidelines for conducting biomedical and behavioral research involving human subjects. The commission fulfilled this responsibility by preparing and releasing the Belmont Report in 1979. The **Belmont Report** is a summary of the basic ethical principles and guidelines for conducting research with human subjects. Following is a summary of the three fundamental ethical principles of the Belmont Report (see the *Resources* section for a Web link to the full report).

Belmont Report

In the Belmont Report, the commission identified three fundamental ethical principles for conducting research with human subjects: (1) respect for persons, (2) beneficence, and (3) justice. These principles have implications for how researchers conduct ethical research today ("Ethical Principles," n.d.). I will discuss each one briefly.

Respect for persons. The first principle in the Belmont Report, **respect for persons,** includes "two ethical convictions: first that individuals should be treated as autonomous agents, and second, that persons with diminished autonomy are entitled to protection," (USDHHS, 1979, Part B, ¶ 2). The first ethical conviction requires that researchers acknowledge that people are autonomous in their opinions and are capable of making and acting on their own choices. However, with respect to research involving human subjects, participants must be provided with adequate information to give their informed consent.

In order to give informed consent, the participants (or their guardians if they are minors) must be fully aware of the purpose and procedures of the study. Thus, researchers should avoid using any methods in the study that involve deception. **Deception** occurs when the researcher omits information about the study or gives false information. If participants are deceived about the purpose or procedures used in the study, even if they agree to participate, they are not giving their informed consent (Drew, Hardman, & Hosp, 2008). Once they are fully informed about the study, then individuals can voluntarily agree to participate (rather than be coerced). Informed consent also means that the participants can voluntarily withdraw from the study at any time, without penalty or negative repercussions (Orcher, 2005). Thus, at a minimum, researchers should disclose information about the study in a language that is comprehensible to the participants in order to obtain their voluntary informed consent. Here are some basic information points that should be disclosed:

- Who is conducting the research and how they can be contacted before, during, and after the study;
- The purpose of the study;
- The potential risks involved; and
- The benefits of the study.

The second ethical conviction of respect for persons refers to protecting those individuals who are not fully autonomous because of age, illness, injury, disability, or in restricted settings such as prison. In research, these individuals are commonly referred to as vulnerable populations. **Vulnerable populations** are children, pregnant women, prisoners, or others who may need additional protection from harm, depending on the risks involved.

Beneficence. The second principle in the Belmont Report, **beneficence,** refers to two general rules: "(1) do not harm; and (2) maximize possible benefits, and minimize possible harms" (USDHHS, 1979, Part B, ¶ 7). The first rule, "do not harm," places an obligation on researchers to guarantee the participants' well-being throughout the study and not to injure or endanger, physically or psychologically, their human subjects, especially vulnerable populations. The best time to examine the proposed research relative to potential risk to participants is early when you are framing your research questions. If you wait until you have progressed into the design of your study, you may find that major changes will be required to eliminate or minimize serious risks. By examining the potential risks early, you save time and also increase your feasibility to conduct the study. Here are some questions to ask yourself to make sure you are not proposing a study that may be harmful to participants:

- Is there potential for the participants to be harmed or be at risk for harm in any way (e.g., physically, psychologically, emotionally, socially, or academically)?

- If so, could I redesign my study so that I could protect the participants from harm but still get the information that I need to answer my research questions?

- Do I need to change my research questions to ensure my participants' well-being?

- Will this research require costly safeguards that require external support?

Sometimes, in order to benefit participants and society at large, it may be necessary to place subjects at risk for harm. Thus, the second rule, "maximize possible benefits, and minimize possible harms," refers to the cost-benefit analysis that researchers must consider when planning and conducting a study. In a **cost-benefit analysis,** researchers must weigh the potential benefits against the anticipated risks and decide whether the benefits are so great that they justify putting subjects at a certain level of risk or the risks are so high that the benefits are not worth the potential harm to subjects. Fortunately, most typical research conducted in educational settings or other agencies involves little or no risk of harm to the participants (Fraenkel & Wallen, 2006). Here are some questions to analyze the cost-benefit ratio when designing your thesis study:

- Do the potential benefits outweigh the anticipated risks?

- Will the information that will be gathered as a result of the study be worth the potential risks placed on subjects?

- Have I designed the study in such a way that the risks have been minimized and the benefits maximized as much as possible?

- Have I explored all potential risks?

Justice. The third principle in the Belmont Report, **justice,** refers to fairness and equity in the selection of participants and the distribution of benefits. To meet this third principle, researchers must first consider if they are recruiting the participants for their study in a fair and equitable manner, making sure not to exploit any one segment of the population. The three historical cases of abuse in human research mentioned earlier were examples where extreme harm was caused to vulnerable populations (e.g., concentration camp prisoners, pregnant women, poor and ill African American men). Thus, researchers need to be careful not to systematically select their participants based on characteristics such as availability. For your thesis study, make sure you are not selecting subjects because they are in a vulnerable position in society (e.g., low income, children) but rather because they are the group most directly related to your research questions.

The second consideration for justice is the fair and equitable distribution of benefits. From the historical examples mentioned, the human subjects in the studies were not the recipients of the benefits of the studies—they were merely the guinea pigs to benefit others. In order to meet the justice principle, researchers must ensure that the results of the study provide benefits equitably. For example, a new drug to prevent diabetes should not be tested on low-income individuals and then once found to be effective, made available only to those with the financial means to afford the drug. For your thesis study, consider whether there are fair and equitable benefits for the participants in your study as well as the larger population that they represent.

In addition to the ethical principles laid out in the Belmont Report, researchers in different fields and disciplines have developed and adopted their own ethical standards specific to the type of research that is conducted with human subjects. For example, the American Educational Research Association (AERA) has a set of ethical standards that focuses on educational research that often involves children and other vulnerable populations (see the *Resources* for a Web link to the AERA ethical standards). The American Psychological Association (APA) also has a set of general principles and ethical standards for psychologists referred to as the Ethical Principles of Psychologists and Code of Conduct (see the *Resources* for a Web link to the APA ethical principles). As a professional, it is important for you to know the ethical standards and principles that guide your field or discipline, especially as it relates to research with human subjects.

Federal Regulations

The three ethical principles in the Belmont Report served as the foundation for the development of federal regulations in 1981 by the USDHHS for the protection of human subjects in research studies. In 1991, the core regulations were formally adopted as the Federal Policy for the Protection of Human Subjects, known as the Common Rule.

Common Rule

The **Common Rule** is a federal policy for the protection of human subjects followed by most of the federal departments and agencies that sponsor research with human subjects (e.g., Department of Education, Department of Justice, Environmental Protection Agency, National Science Foundation, Consumer Product Safety Commission) (USDHHS, 1991). Three of the central requirements in the Common Rule are: (1) any research supported or conducted by any federal department or agency must ensure compliance with the policy; (2) researchers must obtain written informed consent; and (3) institutions must have an Institutional Review Board (IRB) in place to review and approve research studies. The Common Rule also includes three subparts, B through D, that have additional protections for research that involve pregnant women, fetuses, neonates, prisoners, and children as human subjects (see the *Resources* section for a Web link to the full regulation).

In the next section, I will focus on the IRB procedures since this has major implications for much thesis research.

Institutional Review Board (IRB)

As mentioned, all institutions of higher education that receive federal funds (for research or scholarships) must have in place an Institutional Review Board (IRB). In compliance with the Common Rule, the IRB committee is made up of at least five members, representing a diverse group of expertise and backgrounds (e.g., from different schools and colleges within the university). The major role of the IRB is to ensure that all research with human subjects conducted by persons affiliated with the institution (including administrators, faculty, staff, and students) is done ethically and in compliance with federal regulations. In doing so, the IRB adheres to the three principles of the Belmont Report: respect for persons, beneficence, and justice. To apply these principles, the IRB requires that researchers (including undergraduate and graduate students) submit an IRB application for approval. A typical **IRB application** consists of the research plan, a cover letter to the participants, an informed consent letter, all of the measurement instruments that will be used in the study, and your chairperson's signature (it will be his or her responsibility to ensure that you conduct the research in an ethical manner). Your IRB committee may require additional documentation, so make sure you check their requirements.

IRB Application Process

In this section, I will describe the typical IRB application process at a university. Although each IRB committee follows the Common Rule, the actual application process may vary, so it is critical for you to find out the IRB procedures and guidelines at your institution (there should be an IRB manual or Web site available). Typically, universities offering graduate degrees have a staff with responsibilities for assisting researchers in fulfilling their obligations in meeting the requirements related to doing research involving human subjects. I suggest that you meet with a representative of this office early in your thesis planning process. They should also have a training program that you can complete online that will be helpful as well. If you have additional questions about the IRB procedures, you should discuss these with your chairperson and/or the IRB chairperson at your institution.

The IRB application process begins with the initial application. Once the IRB receives the application, it is processed and sent out for review to a member of the IRB committee. In some complicated cases, a secondary IRB member may also review the application. Once the committee members have approved the application, the IRB chairperson must give his or her final approval. This process can take anywhere from three to four weeks with a complete application to six to eight weeks for an inadequate or incomplete application. You should keep in mind that the IRB committee reviews applications from faculty, staff, and students from all over the university, so there will be times when they have a high volume of applications, especially at the beginning and end of the semester (this may cause longer process times). Thus, it is recommended that you start the IRB process well in advance of your anticipated research start date. The IRB approval must be granted *before* any recruitment procedures are enacted, contact with potential participants is made, or data are collected. Getting IRB approval before starting any component of your study is extremely important because the IRB does not retroactively approve applications, and if you start your study without IRB approval, you may not be able to use any of the data that were collected or complete your study. Once you receive approval from the IRB committee, you typically have 12 months to complete your data collection involving human subjects. However, there are processes to renew the IRB application if you need additional time or to modify it if you need to make changes to your study. In the next section, I will describe how to prepare the research plan for the IRB application.

Preparing the IRB Research Plan

The **IRB research plan** describes the need for the study and the research design and may include the following sections: (1) background and rationale, (2) sample, (3) recruitment, (4) consent process, (5) procedures, (6) potential risk to subjects, (7) minimization of potential risk, (8) potential benefits, (9) costs to subjects, (10) reimbursement/compensation to subjects, and (11) confidentiality of records (Institutional Review Board, 2001). Although there are many sections to the research plan, you want to be as succinct as possible and use non-jargon language. I will discuss what you need to include in each of these sections; see Appendix A for a sample initial IRB application that shows an example of each of the components.

1. Background and rationale: In this section, provide the background literature related to the research problem. Include citations from primary and secondary sources to support your claims. You should also provide the rationale (i.e., justification) for the necessity of the study. Adding statistical data (e.g., test scores, crime rates) to show the magnitude of the problem will strengthen the rationale. In addition, describe the purpose of the study and explain how your study is related to the research problem. This section shows the IRB committee that you have done the literature research related to the problem and that your study will make an impact on the problem.

2. Description of sample: In this section, describe the sample group (referred to as participants) in the study. The description should include how many subjects will be in the study and the subjects' age/grade level,

gender, ethnicity, and any special characteristics (e.g., disability, income level, English learner). You should also explain your relationship to the subjects and how you will have access to them. For example, the subjects may be students in your classroom or patients on your caseload. This section shows the IRB committee whether you are researching vulnerable populations (who may require additional safeguards) and that you will have access to subjects (so the study is feasible). The IRB committee may require a letter from the administrator at the school or agency stating his or her permission for you to access subjects at the site.

3. Recruitment procedure: In this section, describe how you will recruit the subjects to participate in your study. This is different from having access to subjects. For example, the manager at a business can give you permission to access his employees, but it will be up to you to recruit them for the study. The recruitment section should explain the procedures that you will use to solicit participation. For example, you may meet with potential subjects face-to-face individually or as a group, send written notices, make phone calls, and so on. Keep in mind that your IRB committee may limit the amount of contact you have with potential subjects during the recruitment process. This section shows the IRB committee that you have a fair and equitable selection of participants. You may also need to include your recruitment materials (e.g., memos, flyers) with your IRB application.

4. Subject consent process: In this section, describe how you will get the participants' informed consent to participate in the study. If the participants are minors (under the age of 18), then you will have to get their parent/guardian's consent. The procedure for obtaining consent may include face-to-face meetings, mailing written notices, phone calls, and so forth. If you are asking multiple groups of individuals (e.g., administrators, teachers, students) to participate, you may need to have a specific informed consent form for each group. This section shows the IRB committee that your participants will provide voluntary informed consent. You will need to include either a cover letter or an informed consent form(s) with your IRB application (see Appendix B for a sample cover letter and Appendix C for a sample informed consent form).

5. Procedures: In this section, describe the full procedures that the participants will be exposed to before, during, and after the study. The procedures include any type of manipulation or intervention that will be conducted (e.g., social skills training), samples of the materials or intervention (e.g., lesson plans, videos), and measurement instruments that will be used to collect data (e.g., surveys, pretest/posttests, interviews). You will also need to describe how the study will be conducted, such as grouping methods (e.g., experimental, comparison), time period (e.g., duration and frequency), and how data will be collected (e.g., face-to-face interviews). If you are tape recording or video recording any of the participants as part of data collection methods, this needs to be stated in the research plan, cover letter, and informed consent form. This section shows the IRB committee that you are conducting ethical

research and not harming your participants. You will need to include the sample materials and all measurement instruments in the IRB application, so make sure that you have compiled these before submitting your application.

6. Potential risk to subjects: In this section, describe the potential risks of harm that subjects will be exposed to in the study. Remember that there are *always* some potential risks, however small. Minimal risks for the subjects could include anxiety, boredom, frustration, fatigue, loss of time, and loss of confidentiality. **Confidentiality** refers to protecting the participants' identity and records. This section shows the IRB committee that you are considering the potential risk of harm to your participants.

7. Minimization of potential risk: In this section, describe how you will minimize the potential risks for the participants. For example, you could give the participants short breaks if they are frustrated or tired. You could also allow the participants to skip questions on a survey or interview that cause them emotional discomfort. If you are unsure as to how to minimize the potential risks specific to your study, discuss this with your chairperson. This section shows the IRB committee that you recognize the potential risks and are trying to minimize them for your participants.

8. Potential benefits to subjects: In this section, describe the potential benefits that will result from your study. The potential benefits should include direct benefits to the subjects (e.g., increased social skills, cognitive skills, time management, vocational skills). You can also include the broader benefits to society, but be careful not to exaggerate the benefits. This section allows the IRB committee to weigh the potential risks against the potential benefits and ensure there is an equitable distribution of benefits.

9. Costs to subjects: In this section, describe any costs that participants will incur. Costs can include monetary costs related to the treatment (e.g., medication) as well as other costs for transportation, child care fees, and so on. Non-monetary costs include the time and effort that participants will expend during the study. In most cases, you should try to keep participants' costs at a minimum. This section allows the IRB committee to make sure that subjects are not unduly burdened by participating in the study.

10. Reimbursement/compensation to subjects: In this section, describe any reimbursement or compensation that will be given to participants and the rationale. This can be very tricky so be careful. If possible, participants should be reimbursed for reasonable costs (e.g., transportation, parking). However, you want to avoid offering a reimbursement/compensation that could look like you are "inducing" participants to agree to the study. You also want to be careful not to offer participants compensation contingent on completion of the study, as this is perceived as coercion. This section allows the IRB committee to make sure that participants are truly volunteering to participate and are not being coerced.

11. Confidentiality of records: In this section, describe how you will keep the study records and files secure and the participants' identities confidential. There are several strategies to maximize participants' confidentiality. First, you need to decide whether the participants will remain anonymous. Anonymous is different from confidential. Anonymous means that there is no way to trace the data back to the individual participant. In order to give the participants anonymity, you need to remove all names and identifying information (e.g., addresses) from the measurement instruments (e.g., survey) and code the measurement instruments so that each participant is assigned a number. Obviously, there are some data collection procedures (e.g., interviews) where anonymity is very difficult to ensure. If you need to know each individual's data in order to answer the research question, then you may prefer to code the data for confidentiality rather than anonymity. For confidentiality, remove all names and identifying information from the measurement instruments and code the measurement instruments so that each participant is assigned a number. Then create a master list that matches the number with the identification of each participant so that you can trace the individual data if necessary. Once the data are collected, only the researcher, research assistants, and the chairperson should have access to the data. In addition, the data should be stored in a secure location such as a locked file cabinet or a computer that is password protected (if possible, personal information should always be encrypted). Remember that it is imperative that before, during, and after the study, the participants' identity and records should not be revealed. This section shows the IRB committee that you are protecting the participants' right to confidentiality.

Once you have received approval from the IRB, make sure to obtain permission from any other necessary agency (e.g., school district, hospital, business). In some cases, you will need to go through a separate application process and in other cases, outside agencies will require a copy of the IRB approval from your institution. Only when you have received approval from all parties can you access participants. If the participants are adults, have them sign a written consent form. Remember that you cannot simply ask the person to sign a consent form that he or she cannot read or comprehend (that would not be informed consent). Thus, if necessary, use an interpreter during a face-to-face meeting with the individual participant if he or she cannot read or hear. Translate the information about the study into the participant's native language if you are sending a written notice. If the participants are minors (under 18), you need to get informed consent from their parents/guardians. The IRB may also require you to give the participants a copy of their Research Subject Bill of Rights. The **Research Subject Bill of Rights** is a list of rights that is guaranteed for every participant in a study. Make sure the participants receive a copy of the informed consent form for their records and keep a copy for your files. After you have received the participants' informed consent, then you may begin your study!

Ethical Behavior

Completing the IRB process and adhering to the requirements when conducting your study is only one element of ethical behavior as a researcher. When conducting and reporting research, it is critical that you demonstrate ethical behavior and integrity at all times. Now is the time to learn as much as you can about ethics in research and internalize the information so it is a natural part of your professional behavior. This includes being honest in your interactions with participants as well as complying with ethical standards in your field for data collection, analysis, and reporting. As a beginning researcher, you will find that unanticipated situations will occur. When this happens, the appropriate solutions will be evident, but there may be less appropriate solutions in the form of shortcuts. These will be equally apparent and need to be avoided. Your master's thesis will be a public document that will be read by many researchers as they search the literature for similar problems. I will not go into all of the situations that might occur but following are some examples. During data collection, do not interfere with, influence, or modify the participants' responses to measurement instruments. This is critical when the participants do not "answer" in the way that you anticipate or want, which happens in the best of research studies. During data analysis, do not inflate, delete, or manipulate the data to obtain desirable results. This too is important. Remember it is not uncommon for your hypotheses to be unsupported by the results. You conduct the research to find that out. Keep in mind that in research, the researcher is also taking risks, and the results may not always be what are expected or desired. Discovering that an intervention does not work for a particular sample is still making a contribution to the literature.

Plagiarism

Finally, in writing the thesis and reporting the results, do not plagiarize. To **plagiarize** refers to using another person's ideas or words without giving them proper credit ("What is Plagiarism," n.d.). Plagiarism can be any of the following: "turning in someone else's work as your own; copying words or ideas from someone else without giving credit; failing to put a quotation in quotation marks; giving incorrect information about the source of a quotation; changing words but copying the sentence structure of a source without giving credit; or copying so many words or ideas from a source that it makes up the majority of your work, whether you give credit or not" ("What is Plagiarism," ¶ 4). For more information about how to avoid plagiarizing, refer to the Plagiarism.Org Web site (http://www.plagiarism.org). You are not expected to know everything about the topic that you are researching, but you are expected to credit the individuals whose work you review and integrate into your study. Plagiarism can be tempting because there is easy access to so much information (e.g., Internet). Thus, it is important to monitor yourself. Just as it has become easy for students to plagiarize, it has also become easier to identify plagiarized material. Informed people are likely to identify content from other sources without a citation, and there is software available that is designed to identify plagiarized material. If a student is caught plagiarizing, this can result in failing a class, expulsion from a program, or even withdrawal of a degree. If a member of a profession is caught plagiarizing, the consequences for his or her career cannot likely be overcome. Thus, it is not worth succumbing to the temptation of plagiarism (even if others around you are doing it), and it is easy to avoid by being professional in your behavior. Based on the definition above, there are several ways to prevent plagiarism: (1) do your own work, (2) give credit to the original source or idea, and (3) paraphrase rather than copy someone's writing. To **paraphrase** is to maintain the gist or essence of the original work (with appropriate citations) but to write it in your own words. Paraphrasing and citing sources are two very important skills that will help you to be successful in writing the thesis.

The purpose of a thesis is to demonstrate research skills and to do original work. Knowing and adhering to ethical practice is as important as knowing and adhering to sound research methodology. By maintaining your ethical behavior and integrity throughout the research process, you will have conducted an original study and written a master's thesis that you can be proud of.

Summary

Understanding the ethical standards and principles related to conducting research with human subjects is a critical part of your formation as a researcher. As you plan and design your study, make sure that you take into consideration the main ethical principles and standards from the Nuremberg Code and the Belmont Report. This will ensure that you prepare an ethical and successful research study application for the Institutional Review Board for the Protection of Human Subjects (IRBPHS). In the next chapter, I will discuss how to write Chapter One, Introduction, for your thesis. Here is a summary of the most critical points from Chapter 4:

- The three main standards of the Nuremberg Code are: (1) voluntary informed consent, (2) avoid all unnecessary mental and physical pain and suffering, and (3) weigh the risks against the expected benefits.

- In 1962, Congress passed the Kefauver-Harris Drug Amendments, which increased the regulatory powers of the Food and Drug Administration.

- The National Research Act of 1974 created the National Commission for the Protection of Human Subjects of Biomedical and Behavioral Research.

- In the Belmont Report, the commission identified three fundamental ethical principles for conducting research with human subjects: (1) respect for persons, (2) beneficence, and (3) justice.

- Researchers in different fields and disciplines have developed and adopted their own ethical standards specific to the type of research that is conducted with human subjects.

- In 1991, the core regulations by the Department of Health and Human Services (USDHHS) for the protection of human subjects in research studies were formally adopted as the Federal Policy for the Protection of Human Subjects, known as the Common Rule.

- Three of the central requirements in the Common Rule are: (1) any research supported or conducted by any federal department or agency must ensure compliance with the policy; (2) researchers must obtain written informed consent; and (3) institutions must have an Institutional Review Board (IRB) in place to review and approve research studies.

- The major role of the Institutional Review Board (IRB) is to ensure that all research with human subjects conducted by persons affiliated with the institution (including administrators, faculty, staff, and students) is done ethically and in compliance with federal regulations.

- The IRB requires that researchers (including undergraduate and graduate students) submit an IRB application for approval *before* any recruitment procedures are enacted, contact with potential participants is made, or data are collected.

- When conducting and reporting research, it is critical that you demonstrate ethical behavior and integrity at all times.

Resources

 ### Common Obstacles and Practical Solutions

1. One of the common emotions that students face at this stage is anxiety about the IRB process. Words that come to mind are, "What if I don't get approval?" Do not worry. Most student research puts participants at minimal risk of harm (unless you are doing something very bizarre or something you shouldn't). However, it is necessary for the IRB committee to review your application to make sure that your study is feasible and you have minimized potential harm with maximum benefit for the participants. Think of the committee as a friendly guard dog.

2. Another common obstacle faced by students is getting approval to conduct research from other related organizations (e.g., school districts,

hospitals, prisons). Most organizations have their own research approval process and this tends to take longer than the university's IRB process. Therefore, it is critical that you find a main contact person, follow their guidelines exactly, and start the process early!

 ## Reflection/Discussion Questions

As you begin to design your study, it is important to consider the effects or consequences of your study on others, especially the participants. In doing so, reflect upon the tragedies and unethical treatment of past research studies. The following reflection/discussion questions will help identify the main standards and ethical principals that must be applied while conducting research with human participants. Remember the wise words of the great philosopher George Santayana who once said, "Those who cannot learn from history are doomed to repeat it."

1. What are the Nuremberg Code and the Belmont Report? Why were these established? What are the main standards and ethical principles from these documents? Give specific examples of how they relate or could be applied to your field or discipline area.

2. What is the Common Rule and who developed it? Which agencies adhere to the Common Rule? What are the implications of the Common Rule for your research?

 ## Try It Exercises

The following exercises are designed to help you successfully complete the Institutional Review Board (IRB) application to conduct research at your institution. Doing this early in the process is critical, as you cannot begin data collection without IRB approval. In Activity One, you will identify the main ethical principals/standards in your field or discipline area. In Activity Two, you will research the IRB process at your specific institution. In Activity Three, you will develop the IRB application for your study.

1. Activity One: For this activity, focus on the resources specific to your field or discipline area.

   • Search the Internet and find the ethical principles/standards from your field or discipline area related to conducting research with human subjects.
   • If there are none, create a list of five ethical principles/standards that are specific to your field or discipline area and aligned to federal legislation (e.g., Belmont Report, Common Rule).

2. Activity Two: For this activity, focus on the Institutional Review Board Web site or campus office at your institution.

- Search your institution's Web site to locate the Institutional Review Board (IRB) Web site or campus address.
- Search the IRB Web site or visit the IRB office and list the name of the chairperson and the other members of the committee (with their respective school/college/department).
- Search the IRB Web site or visit the IRB office and obtain a manual or guide to complete the application process. Get samples of the IRB application, informed consent form, and cover letter if available.
- Read the IRB manual and make a list of all the necessary components of the IRB application.

3. Activity Three: For this activity, focus on the Institutional Review Board procedures and guidelines at your institution from Activity Two.

- Develop an IRB research plan for your study (per IRB application guidelines).
- Develop a participant informed consent form or cover letter for your study (per IRB application guidelines).
- Develop/locate and copy all measurement instruments that will be used for your study (if required by the IRB).
- Copy samples of any materials that will be used for your study (if required by the IRB).
- Obtain a letter of permission to access participants from the research site administrator (if required by the IRB).

Key Terms

- Belmont Report
- beneficence
- Common Rule
- confidentiality
- cost-benefit analysis
- deception
- Institutional Review Board (IRB) application
- Institutional Review Board (IRB) research plan
- justice
- Kefauver-Harris Drug Amendments

- National Commission for the Protection of Human Subjects of Biomedical and Behavioral Research
- National Research Act of 1974 (Public Law 93-348)
- Nuremberg Code
- paraphrase
- plagiarize
- Research Subject Bill of Rights
- respect for persons
- voluntary informed consent
- vulnerable populations

Suggested Readings

- Sales, B. D., & Folkman, S. (2000). *Ethics in research with human participants*. Washington, DC: American Psychological Association.

- Smith-Tyler, J. (2007). Informed consent, confidentiality, and subject rights in clinical trials. *Proceedings of the American Thoracic Society, 4,* 189–193.

Web Links

- American Educational Research Association (AERA) Ethical Standards
  http://www.aera.net/aboutaera/?id=222

- American Psychological Association (APA) Ethical Principles of Psychologists and Code of Conduct
  http://www.apa.org/ethics/code2002.html

- The Belmont Report
  http://www.hhs.gov/ohrp/humansubjects/guidance/belmont.htm

- The Common Rule
  http://www.hhs.gov/ohrp/policy/common.html

- The Nuremberg Code
  http://www.hhs.gov/ohrp/references/nurcode.htm

- Plagiarism.Org: Learning Center
  http://www.plagiarism.org/

- Teaching the Responsible Conduct of Research in Humans (RCRH)
  http://www.ori.dhhs.gov/education/products/ucla/default.htm

5

How to Write
Chapter One, Introduction

Writing Style	97
Chapter One Sections	98
Introduction	99
Statement of the Problem	103
Three Parallel Ladders Strategy	104
Background and Need	107
Three Parallel Ladders Strategy	107
Purpose of the Study	109
Research Questions	112
Significance to the Field	113
Definitions	113
Limitations	114
Ethical Considerations	115
Summary	115
Resources	116
Common Obstacles and Practical Solutions	116
Reflection/Discussion Questions	117
Try It Exercises	117
Key Terms	118
Suggested Readings	119
Web Links	119

The beautiful part of writing is that you don't have to get it right the first time, unlike, say, a brain surgeon. You can always do it better, find the exact word, the apt phrase, the leaping simile.

—Robert Cormier

The rest of this book will focus on the writing process and formatting style for the chapters of the master's thesis. The next five chapters focus on how to write each chapter in the thesis, including writing tips and strategies that will help to facilitate the process. I purposely use the term *process* because for all the chapters in the thesis, you will need to write multiple drafts, edit, revise, and ultimately write more drafts.

There is a tendency for many students to begin the writing process too early. They feel a need to begin writing without having mapped out their thesis and thinking through the content requirements for each chapter. There are risks in beginning to write too soon. The most serious risk is that you may invest energy and time going in the wrong direction. This can be frustrating and cause you to miss important deadlines. Keep in mind that you will write separate chapters entitled Introduction, Review of the Literature, Methods, Results, and Discussion. Before writing Chapter One, you need to have a good feel about what will be included in the literature review and the methodology chapters. This level of planning prepares you to determine what to include in Chapter One. Remember that your goal in Chapter One is to introduce your research.

Although I know you are eager to start writing, before you sit down at your computer, make sure that you have read all of the research and literature resources related to your research problem that you acquired and have your organizational system in place. This will minimize your frustration and help you judge whether you have enough resources or need to do more searching. I have noticed that most of the students who struggle with writing Chapter One do so not because of the writing per se but because they have not read enough literature about the research problem. Only after you have the "mastered" the necessary background information can you begin the actual writing process. In this chapter, I will first discuss the writing style for the thesis and then address each of the required sections for Chapter One.

Writing Style

As you prepare to write, keep in mind that the writing style in a master's thesis is very different from that used in creative writing or narrative writing. The writing style is technical, formal, serious, and impersonal. This can be a very difficult transition for students who are used to writing poetry or stories. For example, the tense must be in third person at all times (e.g., refer to yourself as "the researcher"), and you should not use an informal tone or colloquialisms (i.e., slang). In fact, the thesis should be free of personal biases, judgments, and opinions. As I often tell my students, "There is no room for *you* or *I* in a master's thesis." Thus any "personal positions" that you take throughout the thesis must be supported by the research literature. If you are having difficulty switching or unsure how to use a "technical" writing style, refer to the APA publication manual (APA, 2001). I have also placed general writing tips in Appendix D.

Chapter One Sections

The purpose of Chapter One is to communicate the major elements of the research study and to set the stage for subsequent chapters. Chapter One is the first page after the table of contents, and starts on a new page. The major sections/headings within Chapter One are: (1) *Introduction,* (2) *Statement of the Problem,* (3) *Background and Need,* (4) *Purpose of the Study,* (5) *Research Questions,* (6) *Significance to the Field,* (7) *Definitions,* (8) *Limitations,* and (9) *Ethical Considerations* (see Figure 5.1 for major sections in Chapter One). Keep in mind that these sections are typical of a master's thesis, but there may be slight variations depending on your institution or the preferences of your chairperson. Make sure to check with your department and chairperson for the thesis requirements for your program. You should also keep in mind that these are general guidelines—you may need to write more or less, depending on your chairperson and program's expectations.

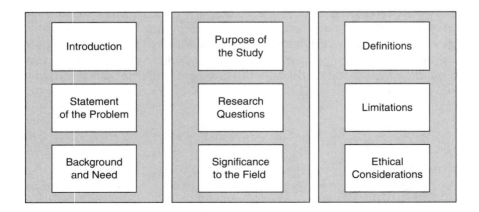

Figure 5.1   Major sections in Chapter One, Introduction.

The format of Chapter 5 will be slightly different from previous chapters since the focus is on how to write. Thus, for each section in Chapter One of the thesis, I will describe what needs to be included and offer examples, writing strategies, and tips. You will need to use citations from empirical research studies, reference materials, and national and state reports with statistical data to support your writing (see Chapter 10 for APA style). After reading the description of each section, I recommend that you read the examples in the appendixes from actual students' master's theses so that you can get a sense of the breath, depth, and style of the writing.

Introduction

The *Introduction* section in Chapter One describes the general problem you will be addressing in your research study. Your goal is to present an overview of the study in a manner that allows the reader to understand the context of your research in terms of the issues it addresses, the importance of the research to be done, and the specific research problem to be studied. Readers will expect the introduction to provide them with the background to understand the subsequent sections of the chapter describing the research. There should be at least four paragraphs in the *Introduction* section, and each paragraph fulfills a different role. For this section, I have found it helpful to use a funnel writing strategy. In an actual funnel, the opening at the top is wide and then it slowly narrows to a small opening. A **funnel writing strategy** is analogous to a funnel where your first paragraph about the problem is broad and every subsequent paragraph narrows the topic toward the specific problem (see Figure 5.2 for a depiction of a funnel strategy for the *Introduction* section in Chapter One).

The first paragraph in the *Introduction* section should be a description of the broad issues related to your study. The purpose of this first paragraph is to give the reader background knowledge and a context for your study (without specifically mentioning your problem yet). Typically, in this paragraph you discuss *broad* societal trends and national or international phenomena that are *related* to your problem. In other words, what is the big picture? One of the problems that students face in writing this paragraph is that they are so immersed in their immediate problem that they cannot see beyond it. Thus, take three steps away from your specific problem and ask, "What are the broad societal issues that have trickled down to cause or influence my specific problem?" For example, if you are focusing on broad issues in education or special education, you might discuss federal mandates, the standards-reform movement, school violence, academic achievement data on large-scale assessments, demographic changes, the overrepresentation of students of color receiving special education services, and so on. If you are focusing on broad issues related to juvenile delinquency, you might discuss gang membership, expulsion and high

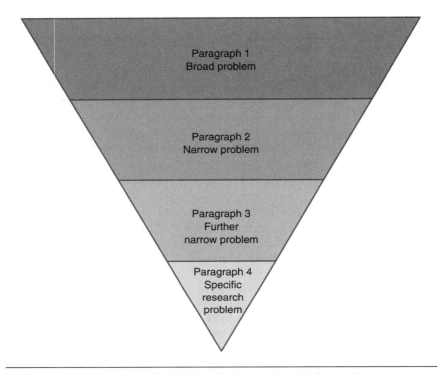

Figure 5.2   Funnel strategy for the *Introduction* section in Chapter One.

school drop out, substance abuse, budget cuts in after-school programs, and so forth. If you are focusing on broad issues related to counseling, you might discuss mental and emotional illness, scarcity of mental health services, drug and alcohol abuse, family conflict, child and spousal abuse, and so on. If you are focusing on broad issues related to business and management, you might discuss globalization in the market economy, outsourcing, corporate social responsibility, climate change, and so forth. Remember to support your claims with citations from the research, especially from national reports with statistical data. No matter which societal or national issue(s) you focus on, keep in mind that it is not enough to discuss the issue; you want to show how the issue manifests into actual problems and the consequences of the problems for society. One of the questions I often ask my students to answer is, "So what? What are the implications of this issue?" By answering this question, you are making the problem(s) explicit for the reader and building a justification and rationale for your study. The key to writing this paragraph is to think broadly—if you are too narrow here, then you will not have any room to funnel in the next few paragraphs (see Figure 5.3 for a sample funnel for the *Introduction* section of Chapter One). Here is an example of a topic sentence for the first paragraph:

The federal mandate, the No Child Left Behind Act (NCLB) of 2001, requires states to create an accountability system, measure student performance through testing, and ensure that teachers are highly qualified.

For the rest of the paragraph, I would describe the NCLB mandate and its implications for the states.

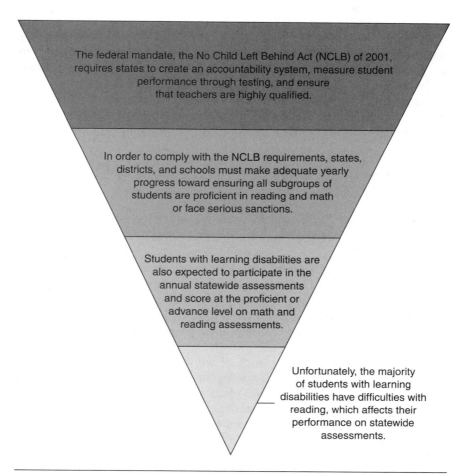

The federal mandate, the No Child Left Behind Act (NCLB) of 2001, requires states to create an accountability system, measure student performance through testing, and ensure that teachers are highly qualified.

In order to comply with the NCLB requirements, states, districts, and schools must make adequate yearly progress toward ensuring all subgroups of students are proficient in reading and math or face serious sanctions.

Students with learning disabilities are also expected to participate in the annual statewide assessments and score at the proficient or advance level on math and reading assessments.

Unfortunately, the majority of students with learning disabilities have difficulties with reading, which affects their performance on statewide assessments.

Figure 5.3   Sample funnel strategy for the *Introduction* section in Chapter One.

The second paragraph is a one-step funnel where you begin to narrow from the broad problem(s) in the previous paragraph. Make sure you have a smooth transition (i.e., segue) from the first paragraph and a topic sentence. In the first paragraph, you focused on societal and national trends. For this paragraph, you will *narrow* the discussion to focus on state, regional, or local issues *related* to your problem. Thus, take two steps away from your specific problem and ask, "What are the state, regional, or local issues that have trickled down to cause or influence my specific problem?" For example, in education or special education, you might discuss state-level mandates, state content standards, academic achievement data on statewide assessments, demographic changes, or the percentage of students of color receiving special education services in specific school districts, and how these issues affect students, parents, schools, and teachers. The same one-step funnel can be applied to other fields and disciplines. Remember that it is critical to discuss how the state, regional, or local issues manifest into problems and the consequences for the communities and neighborhoods. This adds to the justification and rationale for your study. In addition, support your claims with citations from the research, especially from state or regional reports with statistical data. Be careful not to focus too narrowly here; otherwise, you will not be able to funnel for the next two paragraphs. Here is an example of a topic sentence for the second paragraph:

> In order to comply with the NCLB requirements, states, districts, and schools must make adequate yearly progress toward ensuring all subgroups of students are proficient in reading and math or face serious sanctions.

For the rest of the paragraph, I would describe what states are doing to meet the NCLB mandate and implications for school districts, schools, and teachers.

The third paragraph (with a smooth transition and topic sentence) is another one-step funnel where you begin to narrow from the local problem(s) in the previous paragraph. In the second paragraph, you focused on state, regional, and local issues. For this paragraph, you will narrow the discussion to focus on the *specific* group or subgroups of individuals *related* to your problem. Thus, take one step away from your specific problem and ask, "How are the groups or subgroups of individuals related to my problem affected by the national, state, regional, or local issues?" For example, in education or special education, you might want to focus on students in elementary, middle, or high school, students with moderate to severe disabilities, students with specific disabilities (e.g., learning disability), novice or mentor teachers, paraprofessionals, administrators, students from specific cultural/ethnic backgrounds, English learners, and so on. This is the group(s) that will make up the sample group in your study. The same one-step funnel strategy can be applied to other fields and disciplines. Remember that it is critical to discuss how the national, state, regional, or local issues manifest into problems and the consequences for the group or subgroup of individuals targeted in your study. This adds to the justification and rationale for your study and the selection of your sample group. In addition, support your claims with citations from the research, especially from empirical research studies and reference materials. Here is an example of a topic sentence for the third paragraph:

> Students with learning disabilities are also expected to participate in the annual statewide assessments and score at the proficient or advance level on math and reading assessments.

For the rest of the paragraph, I would describe the expectations for students with learning disabilities on statewide assessments and their performance as compared to students without learning disabilities.

Finally, the last paragraph in this section funnels directly to your research problem. Avoid writing, "My research problem is about . . . ," which is the book report method you used in the fourth grade. Instead, this last funnel should be a natural flow from the first three paragraphs. For this paragraph, you will narrow the discussion to focus on your specific problem and how the problem affects the group or subgroups of individuals that you have targeted. Then, you want to expand on the consequences of the problem for this specific group. This is also where you would operationally define terms and phrases that you will be using as part of your study. Remember to support your claims with citations from the research, especially from empirical research studies and reference materials. Here is an example of a topic sentence for the last paragraph:

> Unfortunately, the majority of students with learning disabilities have difficulties with reading, which affects their performance on statewide assessments.

For the rest of the paragraph, I would describe the reading difficulties that students with learning disabilities encounter and the implications for their performance on statewide assessments as compared to students without learning disabilities. This last paragraph is a great lead-in to the next section of the chapter, which focuses on the areas related to your research problem. See Appendix E for a sample *Introduction* section for Chapter One.

Statement of the Problem

The next section of Chapter One, the *Statement of the Problem*, differs from the *Introduction* section where you discussed broad issues related to your problem. In the *Statement of the Problem*, you will delve deeper into your problem using language that is very clear in stating the problem to be researched. You can do this by identifying three areas that are related to your research problem. View each area as a subsection of the *Statement of the Problem*.

Three parallel ladders strategy. One model for doing this is to use the three parallel ladders strategy. The **three parallel ladders strategy** is an organizational writing strategy used in Chapters One and Two of the thesis. For this strategy, imagine three parallel ladders lying side by side. The first ladder will represent the *Statement of the Problem*. The second ladder will represent the *Background and Need*. The third ladder will represent your review of the research literature in Chapter Two. The three rungs in each ladder represent the three common areas throughout Chapters One and Two (see Figure 5.4 for a depiction of the three parallel ladders strategy for Chapters One and Two).

In order to identify the three areas, first thoroughly read the research literature related to your research problem. A good type of article is one that gives you a broad overview of your research problem such as a secondary source, meta-analysis, or literature synthesis. The introduction section of

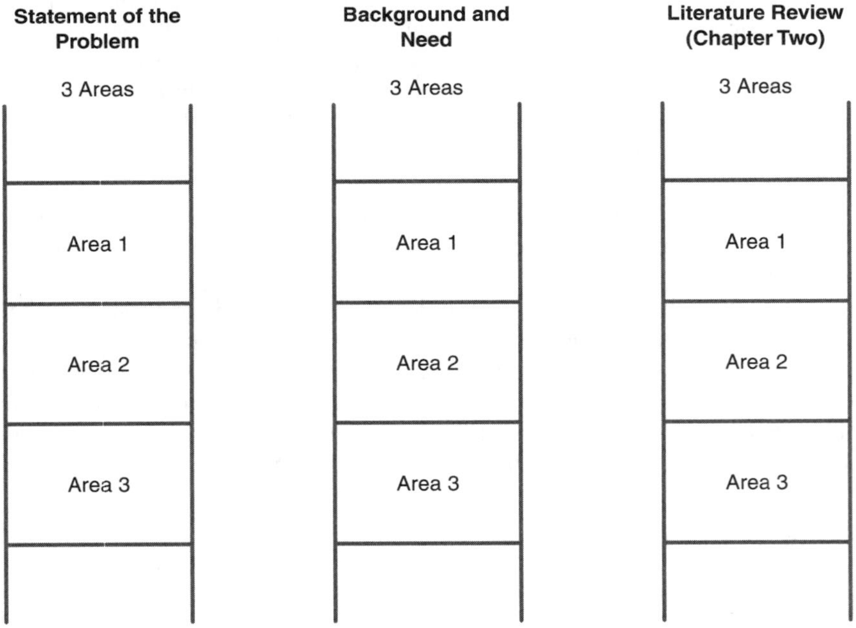

Statement of the Problem	Background and Need	Literature Review (Chapter Two)
3 Areas	3 Areas	3 Areas
Area 1	Area 1	Area 1
Area 2	Area 2	Area 2
Area 3	Area 3	Area 3

Figure 5.4   The three parallel ladders strategy for Chapters One and Two.

empirical research articles is also a good source to find broad issues. Next, select the three areas that are most relevant to your research problem. The areas may be a subarea within your research problem or a parallel area that is influenced by or affects your research problem. Keep in mind that the areas should not be too narrow because you will need to locate at least three empirical research articles relating to each area for your literature review in Chapter Two. For example, from my research problem of students with learning disabilities performing poorly on statewide reading assessments, three related areas and problems are: (1) Teachers are unaware of which accommodations are appropriate for students with learning disabilities on statewide assessments; (2) Students are required to be able to read a variety of genres on the state assessment, including expository and figurative text; and (3) Students with learning disabilities do not have a repertoire of reading comprehension strategies (see Figure 5.5 for a depiction of the ladder for the *Statement of the Problem* section in Chapter One).

Once you have identified the three areas, you can start to write the section. The first paragraph should be a brief introduction to the three areas related to your research problem. This will serve as an organizational tool for the rest of the section. For the three subsections, you will write about each specific

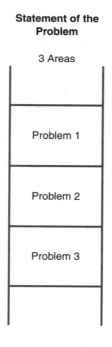

Figure 5.5   Ladder for the *Statement of the Problem* section in Chapter One.

area separately. Do not mix up the three areas because this will confuse your reader; you can use a heading to label each area to help you stay organized and on topic. A **heading** is the name of a section or subsection used to organize the paper. The headings are formatted depending on how many levels of heading there are in the paper (see Chapter 10 for APA style).

Start each subsection with an introduction that briefly describes the area. Next, discuss the relationship between your research problem and the area (make sure you make this connection explicit for your reader). Then, write about the *problems* within the area and how they affect your targeted group and relate to your research problem. Here is where you want to be very specific about the consequences and effects of the problem (i.e., answer the "so what?" question). For example, for the third area, "Students with learning disabilities do not have a repertoire of reading comprehension strategies," you would discuss the problems that students with disabilities have with reading comprehension (e.g., poor fluency, lack of metacognition skills, limited vocabulary) and the consequences (e.g., low motivation to read, failing classes). In this section, you should define any ambiguous terms or phrases that are relevant to your study. Finally, support your writing by paraphrasing (not plagiarizing) information from the research literature and citing the sources using the appropriate editorial format. Include quotes sparingly and only if the author said something so brilliant that you could not paraphrase it without destroying the essence of the quote (see Chapter 10 for APA style).

Remember to focus on the problems within the areas and do not mention any types of interventions or "solutions" to the problems yet—that will go into the next section *(Background and Need)*. If you find new general information, put it in the *Introduction* section. End each subsection with a summary and smooth transition into the next section. At the end of the entire *Statement of the Problem* section, write a brief summary that highlights the three problems related to the research problem. Here is an example of three areas related to a research problem and the problem within each area (see Appendix F for a sample *Statement of the Problem* section):

Research Problem: Students in juvenile delinquent treatment centers have behavior difficulties that affect their academic, social, and emotional development.

- Area #1: Choices and Decision Making
  - Problem: Since the students are in a restrictive environment, they are not given many choices and opportunities to participate in the decision-making process. This will disadvantage them when they return to less-restrictive environments.

- Area #2: Specific and Immediate Praise
  - Problem: Students in juvenile delinquent centers are often victims of child abuse and neglect who did not receive praise and encouragement in their home settings. This has negative consequences for their self-concept and self-esteem (note that both of these terms would have to be defined).

- Area #3: Motivation
  - Problem: Students in juvenile delinquent centers typically have lower levels of motivation, which affects their learning and behavior.

In this example, the first two related areas are components that I would like to include in my behavior management program intervention (independent variable). The third area is what I hope to increase with the behavior management program intervention (dependent variable). Notice that the focus for each area is the problem related to students in juvenile delinquent centers. In the next section, *Background and Need*, I will focus on the solutions to these problems.

Background and Need

As you have explored your research ideas, you have read extensively and given considerable thought to the problem and its importance. In Chapter Two, you will synthesize the literature that supports your research study. That will be an extensive chapter. In the *Background and Need* section of Chapter One, however, you will provide the reader with a clear and concise statement on the background of the study and the need for the research. You want to convince the reader that the problem is important to research and provide a rationale for studying the problem. This is the reason for discussing the background. In essence, you are sharing your perspective on the importance of the study.

Three parallel ladders strategy. In this section, I will use the same three areas that were identified in the *Statement of the Problem* section. In other words, each subsection in the *Background and Need* will match one of the subsections discussed in the *Statement of the Problem* section. Thus, for the *Background and Need* you will also use the three parallel ladders strategy. The second ladder will represent the *Background and Need*. The three rungs in the second ladder represent the interventions and solutions to the problems within the three areas (see Figure 5.6 for a depiction of the ladder for the *Background and Need* section).

Since you have already identified the three areas, it will be easier to write this section. To provide some background information, include a short paragraph here on the historical background related to the areas, if appropriate. Then, include a brief introduction to the three areas related to your research problem that will serve as an organizational tool for the rest of the section.

Each subsection will start with an introduction that briefly describes the area. Then, write about the research-based interventions that help to "solve" the problems within the area. For example, if one of the areas is homelessness, and the problem is that a large proportion of homeless people suffer from mental illness, then you would discuss different research-based programs that have been effective in offering mental health services for this population. Good types of articles to use for this section are ones that give you

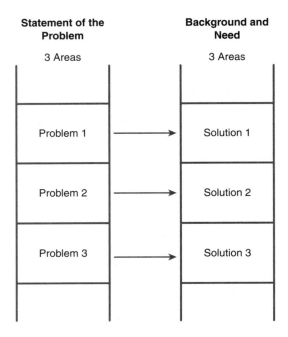

Figure 5.6   Ladder for the *Background and Need* section in Chapter One.

a broad overview of research studies (e.g., meta-analyses, literature synthe-ses) or empirical research articles specific to the problem. Try to avoid just telling what should be done (i.e., do not preach). Instead, provide a brief description of the intervention, the sample group it was conducted with, and the results. Whenever possible, report on interventions that were effective with your targeted group or a similar group. This serves as a justification for you to include these research-based practices in your study.

After you have discussed the solutions reported in the literature, point out the "need" and gaps that still remain in the literature related to this area. This is very critical as it serves as a rationale to conduct your study and shows how your study will contribute to the existing research. For example, a gap would be that the existing studies were not conducted with your spe-cific sample group or in your particular region. Another gap would be if your study proposes to adapt a research-based intervention for a new sam-ple group. Make sure to support your writing by paraphrasing information from the research literature and citing the sources using the appropriate edi-torial format. At the end of the entire *Background and Need* section, write a brief summary that highlights the research-based interventions that have been conducted and the needs that still exist. Here is an example of three areas related to a research problem with the problems and solutions.

Research Problem: There has been an increase in the use of illegal drugs and alcohol by young teens.

- Area #1: Substance Abuse in Families
  - ○ Problem: Children whose parents abuse drugs or alcohol are more likely than children whose parents who do not abuse drugs and alcohol to be abused, neglected, and experiment with drugs and alcohol themselves.
  - ○ Solution: Family therapy can help to identify the family's stage in addiction as well as provide the teens with ways to recover from their family's dysfunctions (Niolin, 2001).

- Area #2: Mental Health Risks
  - ○ Problem: Alcohol and drug abuse may harm an adolescent's physical and brain development and lead to depression and anxiety.
  - ○ Solution: Keepin' It R.E.A.L. is an effective program to prevent middle school students from using drugs by drawing on their traditional ethnic values (Blaum, 2004).

- Area #3: Academic/Social Risks
  - ○ Problem: Alcohol and drug abuse may weaken teenagers' ability to think, concentrate, store information, and impair their judgment, which may lead to risky behaviors.
  - ○ Solution: Project ALERT is a group of lessons designed to teach middle school students about the harmful effects of substance abuse. The results of the study indicated that students who participated in the program had 38% lower marijuana initiation rates and 24% lower scores for alcohol abuse than the control group. (USDHHS, 2004).

In this example, the three solutions would be interventions that I would include in my prevention and treatment program (independent variable) for teens who suffer from family substance abuse (sample group) in order to decrease the teenagers' rates of substance abuse (dependent variable). This leads to the purpose of my study, which is to develop a program that integrates family therapy and lessons from the Keepin' It R.E.A.L. and Project ALERT interventions.

After I have given the reader a broad introduction, described my research problem in detail, and provided the background literature and research, I will connect these sections to the *Purpose of the Study*. By this time, my reader will already be convinced that I have identified a significant problem that needs to be addressed, and I am aware of the most relevant and effective research-based practices to influence the problem.

Purpose of the Study

The *Purpose of the Study* section in Chapter One explains the purpose and goal of your study related to the research problem. The intent of this section is to refine what you have written into a precise statement describing what you propose to research and why. The *Purpose of the Study* has four main parts: (1) purpose statement, (2) need/rationale for the study, (3) description of the study, and (4) expected outcomes. I will explain each part briefly.

The first part of the *Purpose of the Study* is the purpose statement. Here, state the purpose of your study in one sentence! Include in the statement the what, why, who, and where related to your study. Here is a template you can use:

> The purpose of this study was to (what you did) (why you did this/issue) (who was your sample group) (where was the setting).

Here is an example for an intervention quantitative study:

> The purpose of this study was to utilize the See Story visual imagery strategy (what) to improve the reading comprehension (why/issue) for students with learning disabilities (who) in a low-performing public high school (where).

Here is an example for a qualitative study:

> The purpose of this study was to explore how disability was perceived (what) by special education teachers and parents/families with children with disabilities (who) and how special education services were provided (why/issue) in an African primary school for children with disabilities (where).

The second part of the *Purpose of the Study* is the rationale. This briefly explains the need for focusing on this particular problem or issue. Providing a rationale is critical because it provides justification and validation for why it is important or necessary to conduct the study. In qualitative studies, the rationale may also be used to "foreshadow" the design of your study (Creswell, 2007, p. 102). Here, you can summarize some of the main points from the *Introduction* and the *Statement of the Problem*. Include sentences about the problems (broad and specific) and the consequences of not addressing the problems. For example,

> Many high school students with learning disabilities plateau at the fourth grade reading level. If these students are not taught explicit reading comprehension strategies, they will score poorly on statewide assessments, including the high school exit exam. In states where students must pass the high school exit exam in order to receive a high school diploma, poor reading comprehension skills will negatively affect students' with learning disabilities ability to proceed to postsecondary educational settings or obtain employment.

Here is another example:

> Since the first major disability legislation was passed in 1975, the field of disability and special education has progressed tremendously in the United States.

Researchers and educators have made strides in assessment, instruction, service delivery, teacher preparation, and collaboration with families in all disability areas. Despite the progress in the United States, special education services are still at the initial stages in less-developed countries such as in East Africa. Moreover, few research studies have documented how disability and special education services are defined and implemented in these areas through the cultural lens of the parents, families, and teachers in these communities.

The third part of the *Purpose of the Study* is the description. This briefly explains the methods that you used to conduct the study. Include your sample group, description of your study or intervention (if you have one), and how you will collect the data. For example,

In order to improve high school students' with learning disabilities reading comprehension skills (and ultimately their performance on standardized assessments), the researcher implemented the See Story strategy. This strategy teaches the students to use visual imagery before, during, and after they read. Fifteen students with learning disabilities (Grades 9–10) were introduced to and utilized the strategy in their English Language Arts classes on a daily basis over a six-week period. The students' reading comprehension levels were measured before and after the intervention using a standardized reading assessment. The students' attitudes toward reading were also measured with a student survey after the intervention was completed.

Here is another example:

In order to measure the participants' perspectives of disability and special education services, the researcher conducted interviews with 10 parents/families of children with disabilities and the classroom teachers from the primary school. In order to explore and describe how special education services were provided to the children with disabilities, the researcher conducted observations at the school site.

The last part of the *Purpose of the Study* is the expected outcome or goal of the study. This briefly explains the benefits that will result from your study. You can have several expected outcomes. For example,

As a result of the See Story strategy, the high school students with learning disabilities were expected to increase their reading comprehension level. Another goal of the study was to determine whether the students' attitudes toward reading were positively related with their reading abilities.

Here is another example:

The purpose of the ethnography was to explore disability issues and special education services from the perspectives of parents, families, and teachers in a learning community in East Africa. By learning how the members of the community viewed disability and special education services, this provided a cross-cultural context to view these issues through the participants' lens rather than imposing a cultural framework on them. This study also had implications for how special education services were provided to the children with disabilities at the primary school level.

Once you have established the purpose of the study, you need to write research questions that are aligned with the purpose and the methods of the study.

Research Questions

The research question(s) is the question related to the problem that you are attempting to answer with your study. The key is to frame your research questions so that you are addressing the most critical elements of your study. This does not mean that you need to develop an exhaustive list of research questions. Instead, select those questions that are most important to you and can be studied within the available time and resources for doing a thesis. Remember that the more research questions you have, the more data you will have to collect and analyze. The research questions are aligned with the methods of the study and vice versa, so you should consider your research methods as you develop the research questions.

Make sure the research questions are written so that once you collect the data, you will be able to answer them. This might involve including the measured variables in the question. A good strategy is to convert the purpose statement into a question. For example, if I want to know the impact of the See Story strategy, I would convert the purpose statement into a question and ask,

> What are the effects of the See Story visual imagery strategy (independent variable) on the reading comprehension levels (dependent variable) for students with learning disabilities (who) in public high schools (where)?

If I do not have an intervention but want to measure students' attitudes based on a survey, I would still include the dependent variable or other measured variables in my research questions. For example,

> What are high school students' with learning disabilities attitudes toward reading (dependent variable)?

or

> What is the relationship between the students' attitudes toward reading (measured variable) and their reading comprehension abilities (measured variable)?

Here is an example for a qualitative study:

What are the perceptions toward disability by special education teachers and parents/families with children with disabilities? How are special education services provided in an East African primary school for children with disabilities?

When developing research questions, try to avoid writing research questions that have a yes/no answer such as,

Can high school students with learning disabilities improve their reading comprehension abilities?

or why questions such as,

Why do the parents have these feelings toward their children with disabilities?

These questions are more rhetorical (or not answerable) and do not tell the reader or the researcher anything about the design of the study. In addition, a yes/no research question does not allow much room for discussion and interpretation. An open-ended question (with parameters) allows you to answer the research question but also discuss the implications of the results.

Significance to the Field

The next section is the *Significance to the Field* (also referred to as *Significance of the Study*). In this section, describe the benefits (short and long term) for the participants in the study as well as the contribution that the study made to the research literature in your field. For example, if you conducted an intervention, you may have made a positive impact on the participants' academic, social, physical, or emotional well-being. If you conducted surveys, interviews, or observations for your study, you may have discovered important information about the participants' attitudes, perceptions, and behaviors. Although this section is typically included in Chapter One, you may want to add to this section after you have completed the study.

Definitions

The next section in Chapter One is *Definitions*. This section is where you will define terms or phrases that need a more detailed explanation than the ones that were provided earlier in the chapter. Remember to use consistent terms to convey the same meaning as you present in your definitions. Thus, if you have labeled a concept or variable with a specific term, use this term consistently throughout the entire text. Once you formally define the term in this section, the reader will know exactly what you are referring to.

Perhaps the most difficult part of writing this section is determining which terms to define. There are three rules that I use in selecting terms to define. The first rule is to define all terms that a person outside of the field would not be familiar with (i.e., technical jargon). For example, if I am a noneducator, I may not know the definition of a *learning disability* or my definition might be different from the standard definition in the field. Thus, *learning disability* is a term that I would have to define in this section. Whenever possible, I would also use the legal, standard, or recognized definition from the literature and provide the appropriate citations. A second rule is to define all terms that have been "coined" by their users. This refers to familiar terms that may have new definitions because of changing cultural context. These terms would need to be operationally defined because the standard dictionary definition is not accurate for how the term is defined by the users. For example, *Response to Intervention* is a very critical term in education today, but might not be understood in other fields. Finally, the third rule is to define all terms that may be ambiguous to the reader because the definition of the word is dependent on the context or the participant's interpretation. For example, *transition* has multiple meanings depending on the context. In counseling, *life transition* refers to moving from one life stage to another such as from work to retirement. In education, *transition* refers to moving between elementary, middle, high school, and postsecondary settings. In business, a *business transition* could refer to a change in ownership or management. In sociology, a *criminological transition* refers to changes in society that lead to increases in crime rates ("Criminological transition," n.d.). By defining the term (with a citation from the literature), this clarifies the concept for the reader and ensures that everyone is on the same page. After you have defined all the terms, list them with bullets and arrange them in alphabetical order, so that it will be easy for the reader to find specific terms.

Limitations

The next section is *Limitations*. This section is where you will discuss all the limitations in the study. Limitations can be inherent to the research design, data analysis, time and resources, or a condition that was set by the researcher. For example, lack of a control group is a common limitation in students' theses because of the limited access to participants. Another common limitation is small sample size (in a quantitative study). A limitation is a flaw or weakness in the study that affects the internal validity and external validity of the results. **Internal validity** (within the study) refers to whether the changes in the dependent variable were due to the independent variable or some other variable. If there is no control group in an experimental study, this will reduce the internal validity because it is uncertain whether the changes in the dependent variable were due to the treatment or some other factors.

External validity (outside the study) refers to whether the results of the study are applicable or can be generalized to other settings and groups (Gay et al., 2006). Having a small sample size would reduce a study's external validity because of the limited generalizability to other groups. However, depending on the research design, this would not necessarily be a limitation in a qualitative study. Keep in mind that all studies have limitations, and it is not a personal reflection on you as a researcher. Thus, the best way to deal with limitations is to be up front about them and explain how they affect the results of the study; trying to hide or cover the limitations of a study will only further weaken the study. We will discuss these in more detail in Chapter 9.

Ethical Considerations

The last section in Chapter One is *Ethical Considerations*. This section is where you will describe the procedures that you followed to ensure that the research was conducted in an ethical manner. This includes following the Institutional Review Board process for informed consent, obtaining permission from other agencies to access participants, and minimizing the potential risks to your participants. You may need to include a blank copy of the cover letter and/or informed consent form in the appendix of your thesis, so make sure you keep a copy.

Summary

Chapter One is perhaps the most important chapter in the thesis because it provides a rationale for your study and establishes a structure for the rest of the chapters in the thesis. Once you have described the research problem (and related areas), background literature, purpose of the study, and research questions, this will give you a structure for how to write Chapter Two, Review of the Literature, and plan for Chapter Three, Methods. Chapter One, however, is probably the most difficult chapter to write, so try not to become frustrated if it takes a long time or if you have to write multiple drafts. In the next chapter, I will discuss how to write Chapter Two, Review of the Literature, for your thesis. Here is a summary of the most critical points from Chapter 5:

- The *Introduction* section in Chapter One describes the general problem in the study.

- A funnel writing strategy is analogous to a funnel where your first paragraph about the problem is broad and every subsequent paragraph narrows the topic toward the specific problem.

- The *Statement of the Problem* section describes the three problem areas related to the research problem.

- The *Background and Need* section describes the interventions and solutions to the problems in the *Statement of the Problem* and the gaps that still exist.

- The *Purpose of the Study* section has four main parts: (1) purpose statement, (2) need/rationale for the study, (3) description of the study, and (4) expected outcomes.

- The *Research Questions* section outlines the questions related to the problem that you are attempting to answer with your study and will determine the methods and data analysis that you use.

- The *Significance to the Field* (also referred to as *Significance of the Study*) section describes the benefits (short and long term) for the participants in the study as well the contribution that the study made to the research literature in your field.

- The *Definitions* section is where you define terms or phrases that need a more detailed explanation.

- The *Limitations* section is where you discuss all the limitations in the study. A limitation is a flaw or weakness in the study that affects the internal validity and external validity of the results.

- The *Ethical Considerations* section is where you describe the procedures that you followed to ensure that the research was conducted in an ethical manner.

Resources

Common Obstacles and Practical Solutions

1. A common obstacle that students face at this stage is starting the actual writing of Chapter One. Words that come to mind are, "I have major writer's block." This is a very natural feeling because up to this point, you have been focused on reading and conceptualizing your study. The best way to tackle writer's block is to sit down and write (or in most cases, type on the computer). Believe me—I have been there many times. Start your writing by opening a new Word document and putting in the major headers for the chapter. Next write an outline of the major topics that you will discuss in the Introduction—do not forget to use the funnel strategy! Once you begin to flesh out the outline and pull information from the research, the ideas will flow. If you do not have time to write it all out, make notes to yourself about what information needs to be included and where to find it.

2. Another common obstacle faced by students is formulating the *Statement of the Problem* and the *Background and Need* sections. Words that come to mind are, "I don't know what my three areas are." If your three areas have not emerged yet, a good place to look for them is in your organizational filing system. Look to see how you organized your research articles and especially if you created a literature matrix. If neither is available, do a quick scan of the abstracts and try to put the articles into three piles and label each one with a broad heading. This will also inform you of whether you have enough articles or the most applicable research articles.

 ## Reflection/Discussion Questions

Before you write Chapter One, it will save you much time and frustration if you discuss "the big picture" with a colleague or your chairperson. Often, students get so focused on their own study that they lose sight of the broad context in which the study is situated (the rationale for why you are doing the study in the first place). The following reflection/discussion questions will help to identify the broader issues in your field or discipline related to your research topic and also how to narrow your research topic into the three related areas.

1. What are the foci of the first two paragraphs in the *Introduction* section? Brainstorm different types of problems and issues related to your field or discipline area that would be relevant for these two paragraphs. Discuss how you could use the funnel strategy to transition between paragraphs in the *Introduction* section.

2. What are the similarities and differences between the *Statement of the Problem* and the *Background and Need* sections? What is the focus of each section? Give examples of how you could use the three parallel ladders strategy to organize the writing for these two sections.

 ## Try It Exercises

The following exercises are designed to help you write Chapter One. In Activity One, you will begin to write the *Introduction* using the funnel method. In Activity Two, you will begin to identify the three problems in the *Statement of the Problem*. In Activity Three, you will begin to develop the *Purpose of the Study* and the *Research Questions*.

1. Activity One: For this activity, focus on the issues related to your research problem.

   • Make a list of the major *national* and *societal* issues related to your research problem. Describe the manifestations and consequences of these issues

• Funnel (narrow) one step and list the major *state, regional,* and *local* issues related to your research problem. Describe the manifestations and consequences of these issues

• Funnel (narrow) one step and list the *specific* group or subgroups of individuals *related* to your research problem. Describe the manifestations and consequences of the *national* and *state* issues for this group.

• Funnel (narrow) one last step and list your research problem and the specific group related to your research problem. Describe the manifestations and consequences of the research problem for this group.

2. Activity Two: For this activity, focus on the specific areas related to your research problem.

• Imagine that this ladder represents the *Statement of the Problem* section. Write an area that is related to your research problem inside each rung (total of three).
• Then list the problem(s) within each area.

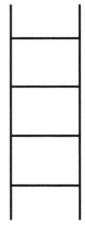

3. Activity Three: For this activity, focus on the purpose of your research study.

• List the four parts that need to be included in the *Purpose of the Study* section.
• Write your purpose statement using the model template from the chapter:

The purpose of this study is to (what do you want to do?) to (why do you want to do this?) for (who is your sample group?) in (where is the setting?).

• List three main points for the rationale of the study.

- Write a brief description of the methods that will be used in the study.
- List the expected goals and outcomes of the study.
- Convert the purpose statement into a research question.

Key Terms

- external validity
- funnel writing strategy
- heading
- internal validity
- three parallel ladders strategy

Suggested Readings

- American Psychological Association. (2001). *Publication manual of the American Psychological Association* (5th ed.). Washington, DC: Author.

- Creswell, J. W. (2007). *Qualitative inquiry and research design* (2nd ed.). Thousand Oaks, CA: Sage.

- Szuchman, L. T. (2008). *Writing with style: APA style made easy* (4th ed.). Belmont, CA: Wadsworth.

Web Links

- APA Style

  http://apastyle.apa.org/

- APA Formatting and Style Guide: The OWL at Purdue

  http://owl.english.purdue.edu/owl/resource/560/01/

- The Chicago Manual of Style Online

  http://www.chicagomanualofstyle.org/home.html

- The Elements of Style, William Strunk, Jr.

  http://www.bartleby.com/141/

- Modern Language Association (MLA)

  http://www.mla.org/

6

How to Write Chapter Two, Review of the Literature

Preparation and Organization 122

Chapter Two Sections 123

    Introduction 123

        Advance Organizer 124

    Body of the Review 124

        Research Synthesis 125

        Section Summary 131

    Chapter Summary 131

Summary 132

Resources 133

    Common Obstacles and Practical Solutions 133

    Reflection/Discussion Questions 134

    Try It Exercises 134

    Key Terms 135

    Suggested Readings 136

    Web Links 136

It does not matter how slowly you go so long as you do not stop.

—Confucius

Bravo on getting through Chapter One of the thesis! This chapter will focus on how to write Chapter Two, Review of the Literature (also referred to as the Literature Review). The Review of the Literature is an important component of a thesis. While it does not describe your research or the methodology that you employed, it provides the reader a context for understanding why and how you conducted your study. Additionally, it communicates your knowledge of related research and of the conditions surrounding the justification for your research.

By now, you are knowledgeable of the literature related to your study. You have translated your knowledge into a statement of your research problem. In addition, you have had the advantage of examining research conducted and reported by other researchers with interests similar to yours and are aware of the gaps that still remain in the literature. The purpose of writing Chapter Two is to provide the reader with an overview of the *significant* research related to your research problem. In doing so, Chapter Two provides contextual background information for your research problem as well as justification and rationale for your research design.

For some researchers, this chapter is difficult to write. There are several reasons for this. First, it may be difficult to determine what literature to report and what to exclude. A common misconception is that the literature review is a comprehensive or chronological summary of every research article that has been written about the topic. If this were the case, you would never finish reading all the articles or have time to write about them! This can be a serious problem as you will have read an extensive amount of material and may feel that it is all important. Yet you cannot include it all and judgments will need to be made on what is most relevant to convey the significance of how your research fits with prior work. You should select only the research articles that are most relevant to your research problem and/or study. Another common misconception of the literature review is that it is simply a summary or description of research articles around a particular topic. Although you will need to write a summary of the selected research studies you reviewed, your task is to evaluate and critically analyze the research that has been conducted and connect it to your research study. I will discuss this in more depth in the research synthesis section. Unlike the term papers you wrote as an undergraduate, Chapter Two is not one of those assignments that you can do the night before it is due (and still get an A!). You can anticipate spending more time on this chapter than any of the others. The time required to review the literature will be extensive as well as the time devoted to writing this chapter. You must research the literature, make decisions on which studies are most relevant, critique those studies, and describe how they relate to your research. In other words, your writing is specific to individual studies reported in the literature and not an overview of what has been done. Additionally, the chapter tends to be the longest one in the thesis, so remember to pace yourself and use the chunking method (i.e., one bite at a time). In this chapter, I will discuss how to organize your empirically based research articles, write each of the required sections, and synthesize a research article.

Preparation and Organization

In Chapter Two, you will retain the same three areas related to your research problem that were identified in Chapter One. Thus, you will use the same three parallel ladders strategy as before. For Chapter One, the first ladder represented the *Statement of the Problem* section where you wrote about the problems within the three areas. The second ladder represented the *Background and Need* section where you discussed the existing solutions and interventions for the problems. For Chapter Two, the third ladder will represent your literature review (see Figure 6.1 for a depiction of the three parallel ladders for Chapters One and Two). The three rungs in the ladder represent the empirical research articles about the three areas. Each area will consist of at

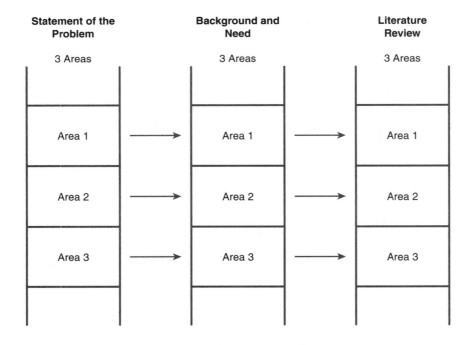

Figure 6.1   The three parallel ladders strategy for Chapters One and Two.

least three empirical research articles. Thus, you will need to have a total of at least nine empirical research articles in order to write Chapter Two.

The first step in preparing the literature review is to read and organize your empirical research articles. You will need to group your research articles according to the three areas. This will indicate whether or not you have the most significant empirical research articles in each area. Remember that empirical research articles are those in which data are collected through quantitative or qualitative methods. Keep in mind that you will not use position papers, literature syntheses, technical reports, and so on, to write Chapter Two (although this may depend on the preferences of your chairperson). Thus, you will need to retrieve articles from research journals (preferably refereed journals). Depending on your field, the research literature changes very quickly, so you want to get the most recently published articles. I would not recommend using an article that is more than five to seven years old unless it was a seminal article. A **seminal article** is one that was significant to the topic (e.g., classic) or created a change in the field. If you are having difficulty finding recent research articles, try the following quick search strategies in relevant search engines or electronic databases: (1) set a limit on the dates, (2) set a limit to journals or research only, (3) search the table of contents in high-quality journals in your field, (4) search the reference lists of good articles, and (5) search for authors who have written extensively on your research problem.

Chapter Two Sections

Once you have reviewed your research articles, you can start to write the literature review. Chapter Two starts on a new page in the thesis. Chapter Two has three main sections: (1) introduction, (2) body of the review with research syntheses, and (3) summary. I will discuss what needs to be included and how to write each section.

Introduction

The introduction in Chapter Two has two purposes. The first purpose is to remind the reader about your research problem, and the second purpose is to inform the reader of the research areas that will be addressed in the chapter. The first paragraph in the introduction is the opening. In this paragraph, revisit the broad problem and research problem from Chapter One. Remember you want to refer to these problems in general terms. Do not write, "My research problem is . . ." Instead, briefly describe the broad problem (e.g., national) and then funnel to the research problem that your study is addressing. This paragraph may seem a bit redundant because it is. As you continue writing, you will notice that there will be a respectable level of redundancy throughout the thesis, especially at the beginning of each chapter.

However, the redundancy is purposeful rather than random. In this context, **purposeful redundancy** refers to intentionally reiterating main points about the research problem and study throughout the thesis. This serves two purposes. First, purposeful redundancy allows each chapter to "stand alone." This means that a reader can begin reading the thesis at any chapter and understand the gist of the research problem and your study. Second, purposeful redundancy links the chapters together so that there is a seamless connection between them. This gives the writing fluidity and unity, and the reader is not left trying to fill in gaps. However, you want to avoid simply repeating verbatim what has already been written unless it is serving a strategic purpose. In other words, you do not want the reader to have a déjà vu, I've-read-this-before moment.

Advance organizer. The next paragraph in the introduction is the advance organizer. In this context, an **advance organizer** is an outline for the literature review and informs the reader of what will be addressed in the chapter. The advance organizer should be based on the three areas related to the research problem from Chapter One. In the advance organizer, explicitly state the areas that will be discussed in the body of the literature review. For example, here is an advance organizer for the three areas from Chapter One:

> The literature review will address three areas of research related to students' with learning disabilities low performance on statewide reading assessments. In the first section, research studies related to the impact of teachers providing students with test accommodations will be addressed. In the second section, there will be a discussion on the difficulties that students with learning disabilities have reading complex genres. Finally, the last section will focus on research-based strategies that have been effective in improving students' reading comprehension.

Here is an example template that you can use to write the advance organizer:

> The literature review will address three areas related to (the research problem). The first section will address research related to (the first area's problem/solution). The second section will focus on research studies about (the second area's problem/solution). Finally, the third section will discuss research related to (the third area's problem/solution).

Once you have the advance organizer, follow this outline and organize the text for the body of the review around each of the sections.

Body of the Review

The body of the review is the heart of the literature review. This is where you will discuss the research in each of the three areas related to your research problem. Remember to label each section with an appropriate level heading (see Chapter 10 for APA style). For example, my heading for the first section would be, *Test Accommodations for Students With Disabilities.* Then, at the beginning of each section, write a brief description about the research topic. Finally, provide a synthesis for each of the individual research studies. Although each article will be synthesized separately, it is important to connect the research articles within each area as well as establish the connections between the three areas. You should also inform the reader how each research article is related to your research problem and/or study (i.e., supports what you are doing or how your study fills a gap).

Research synthesis. The synthesis of an empirical research article is part summary, part analysis, and part critique. In other words, your job is to summarize the study and apply your knowledge of research methods and quantitative/qualitative data analysis to critique the study. Providing a summary of the research article contributes to the body of information about your research problem. Providing a critical analysis of the research article strengthens the justification and rationale for your research study. Thus, you need to do both in order to synthesize the literature and relate it to your research problem. There are 10 basic components included in the research synthesis: (1) introduction, (2) purpose, (3) setting/sample, (4) intervention/issue, (5) procedures, (6) variables/measurement instruments, (7) data analysis, (8) results, (9) conclusions/implications, and (10) limitation/weaknesses (see Figure 6.2 for major components in a research synthesis). Although there are 10 separate parts, some of them may be only one to two sentences while others may be one to two paragraphs, depending on the complexity of the study. I will describe how to write each part with an example research synthesis adapted from a former student's master's thesis (Ho, 2006); there are additional sample research syntheses in Appendix G.

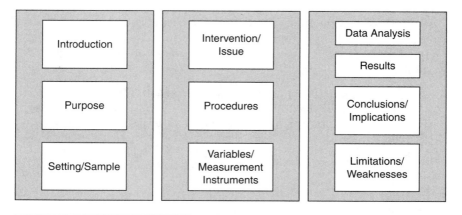

Figure 6.2   Major components of a research synthesis.

1. Introduction: Provide a brief introduction about the topic in the study. You should also define any new terms, if necessary. This information is typically found in the first section of the article where the authors discuss the findings from their literature review. For example,

> Teachers often have difficulty promoting students' knowledge and interpretation of historical events. This is especially true in diverse inclusive settings where students with and without disabilities are taught in the same classroom setting. One alternative method to teach history is through project-based learning. This type of teaching technique utilizes a project-based activity to help students comprehend and apply their understanding of subject matter content.

2. Purpose: Briefly state the purpose of the study and reference the authors in the text with the year of publication (the full citation belongs in the references section; see Chapter 10 for APA style). This information is typically found in the first section of the article right before the "Methods" section. If you are lucky, the authors will explicitly state their purpose; other times you will have to infer the purpose of the study from the given information. For example,

> The purpose of the study was to investigate the effects of a curriculum model entitled supported project-based learning (SPBL) on students' historical knowledge, historical inquiry, and attitudes in inclusive fifth-grade classrooms (Ferretti, MacArthur, & Okolo, 2001). The model was based on both national and state standards for social studies.

3. Setting/sample: Identify the setting where the research was conducted including the state and/or region. Then, describe the participants of the study including their demographic data (e.g., age, grade level, disability, and ethnicity). In some cases, you will need to explain how the participants were selected. This is especially critical if the study used a survey or qualitative design because the sampling procedures are a critical component of the data collection process. This information is typically found in the "Methods" section of the article (sometimes there is a subheading for "Participants"). For example,

> The study took place in two urban elementary schools in Delaware. The participants included three fifth-grade classrooms of 59 students without disabilities and 28 students identified with mild disabilities (24 were identified with learning disability). Sixty-nine percent of the sample group was Caucasian, 28% was African American, and 3% was Hispanic. Four classroom teachers (two general education and two special education) also participated in the study.

4. Intervention/issue: Describe the intervention that was implemented in the study. This is a brief description of *what* treatment the participants

experienced including the materials that were used, professional development or lessons that were taught, strategies or testing conditions, and so on. This information is typically found in the "Methods" section of the article (sometimes there is a subheading for "Materials"). If the study did not involve an intervention, such as in a survey or qualitative study, discuss the issue or phenomenon that was explored. Here is an example of an intervention:

> The students were given a task to investigate the experiences of miners, farmers, or Mormons during the westward expansion period in U.S. history to determine whether or not the group should have gone west. They were first shown a video of an emigrant group during westward expansion in order to pique interest and to build background knowledge. The students were then given primary sources consisting of diaries, journals, photographs, letters, and drawings to read and interpret and were assigned to put together a multimedia technology presentation of the results of their investigation. As part of the intervention, the students were taught lessons on how to analyze and interpret historical evidence. They were also given questions that they could ask each other to help with the examination of the evidence. The questions focused around the people, the problems the immigrants faced, reasons for leaving for the west, and the outcomes that occurred once they arrived. Finally the students were given a narrative framework to organize their information.

5. Procedures: Describe the procedures that were used to conduct the study. This is a brief description of *how* the treatment was administered including the length of the intervention, how participants were put into groups, and under what conditions the intervention was implemented. If the study did not involve an intervention, describe other research procedures that may have been used. This information is typically found in the "Methods" section of the article (sometimes there is a subheading for "Procedures"). For example,

> The intervention lasted for eight weeks over 25 to 29 class periods. The history unit consisted of 14 lessons. The students worked in heterogeneous cooperative groups. The researchers placed students into groups so that there were a comparable number of students with and without disabilities as well as students with average, above average, and minimal knowledge on the topic being studied in each group. As part of the intervention, the students were given instruction on a strategy to help facilitate the analysis, interpretation, and communication of the information they gathered. Each student was given a primary source that he or she would read aloud, describe orally and in writing, discuss within his/her group, fit into the narrative framework, and then transfer to the computer. Once the groups finished their research, they worked on completing the presentation that consisted of both written text and pictures. The students worked on their presentations over eight class sessions. When all groups completed their presentations, each group presented their findings to their peers, teachers, and parents at the school's Open House.

6. Variables/Measurement instruments: Describe the variables that were measured and how the data were collected. This is a brief description of the type of data the researcher collected and the types of measurement instruments used to collect the data. In a quantitative study, report the independent and dependent variables and describe the measurement instruments such as surveys, tests, and so on. In a qualitative study, report how the researcher collected data such as observations, field notes, interviews, and so forth. This information is typically found in the "Data Collection" or "Measurement Instruments" sections of the article. For example,

> There were four dependent variables that were measured in this study: content knowledge, historical knowledge, historical inquiry, and students' attitudes. The first variable was the content knowledge of the unit, which was measured by a 16-item multiple-choice test on westward expansion. A pretest was administered prior to the start of the unit, and a posttest was administered after the conclusion of the unit. To measure historical knowledge and inquiry, interview questions were administered before and after completion of the unit to 18 students with disabilities and 27 students without disabilities. Nine of the interview questions measured historical knowledge, which was based on the students' understanding of the unit in terms of the narrative framework. Eleven interview questions measured historical inquiry. Historical inquiry was defined as the knowledge of why historians study history, how historians know what happened, what types of evidence they use, why historians have different opinions, and why and what types of bias can arise in evidence. Scoring guidelines were developed for the interview questions and interrater reliability on the students' responses was high. The fourth measured variable was students' attitudes including self-efficacy, intrinsic motivation, and attitudes toward cooperative learning and collaborating with peers. This variable was measured through an attitude scale. No information was given about the structure, format, or scoring of the attitude scale.

7. Data analysis: Explain how the data were analyzed. For a quantitative study, this can include the type of statistics or statistical tests that were used. For a qualitative study, this can include the procedures for transcription (for interviews), organization of field notes (for observations), and the methods used for data coding. **Data coding** is a data analysis process used in qualitative research to categorize and label the major themes. This information is typically found in the "Methods" section of the article (sometimes there is a subheading for "Data Analysis") or in the "Results" section. For example,

> After the intervention was completed, several statistical tests were used to analyze the data. A 2 x 2 repeated measures analysis of variance (ANOVA) and a univariate ANOVA test were conducted to determine students' gains from pretest to posttest and if there were any statistically significant differences between students with disabilities and students without disabilities. Differences from pre- to posttest on the attitude scale were analyzed through a MANOVA test.

8. Results: Discuss the results of the study. For a quantitative study, this would include numerical data such as percentage scores, mean scores, or results from statistical tests (e.g., *t* tests). Remember to report the results for each of the variables from the measurement instruments that are relevant to your research problem and/or study. For qualitative data, report the major themes and significant quotes from the participants that support the major themes (remember to include page numbers for quotes). This information is typically found in the "Results" section of the article. For example,

> The results indicated that students in both groups improved their content scores as a result of the intervention. On the content knowledge test, both groups of students had a significant increase in mean scores from pretest to posttest. Students with disabilities had a mean score of 5 (*SD* = 2.1) on the pretest and 9.3 (*SD* = 2.5) on the posttest. Students without disabilities had a mean score of 5.7 (*SD* = 2.5) on the pretest and 11.4 (*SD* = 2.4) on the posttest. The students without disabilities scored significantly higher on the posttest than the students with disabilities. The results were similar for the historical content and historical inquiry questions. For historical content, students with disabilities had a mean score of 2.8 (*SD* = 2.1) on the pretest and 9.4 (*SD* = 4.6) on the posttest. Students without disabilities had a mean score of 5 (*SD* = 3.2) on the pretest and 14 (*SD* = 3.2) on the posttest. The students without disabilities scored significantly higher on the posttest than the students with disabilities. For historical inquiry, students with disabilities had a mean score of 4.3 (*SD* = 2.4) on the pretest and 5.8 (*SD* = 3.2) on the posttest. Students without disabilities had a mean score of 6.5 (*SD* = 1.8) on the pretest and 9.3 (*SD* = 2.5) on the posttest. Once again, the students without disabilities scored significantly higher on the posttest than the students with disabilities. On the attitude scale, both groups improved slightly on the self-efficacy portion, but the students without disabilities made greater gains than the students with disabilities.

9. Conclusions/implications: Discuss the main conclusions and implications based on the results. This information is typically found in the "Discussion" section of the article. However, it is important that you make your own interpretations about the conclusions based on the actual results as authors have a tendency to overstate their conclusions beyond the results. For the implications part, this is where you should make an explicit connection to your research study. Basically, answer the "So what?" question and discuss why these results are important for your research problem or study. For example,

> Several conclusions can be made about the students' learning in response to the SPBL model. First, both students with and without disabilities improved significantly on the content test, and interview questions based on historical knowledge and historical inquiry. The results indicated that students with disabilities had a basic knowledge of history and evidence and that historians conducted investigations. After the intervention, students

with disabilities were able to comprehend the concept of bias and why the interpretations of historians may differ. This provides support for both general and special education teachers to implement a project-based curriculum to improve their students' understanding of social studies content, especially in inclusive settings. However, some of the mean gains on the test and interview questions were relatively small, and the students with disabilities scored significantly below the students without disabilities on all measures. These results indicate that these students may need explicit instruction on the core content in addition to the project-based curriculum. Additionally, the researchers noted the challenges that regular classroom teachers faced with the multimedia component, which questions the feasibility of this type of model in a classroom setting with limited resources and technological support. For future research in this area, providing an additional component using explicit instruction on the narrative framework with less technological demands might strengthen the intervention for teachers and students with disabilities.

10. Limitations/weaknesses: Address limitations or weaknesses of the study. This information is typically found in the "Discussion" section of the article (sometimes there is a subheading for "Limitations"). Similar to the "Conclusions" section, it is important for you to form your own criticisms of the study's design, methods, results, and so on rather than relying on the researcher's stated limitations. Just as researchers have a tendency to overstate their conclusions, they will also often understate the limitations and weaknesses of their study. The limitations and weaknesses section is another area where you should make an explicit connection to your research study. Basically, identify the limitations of the study and discuss how these weaknesses or gaps could be addressed in your study. For example,

There were several limitations and weaknesses in this study. Among the limitations was the unequal participation from the students in the cooperative groups. The students with disabilities struggled to decode words while the students without disabilities quickly read through books on westward expansion. This could have been a decisive factor in their lower test scores and interview questions. Future studies could ensure that students' participation be more equal by having the text read aloud. Another limitation was the consistency of each of the instructional periods due to students with disabilities entering/exiting the class for supplemental services. Future studies would need to control the instructional time and practice to ensure that all students received comparable time. Another limitation of the study was the fact that some of the students could not comprehend the events of another time period. For example, some students had difficulties understanding how it could be that there was not enough land in the Midwest or that during that time, few people lived in Oregon and California. Future studies should incorporate activities that would personalize the events for students so they have a context to draw upon. Finally, a weakness of the study was that the students' difference in background knowledge was not addressed. A future intervention on project-based curriculum models should incorporate explicit instruction on necessary background knowledge.

The research synthesis process that was described is one model to summarize, analyze, and critique each of the research studies related to the three areas of your research problem. If you choose this format, be sure to include transition phrases (segues) between the research syntheses and the three areas so that they are seamlessly connected. However, your chairperson may have additional expectations or prefer a different organizational format, so it is a good idea to check with him or her before you begin writing the body of the literature review. For example, your chairperson may want you to organize each section of the literature review around one specific topic or issue. Rather than discussing each study individually, you would synthesize a group of studies on one specific topic or issue and make references to specific studies to support your claims.

Section summary. After you have synthesized the three articles in each area, provide a summary paragraph for the section. The purpose of this paragraph is to summarize and connect the main points from the three studies. The section summary should also highlight the main limitations of the three articles. For example,

> The research literature indicates that students with learning disabilities continue to struggle with instruction that is delivered in a traditional lecture format. The three research articles that were evaluated in this section provide support for utilizing different types of instructional techniques, particularly project-based and authentic learning experiences that involve technology and cooperative groups. The students with disabilities in these studies who were taught history using these teaching techniques benefited from the instruction, as evidenced by their increase in test scores and attitudes. However, there were several weaknesses to the studies that limit their generalizability to other settings and populations. These limitations included small sample sizes and the limited age groups. Since all the studies were conducted with middle school students, it is unclear whether these results would be transferred to high school students, which is the sample group of this current study. Additionally, other limitations included the consistency of the instruction due to behavior and/or attendance of the students, which could have been a factor that affected the results. These weaknesses will be controlled for in the current study.

Chapter Summary

The last section in Chapter Two is the *Summary*. The *Summary* should have its own level heading. In this section, summarize the key points from the three areas of research as well as the limitations. For example,

To ensure that students with disabilities succeed, it is imperative that these students do not fall further behind in proficiency levels, especially in core content areas such as history. The current materials and traditional lecture methods of instruction in today's high schools seem to put students with disabilities at a disadvantage. Students with disabilities have a particularly difficult time comprehending expository texts, which is the dominant form used in history textbooks and curriculum. The research studies reviewed in this chapter indicated that students with disabilities benefit from direct and explicit instruction in different types of expository texts to assist in their comprehension of their textbooks. Additionally, researchers found that utilizing and activating students' prior knowledge helped in their reading comprehension, memorization, and recall of information and text. Another area that has been studied and shown to be beneficial for students' comprehension was utilizing different types of instructional techniques, particularly project-based and experiential learning strategies that involved technology and cooperative groups. Although these studies showed beneficial methods for the students involved, the studies used small sample sizes and a narrow range of student ages, particularly middle school ages, which made it difficult to generalize across the population. Additionally, some of the studies did not include students with disabilities in their sample groups. More research with a more diverse sample of students at different grade levels is needed to determine if these strategies would be successful across student populations. This current study will contribute to the existing research literature by measuring the effects of a project-based experiential learning strategy on the comprehension of historical content for high school students with disabilities.

In essence, the *Summary* provides a picture of the most pertinent research in the literature related to your research problem as well as a rationale for how your study contributes to the literature. Thus, you should conclude the summary with a brief statement of how the literature supports what you are addressing in your study. Writing a strong summary at the end of the chapter is vital because you want to leave a lasting impression on the reader and convince him or her that your study is absolutely essential.

Summary

Chapter Two is a critical chapter in the thesis because it provides an overview of the research literature related to your problem and study. In doing so, you show the reader that you are knowledgeable about the existing research and that your study fills a much-needed gap. In synthesizing the empirical research articles, you have provided both a summary of the studies as well as a critique (which provides a rationale for your study). Keep in mind that Chapter Two is probably the most time-consuming and longest chapter in the thesis so make sure to pace yourself. In addition, give yourself the time to read the research before you start to write. This may be the only chance you have to delve into a specific research topic and you might actually find yourself enjoying the process! In the next chapter, I will discuss how to write Chapter Three, Methods, for your thesis. Here is a summary of the most critical points from Chapter 6:

- The purpose of writing Chapter Two is to provide the reader with an overview of the *significant* research related to your research problem.

- A common misconception is that the literature review is a comprehensive or chronological summary of every research article that has been written about the topic.

- A required skill to write Chapter Two is to be able to evaluate and critically analyze the research that has been conducted and connect it to your research study.

- In Chapter Two, you will retain the same three areas related to your research problem that were identified in Chapter One.

- You will need to have a total of at least nine empirical research articles in order to write Chapter Two.

- Chapter Two has three main sections: (1) introduction, (2) body of the review with research syntheses, and (3) summary.

- Purposeful redundancy allows each chapter to "stand alone" and links the chapters together so that there is a seamless connection between them.

- To synthesize an empirical research article, you will need to summarize the study and apply your knowledge of research methods and quantitative/ qualitative data analysis to critique it.

- Make your own interpretations about the conclusions based on the actual results as authors have a tendency to overstate their conclusions beyond the results.

- Form your own criticisms of the study's design, methods, results, and so on, rather than relying on the researcher's comments.

Resources

Common Obstacles and Practical Solutions

1. A common obstacle that students face at this stage is selecting the articles to include in Chapter Two. Words that come to mind are, "I have over

30 articles!" Although it seemed like a good idea at the time to collect as many as possible, having 30 research articles for Chapter Two is 20 too many. Remember that the purpose of the literature review is to synthesize the most critical and relevant articles for your research topic; the purpose is not to write the historical chronicle of your research topic. With that said, pick only the research articles that fit the three related areas and can support, justify, or reveal a gap related to your research topic.

2. Another common obstacle faced by students is synthesizing all the research articles. Words that come to mind are, "I don't have time to read and critique all these articles!" If you took my advice in the first tip above, you should only have to synthesize between 9 and 12 articles. This is where the chunking method is critical. Plan a schedule where you tackle one article per day (or one per thesis session). At the first session, read the article carefully and highlight the 10 main components (see Figure 6.2). Make notes on the article where you can critique the study's design, methods, results, and conclusions/implications and also note how the article relates to your study. At the next session, use your notes to summarize and synthesize the article. Take a much deserved break and start the next article.

 ## Reflection/Discussion Questions

Before you write Chapter Two, it is important to identify the common thread that will be carried over from Chapter One so that the thesis appears to be seamless. Chapter Two also requires you to extract your prior knowledge of research methods as you synthesize the articles. The following reflection/discussion questions will help guide you through these two processes.

1. What is purposeful redundancy? What is the goal of using purposeful redundancy in the thesis? How is it different from repetition? Give examples of how and where purposeful redundancy would be appropriate to use in Chapter Two.

2. What is a research synthesis? How does a research synthesis differ from a summary? Use an empirical research article and locate/describe the parts that should be included in the research synthesis.

 ## Try It Exercises

The following exercises are designed to help you write Chapter Two. In Activity One, you will identify the empirically based articles that are related to your three areas. In Activity Two, you will write the introduction and advance organizer paragraphs for Chapter Two. In Activity Three, you will synthesize one of the research articles for Chapter Two.

1. Activity One: For this activity, focus on the research literature related to your research problem and study.

- List the three areas from Chapter One that are related to your research problem or study.
- For each area, write the full citation of three empirical research articles that can be included in Chapter Two (you should have a total of at least nine articles).

2. Activity Two: For this activity, focus on your research problem and study and the three related areas.

- Write an introduction paragraph to Chapter Two, Review of the Literature. Remember to use purposeful redundancy when you address the broad issues and then funnel to your specific research problem.
- Write an advance organizer for Chapter Two, Review of the Literature. Remember to outline the three areas of research that will be discussed. You can use the following template:

The literature review will address three areas related to (the research problem). The first section will address research related to (the first area's problem/solution). The second section will focus on research studies about (the second area's problem/solution). Finally, the third section will discuss research related to (the third area's problem/solution).

3. Activity Three: For this activity, focus on one of the empirical research articles from the three related areas.

- Write a research synthesis for one article for the literature review. Remember to include the following parts: (1) introduction, (2) purpose, (3) setting/sample, (4) intervention/issue, (5) procedures, (6) variables/measurement instruments, (7) data analysis, (8) results, (9) conclusions/implications, and (10) limitations/weaknesses. Then, submit the synthesis to your chairperson for review to make sure you are on the right track!

Key Terms

- advance organizer
- data coding

- purposeful redundancy
- seminal article

Suggested Readings

- Fenton, P. (2002). *Literature reviews and thesis structure: For master's and doctoral students*. Unpublished manuscript, Massey University, Auckland, Australia.

- Galvan, J. L. (2006). *Writing literature reviews* (3rd ed.). Glendale, CA: Pyrczak.

Web Links

- Garbl's Writing Center
  http://garbl.home.comcast.net/~garbl/

- Guide to Grammar and Writing
  http://grammar.ccc.commnet.edu/grammar/

- Sample APA literature review
  http://owl.english.purdue.edu/media/pdf/20070515025950_667.pdf

7

How to Write
Chapter Three, Methods

Preparation and Organization	138
Chapter Three Sections	139
Introduction	140
Setting	142
Sample/Participants	142
Intervention and Materials	144
Measurement Instruments	146
Validity and Reliability	149
Data Collection/Procedures	150
Data Analysis	153
Summary	155
Resources	156
Common Obstacles and Practical Solutions	156
Reflection/Discussion Questions	157
Try It Exercises	157
Key Terms	158
Suggested Readings	158
Web Links	159

The discipline of the writer is to learn to be still and listen to what his subject has to tell him.

—Rachel Louise Carson

If you have successfully completed Chapter Two, Review of the Literature, of your master's thesis—well done! Feel free to take a short break and reward yourself for the hard work up to this point. Then roll up your sleeves, grab the coffee mug, and wipe the dust off the computer! This chapter will focus on how to write Chapter Three, Methods (also referred to as Methodology), of the research study and thesis. After sweating through Chapters One and Two, Chapter Three will probably be the most enjoyable to write because this is where you describe your research design and the procedures implemented in your study. In doing so, you will apply what you have learned in your research preparation and in the review of the literature. Chapter Three is very important because your chairperson and committee members will review this chapter carefully to determine if the research design is appropriate and identify areas that need to be improved.

Chapter Three, Methods, is a critical component of the master's thesis. In this chapter, you will describe in detail how you conducted your research study (i.e., the methodology that you employed). The Methods chapter describes and explains the research design: setting/sample, measurement instruments, procedures, and analysis that were used to complete the study. The Methods chapter needs to be written with sufficient detail to provide a context for the results in Chapter Four and for replicability purposes. **Replicability** refers to the ability to replicate (i.e., copy) the study in order to verify and interpret the results or adapt and expand the study. Do not worry, replicability does not mean you have to redo your study, but others may want to. If you have selected a research problem that has wide interest, it is likely that someone will want to conduct a study in hopes of confirming or expanding your results. For this reason, you want to be certain that the full details of your design are sufficiently described so that someone can independently replicate your study as you conducted it. Since Chapter Three focuses on the methodology of *your* study, it will be based on what you have already done. Now, it is just a matter of writing it in a systematic and comprehensive way.

Preparation and Organization

There are several items that need to be prepared and organized before you begin to write. First, if you have not already done so, it is critical that you prepare a "draft" or "proposal" of Chapter Three before you actually conduct the research. At a minimum, the proposal is a blueprint of the research design and should include the research site, participants, intervention/materials (if appropriate), measurement instruments that will be used to collect data, procedures, and a plan for data analysis. This should be very similar to the research proposal that you submitted as part of your application for the Institutional Review Board. During the proposal stage, your chairperson and committee members will typically want and need to be very much involved. In many ways this is an opportunity for them to teach and for you to learn. If the design is not appropriate for the study, then your work in carrying out the study may not meet the requirements for an acceptable thesis. Sometimes, your chairperson may ask another colleague to assist you on some component of the research design such as the data analysis. Just make sure that Chapter Three's proposal is approved by your chairperson and committee members before you actually begin to collect data!

Chapter Three Sections

Once you have received approval from your chairperson and committee and have organized all of your research materials, you can start to write Chapter Three. Chapter Three starts on a new page in the thesis. Chapter Three is divided into eight main sections: (1) *Introduction*, (2) *Setting*, (3) *Sample/ Participants*, (4) *Intervention*, (5) *Materials*, (6) *Measurement Instruments*, (7) *Data Collection/Procedures*, and (8) *Data Analysis* (see Figure 7.1 for major sections in Chapter Three). If you remember the research synthesis structure from the literature review, the sections in Chapter Three are very similar to a research article. Keep in mind that although they are written and discussed separately, the sections are intertwined and collectively they form the methods of the study.

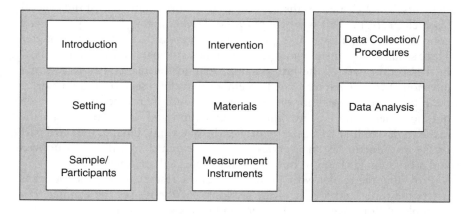

Figure 7.1   Major sections in Chapter Three, Methods.

Depending on your research design, some of the sections listed above may have different titles or may not apply to your thesis. For example, *Intervention* would only be applicable if you conducted an intervention (i.e., experiment) as part of your study. Thus, before you start writing, check with your chairperson for which sections to include. When writing Chapter Three, keep in mind that it is similar to storytelling. You want to tell the reader the "story" of how you conducted your research study, so it should include a setting, characters, and main events (the conclusion of the story will be told in Chapters Four and Five). However, remember that the writing style must be technical in nature, and you must describe the critical elements of the research methods you employed. Consider that the broad audience (readers) may be experienced researchers and/or practitioners. Thus, they will expect to see the elements of your research described in a manner that is accurate but easily understood.

To guide you in writing Chapter Three, I will first discuss how to write each section in general. Then I will provide examples of written work adapted from former students' completed master's theses. I will include examples from both quantitative and qualitative studies when a distinction between the two approaches is necessary. You will notice that the examples are written in the past tense to indicate that the studies have already been completed. Most likely, you will write the Chapter Three proposal in future tense (to indicate what you plan to do) and then come back after the research has been completed to rewrite the chapter in the past tense. However, I recommend consulting with your chairperson to make sure that this is the advised approach.

Introduction

Chapter Three opens with an introduction. The introduction has several elements. The first part of the introduction is a brief reminder of the general research problem. This is where *purposeful redundancy* (see Chapter 6) is a good writing technique. Use purposeful redundancy to connect Chapter Three seamlessly to the previous chapter but also to enable it to "stand alone." In the second part of the introduction, remind the reader of the research question(s) from Chapter One. Remember that the research questions drive the research design and not the other way around. By revisiting the research questions here, you are providing a justification and bridge to the specific research design that was used to answer the questions. Finally, the third part of the introduction is an overview of the research design that was utilized and a brief explanation of how data were collected and analyzed.

Providing the reader with an overview of the research design is critical as it sets the tone (and layout of the sections) for the rest of the chapter. For example, if you used a quasi-experimental research design, the reader will expect to see large groups of participants, independent and dependent variables, and hypothesis testing. If you used a qualitative case study design, the reader will expect to see a small group of participants, description of observation forms or interview questions, and coding of narrative data.

Here is an example of research questions and an overview of a quantitative research design adapted from a former student's master's thesis (Williams, 2006):

The following research questions were addressed in this study:

1. What are the effects of a self-directed learning program on the behavior of high school students with learning disabilities?

2. What are the effects of a self-directed learning program on the levels of self-determination for students with learning disabilities?

This study followed a quantitative pre-experimental model, using a one-group pretest-posttest design. Self-directed learning strategies were embedded into the curriculum of the participating teacher's high school special education English classes. The effects of the self-directed learning program on students' behavior and self-determination levels were then measured through a survey. Self-directed learning tasks implemented in the classroom included writing assignments designed to encourage self-reflection on the student's approach to his or her education, a weekly self-evaluation form that allowed students to self-monitor academic and behavioral performance, and goal development strategies that incorporated appropriate feedback and attributional perspective. Pre- and post-intervention data were collected and analyzed using descriptive and inferential statistics.

Here is an example of research questions and an overview of a qualitative research design adapted from a previous student's master's thesis (Kendall, 2006):

The research questions of this study included the following:

1. What are the factors of communication (verbal or nonverbal) that trigger behavioral outbursts or promote positive behavior/effective communication in a classroom serving students with emotional/behavior disturbances, and learning disabilities?

2. What are the cultural differences in communication (verbal or nonverbal)?

3. What are the factors leading to positive student-teacher relationships?

4. What are the factors that promote a high degree of instructional efficacy?

This qualitative case study described the cultural views of high school teachers and staff and students with emotional and learning disabilities. Interviews and observations were used to collect data in the areas of effective communication, with the primary goal of revealing the relationship between positive and negative verbal/nonverbal communications and students' behavior. The narrative data were transcribed, coded, and categorized into four themes related to the research questions.

Setting

The second section in Chapter Three is the *Setting* (this is the first section that requires a level heading). In this section, describe the research site(s) where the research was conducted. Similar to the setting in a story, the setting in the thesis is where the study took place (i.e., data were collected). The setting could be in a number of locations such as a school, hospital, church, prison, office, home, or even on a bus. In writing about the setting, first provide a description of the broad setting (e.g., school, hospital, juvenile detention center, community center). Remember to include any background or historical information about the setting so that the reader can situate your research site in the broader context. In addition to the broad setting, include a description of the specific area(s) where the data were collected (e.g., classroom, a person's home, office). Include any demographic data related to the setting as appropriate.

Here is an example of a research setting adapted from a former student's master's thesis (Irey, 2008):

> This study took place in an urban elementary school with 241 students located in Northern California. Fifty-nine percent of students at this school qualified for free lunch, and almost 16 percent of the total school population was made up of students with limited English proficiency. Thirty percent of students were Hispanic or Latino, 28 percent were African American, not Hispanic, 17 percent were White, not Hispanic, 9 percent were Asian, 3 percent were Filipino, 2 percent were American Indian, less than one percent were Pacific Islander, and 11 percent declined to state or claimed multiple ethnicities.
>
> The intervention was conducted on a pull-out, individual basis. Instruction was provided in the resource room at the participants' elementary school during the regular school day. The resource room is a small classroom containing a kidney table with a half-sized chalkboard posted at the front wall. There is also a long rectangular table in the back of the room, which is where students received the intervention.

Sample/Participants

The third section is the *Sample/Participants*. There are two parts to this section. The first part describes the sampling plan that was used in the study. **Sampling** refers to the process of selecting participants for a study (Gay et al., 2006). In this part, explain how the participants were selected from the broader population.

The sampling plan will vary depending on the research question and design of the study. For example, if you are utilizing a quantitative research design, you will want to select a large, representative sample group from the specified population. Again, depending on the research question and design, you may need to have a random sample. In a **random sample**, every individual in the population has an equal and independent chance of being selected.

Be careful not to confuse random selection with random assignment. Random selection refers to selecting participants from the population. Random assignment refers to how the participants are put into groups. In **random assignment,** each participant in the sample has an equal and independent chance of being selected for the treatment group. If you are conducting a true experimental study, participants are randomly assigned into different treatment groups. This helps to eliminate the potential bias of having one group (e.g., experimental group) be "stronger" than the other and helps to level the playing field before the intervention begins.

Since it is not always possible or necessary to randomly select from the population, a nonrandom sample is more commonly utilized in a master's thesis. One example of a nonrandom sample is a convenience sample. In a **convenience sample,** the researcher selects the individuals who are available and accessible at the time. An example of a convenience sample is a teacher who includes all the students in his or her classroom. People with clipboards at the shopping mall (the ones that you avoid eye contact with and run away from) are also using a convenience sample when they select shoppers at the mall.

Another type of nonrandom sample is a purposive sample. In a **purposive sample,** the researcher selects individuals who are considered representative because they meet certain criteria for the study. For example, some important criteria for selection are whether the participant is willing and able to contribute to the understanding of the research problem, issue, or phenomenon being explored. In some cases, a specific site might be selected for the sample (Creswell, 2003). This is very common in qualitative studies.

Here is an example of a nonrandom sample from a qualitative study (Kendall, 2006):

> The sampling procedure used by the researcher was convenience sampling. The participants were restricted to those at the researcher's school site who attended or worked at the high school and the participant's willingness to partake in the study. Participants of this research study included twelve high-school students, and one teacher, two paraeducators, and one therapist who worked at a public high school in Northern California. The participants were also selected because they were from diverse cultural backgrounds and part of the same classroom environment where they had multiple opportunities to display and observe communicative behaviors [the focus of the study].

The next part of the *Sample/Participants* section is the description of the participants. In this section, include the participants' demographic data such as age, gender, grade level, race/ethnicity, language, disability, socioeconomic status, occupation, years of experience, and so on. There are several reasons why the reader needs to have demographic information about the individuals who were involved in the study. First, if a researcher wants to replicate the study with the same type of participants, he or she needs to select participants who are comparable to yours. Similarly, if a researcher wants to replicate the study with a slightly different type of participant (e.g., age group), he or she would also need to know exactly who was included in your study in order to make modifications. Another reason for describing the participants is for generalizability purposes. **Generalizability** refers to the extent to which the results about a sample group from a study are applicable to the larger population. This is especially important in quantitative studies. By having a greater understanding of the sample group, the reader can make interpretations about whether or not the results apply to the larger population (assuming that the sample group is representative of the larger population). In qualitative studies, having a detailed description of the participants lends credibility to the researcher (and the results) and helps the reader understand the phenomenon or issue that was explored. Since there is typically a smaller sample size in a qualitative study, each individual's contribution is heavily weighted in terms of shedding light on the research problem(s). Usually there is a table of participants' demographic data included as part of the thesis (see Chapter 10 for APA style).

Here is an example of the description of participants (Kendall, 2006):

> The participants in the study were from diverse ethnic backgrounds. There were 12 high school students. Eight students were African American; 5 were males, and 3 were females. Of the five African American males, there was one 9th-grade student, two 10th-grade students, one 11th-grade student, and one 12th-grade student. Of the three African American females, one was a 10th-grade student, and two were 12th-grade students. The three Latino students were all males and in the 11th grade. The one Caucasian male student was in the 11th grade. All of the students were enrolled in the special day class and were previously diagnosed with emotional disturbance (ED) and/or learning disability (LD). The participating teacher and therapist were Caucasian; the teacher was from the U.S., and the therapist was originally from England. They were both in their mid-fifties and had over 10 years of professional experience. The two male paraeducators were African American and Latino, respectively.

Intervention and Materials

The fourth and fifth sections are the *Intervention* and *Materials*. In these sections, describe the intervention and instructional materials that were used in the study and how the intervention/instructional materials were developed (if appropriate). These sections are necessary only if you included some sort of intervention (i.e., experiment) in your study. In writing about the intervention, you should describe both the independent and dependent variables. Remember that the independent variable is the cause or treatment that is expected to influence the dependent variable (i.e., the outcome or effect). For example, pretend a researcher implemented an algebra intervention with middle school students to prepare them for a statewide assessment. In this study, the algebra intervention is the independent variable and the dependent variable is the students' scores on the statewide assessment.

In a different study with two groups, a researcher compared the effectiveness of motivational interviewing (Spader, 2008) versus traditional nutritional counseling on the eating behaviors of patients with diabetes. In this study, the independent variable was the type of counseling treatment received, and the two levels (e.g., groups) of the independent variable were motivational interviewing and the traditional nutritional counseling. The dependent variable was the eating behaviors of the patients. When describing the intervention, the researcher would include a detailed description of *what* motivational interviewing and traditional nutritional counseling consisted of (the components) and how the two treatments differed.

Here is an example of an intervention adapted from a former student's master's thesis (Kornhauser, 2006):

> The independent variable measured by this study consisted of the intervention program: self-awareness training, social skills training, and increased transition planning involvement. The component of self-awareness training was intended to increase students' understanding and awareness of their specific disabilities, including knowledge of their individual strengths and weaknesses, and ways in which they could compensate for their disabilities. Social skills training involved the examination of conflicts frequently encountered by students, and the development of alternative, positive solutions to these conflicts through direct skill instruction. Lastly, interventions in the area of transition planning required students to participate in activities that would prepare them for a smooth transition into adult life after high school.
>
> The dependent variable measured by this study consisted of students' perception of their own levels of resiliency, as defined by the researcher. Within the dependent variable there were three categories of student perceptions that consisted of self-awareness, social skills, and transition planning.

In the materials section, describe the materials that were used as part of the intervention. Sometimes these materials are from a commercial program and sometimes they are researcher made. Remember to describe the materials in enough detail so that the reader could replicate or adapt the intervention. A good idea is to include a sample of the materials in the appendix of the thesis, so be sure to keep records and clean copies of everything that you used (see Chapter 10 for APA style).

Here is an example of a description of materials (Kornhauser, 2006):

> Three main types of instructional materials were used during the intervention for self-awareness, social skills, and transition planning. Instructional materials to improve students' levels of self-awareness were developed by the researcher. These lessons focused on the study and understanding of students' disabilities, including strengths and weaknesses presented by the disabilities, and ways in which they could compensate for their weaknesses. In addition, students watched a video and used Internet resources to help them understand and gain insight into their disabilities.
>
> Curriculum used in the social skill development lessons was taken from "Skillstreaming the Adolescent" (Goldstein & McGinnis, 1997). Lessons in this

area consisted of activities in which students were required to examine their behaviors in situations involving conflict and discover positive ways in which they could approach these situations. Social skills instruction during these lessons involved components of modeling, discussion, role-play, and feedback.

The transition planning series of lessons was developed by the researcher and drawn from the transition planning curriculum mandated by the school district for all students receiving special education services. The curriculum involved direct instruction that focused on services available to individuals and use of the Internet as a tool to gather information. The curriculum also focused on career planning and independent living after graduation from high school (see Appendix B for sample lessons and materials).

Measurement Instruments

The sixth section is the *Measurement Instruments*. In this section, describe each of the measurement instruments or tools that were used to collect data. There should be a title and brief description of each measurement instrument and how the instrument was scored or interpreted. You can decide the order of presentation of the measurement instruments although I typically discuss the most important instruments first. Keep in mind that you will keep the same order for Chapters Four and Five. To represent this visually, I use the three parallel ladders strategy from Chapters One and Two to represent the order of the measurement instruments (see Figure 7.2 for a depiction of the three parallel ladders strategy for Chapters Three, Four, and Five). The presentation of the measurement instrument in Chapter Three represents the first of the three ladders and each rung represents one measurement instrument (see Figure 7.3 for a depiction of the ladder for Chapter Three). The actual measurement instruments will be included in the appendix of the thesis, so be sure to keep clean copies of all the instruments that you use (see Chapter 10 for APA style).

There are many different kinds of measurement instruments that can be used, and the one(s) that you select depends on the research design and research question in your study. For example, in quantitative studies, researchers commonly use cognitive tests, attitude scales (e.g., surveys), and structured observation checklists (especially for studies that measure changes in behaviors). In qualitative studies, observations and interviews are commonly used.

There are at least three kinds of measurement instruments that can be used to collect data. The first kind is a standardized instrument. This would be an instrument that has been used widely in the field and validated for a particular purpose. For example, in education, the Woodcock Johnson III Tests of Achievement (Woodcock, McGrew, & Mather, 2000) is a standardized battery of tests that measure academic achievement. The second kind of measurement instrument is a researcher-made instrument. This is very common in students' master's theses and sometimes preferable to standardized measures because it can be developed to be more "sensitive" to

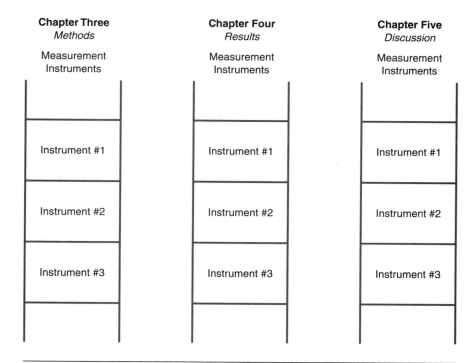

Chapter Three *Methods*	Chapter Four *Results*	Chapter Five *Discussion*
Measurement Instruments	Measurement Instruments	Measurement Instruments
Instrument #1	Instrument #1	Instrument #1
Instrument #2	Instrument #2	Instrument #2
Instrument #3	Instrument #3	Instrument #3

Figure 7.2   The three parallel ladders strategy for Chapters Three, Four, and Five.

what is being studied. For example, a marriage and family therapist might want to develop her own survey to measure clients' satisfaction around a new communication technique she developed for family members. The third kind of measurement instrument is collecting data that are normally collected or already exist. This is also helpful for students' master's theses because it saves time and resources since the data are already being collected for other purposes. For example, in business and management, companies often keep records of employee absences. A researcher might want to explore the relationship between the frequency of employee absences and their level of personal productivity.

In describing the measurement instruments, provide enough information so that the reader is able to replicate the study and/or interpret the results. For a quantitative measure such as a test or survey, this includes a title, description of what the instrument measures, how it is administered, how many items and format of items, sample items, how it is scored, and any standardized benchmarks or norms. For a qualitative measure such as an observation or interview protocol, include a description of what it measures, how it is administered, type and number of questions asked, and sample items. Sample measurement instruments are typically included in the appendix of the thesis, so be sure to keep clean copies (see Chapter 10 for APA style).

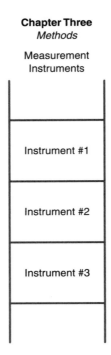

Chapter Three
Methods

Measurement
Instruments

Instrument #1

Instrument #2

Instrument #3

Figure 7.3   Ladder for Chapter Three.

Here is an example description of one standardized test measure (Irey, 2008):

> The Dynamic Indicators of Basic Early Literacy Skills Oral Reading Fluency (DORF; Good & Kaminski, 2002) assessment was used to measure students' fluency scores both before and after the intervention. The DORF is a standardized test that measures students' fluency and accuracy with leveled reading material. Students are given the test individually, and they read three passages aloud for one minute each. During this time the administrator marks any omissions, substitutions, or hesitations (longer than three seconds) as errors. Self-corrections that are made within three seconds are not counted as errors. The median number of correct words per minute read on all three passages constitutes the student's oral reading fluency rate.
>
> The DORF has benchmarks for each grade level. The benchmark goal for students in spring of first grade is 40 words per minute, the goal for students in spring of second grade is 90 words per minute, and the goal for students in spring of third grade is 110 words per minute. Students scoring below 10 in spring of first grade, below 50 in second grade, and below 70 in the spring of third grade are considered at-risk and require intensive instruction.

Here is an example description of an observation checklist (Kendall, 2006):

> The researcher utilized an observation checklist to collect data. The purpose of the observation checklist was to describe the students', therapist's, teachers' and paraeducators' communicative behaviors. The observations were conducted at five different times for an hour and a half for each observation, totaling 7.5 hours of observation. The behaviors observed for the school staff were: yelling, frowning, smiling, laughter, physical contact, close proximity to student, medium proximity to student, long range proximity, fat words, muscle words, negative comments, positive comments, rejection to requests, positive ultimatums, negative ultimatums, negative consequences, positive consequences, directives with no choice, and directives with a choice. The behaviors observed in the students were: yelling, frowning, smiling, laughter, physical contact, close proximity to staff, medium proximity to staff, long range proximity to staff, fat words (i.e., directives that are low in contextual cues), muscle words (i.e., directives that are high in contextual cues), negative comments, positive comments, posturing, horse play, or physical violence. Physical contact, rejection to requests, posturing, horse play, and physical violence all required a detailed description, including antecedent and subsequent behaviors, in order to describe the effect and nature of the behaviors (including verbal/nonverbal, voice tone, laughter, frowning, etc.). The communicative behaviors were tallied to produce a frequency count of each type of behavior. In addition, descriptive and reflective comments with regards to the communicative behaviors were noted on the observation checklist.

Validity and reliability. The last part of this section is a description of the measurement instrument's validity and reliability. **Validity** refers to the extent to which the instrument measures what it was intended to measure. If a measurement instrument is not valid for the intended purpose, then it will be difficult to interpret the results in a meaningful way. A standardized achievement test such as the Woodcock Johnson III is a good example of a measure that would have strong validity data. Just be sure to follow the procedures for administration and scoring, as straying from these procedures will decrease the validity of the results. If you create your own measurement instrument, two ways to increase the validity is to "pilot" it with a small group or have "experts" in the field review it and make any necessary adjustments.

Reliability refers to the extent to which an instrument *consistently* measures what it was intended to measure. If the measure (or individual scoring the measure) has strong reliability, then you should get similar results every time it is administered. Reliability is very important when using two alternate forms of a test or when the scoring or interpretation of the measure is subjective (e.g., coding observations or open-ended questions). If you have two or more people scoring or coding the measures, it is especially critical to have a rubric and do some interrater reliability training beforehand to increase reliability. Keep in mind that a valid measure is always reliable but a reliable measure is not always valid. In other words, you could consistently be measuring the wrong thing over and over. In writing about the validity and reliability of a measurement instrument, be sure to describe how you considered these two issues and amended the instruments if necessary.

Here is an example description of the validity and reliability of some measurement instruments (Irey, 2008):

> The validity and reliability of the DORF and the McLeod Assessment of Reading Comprehension assessments have previously been established (Good & Kaminski, 2002; McLeod, 1999) and each measure has been tested to ensure that the passages are correctly leveled to each grade level. To establish that the prosody checklist was valid, it was used prior to the intervention with students at different reading levels to ensure that it measured all of the aspects it was intended to measure and was appropriate for all reading levels. To check its reliability it was administered multiple times with the same students during a short period of time (so their skill level did not change) and modified as needed until it yielded similar scores on multiple trials. The same procedures were completed with the attitude survey.

Here is an example description of interrater reliability procedures adapted from a former student's master's thesis (Gomes, 2008):

> Another teacher from the researcher's school was enlisted to grade 25% of the reading comprehension tests to ensure interrater reliability. The teacher was chosen because he had read all of the graphic novels used in the study, had taught each of the students, and had a good relationship with the researcher. The teacher was given one test from each group for each phase, totaling 8 tests, which were chosen at random by the researcher. He was blind to the conditions of the study. The teacher was instructed by the researcher to use the rubric to grade each test. The researcher trained him to use the rubric by providing him with a sample test and guiding him in using the rubric to answer each question. He was also instructed to mark items as correct when the participants' answers contained synonyms to the rubric answers. Moreover, he was shown by the researcher where and how to mark the scores of each test. Interrater reliability was established using a point-by-point analysis. The teacher scored 8 reading comprehension assessments using a rubric given to him by the researcher. The researcher compared her scores of the same 8 assessments to the scores of the teacher. For each question the researcher and the teacher matched, a percentage point was awarded. A percentage of agreement was assigned to each assessment.

Data Collection/Procedures

The seventh section is the *Data Collection* or *Procedures*. In this section, describe the data collection or procedures used to conduct the study. In other words, explain *how* the data were collected and/or the procedures that were followed throughout the study. This includes procedures for administering measurement instruments, details of implementation for any intervention (e.g., length of treatment, time of day), and difference of conditions in treatment groups (if there were multiple groups). As mentioned, there are many different ways to collect data depending on the research design and research question. However, detailed descriptions in this section are extremely important for both credibility and replicability purposes.

For a qualitative study, data collection could involve conducting observations, interviews, focus groups, or researching documents, artifacts, and audiovisual materials (Creswell, 2007). In writing this section, you need to explain exactly *how* these data collection activities were conducted. For example, if you conducted observations, describe the conditions in which you conducted the observations (e.g., time, place, frequency), your role as the observer (e.g., participant or nonparticipant observer), and how field notes were recorded.

Here is a description of data collection from a qualitative study (Kendall, 2006):

> The data were collected through observations and interviews. The observations were collected under natural, non-manipulative settings using an observation checklist (see Appendix B). The observations of the participants were conducted in their classroom which was the natural setting. The researcher was a non-participant observer and sat in the back of the room to avoid any interference to the setting. The data collection process took place over a 5 week time period. Observations took place once per week for a one and a half hour time period, totaling 5 observations (7.5 hours of observation time). The interviews were conducted at the school site, and the procedure did not disrupt the participants' normal, daily, classroom activities. The interviews were conducted with the participants individually during their lunch or preparation period in a different classroom, using the interview protocol (see Appendix B). Each interview was tape-recorded for accuracy and lasted between 30 and 45 minutes.

To describe the data collection procedures in a quantitative study, it is easiest to describe each phase of the study. For example, in an experimental study, you could divide the procedures into three phases using the following subheadings: *pretest, intervention,* and *posttest.* In the pretest phase (also referred to as *baseline*), describe any procedures that were implemented prior to the intervention. This includes any measurement instruments that were administered as a pretest or pre-intervention actions such as meeting with the participants or training service providers.

Here is an example of the pretest phase adapted from a former student's master's thesis (Nixon, 2004):

> Each of the measurement instruments was administered to students two weeks prior to the intervention. The two reading comprehension measures were administered individually. The student was given a story to read silently (see Appendix B). Before the student began to read, the researcher prompted,

"Please read this story carefully to yourself. As you read try to remember as much as you can. When you are done, I will ask you to retell the story back to me in your own words. I will also ask you some questions about the story." After the student read the story silently, he or she was prompted, "Now, please tell the story back to me in your own words." The student's retelling was tape-recorded, then transcribed, and used to score the story retelling checklist. At the conclusion of the retelling, the student was then prompted, "Now I am going to ask you some questions about the story." The researcher completed the story grammar checklist as the student responded to the questions. All responses were also tape-recorded in case they needed to be reviewed by the researcher later. The motivation survey was administered to the students as a whole group. Before each administration, the students were prompted, "This is a survey about reading. Each question will tell you the way some people feel about reading. Under each question are five statements . . . a lot like me, a little like me, not sure, a little different from me, and very different from me. Fill in the bubble that shows how **you** feel about the question. Stop and think about each question before you answer. You will have as much time as you need to finish all of the questions. This is not a test and does not count toward your grade. Please take each question seriously and answer it as honestly as you can." At the completion of the administration, surveys were collected and scored by the researcher.

In the intervention phase, describe any procedures that were implemented during the intervention. This includes the frequency and duration, the stages of the intervention, and any measurement instruments that were administered.

Here is an example of a description from one unit of instruction during the intervention phase (Nixon, 2004):

The intervention occurred during the students' Resource Reading/Academic Support class (50-minute sessions) four times per week over the course of 6 weeks. The intervention consisted of three units each designed to incorporate a specific dramatic element into reading instruction. Unit One focused on script-writing, Unit Two focused on the use of props, and Unit Three focused on role-playing. The stories used in each unit were taken from the class textbook adopted by the district for all reading classes and were written at the students' instructional reading level.

The general procedures for each unit were very similar. On Day One of each unit, students read the story independently and wrote written responses to a series of comprehension questions provided by the textbook. On Day Two, the teacher read the story aloud as the class followed along. The responses to the questions written the previous day were then discussed. At the conclusion of the discussion, the teacher would review all group rules, roles and procedures with the class (these were posted on the classroom wall) (see Appendix B) and announce the members of each group, which were selected by the teacher. Group members changed for each unit. The teacher would also introduce the rubric and guidelines for the project the groups would be working on. The rubric would be used by the researcher to evaluate student learning.

On Day Three, students would sit in their designated groups and complete a story outline, including the introduction, rising actions, climax, and conclusion for the story (see Appendix C). They would also begin working on the tasks specific to the unit objective. On Day Four and Day Five they would continue to work in groups. On Day Six, the groups would rehearse their performances. On Day Seven, the groups would present their projects to the class and their performances were videotaped. On Day Eight, the class would view the footage from the performances and receive their project grades based on the rubric and project guidelines established on Day Two. Each student received an individual grade and a group grade for each unit project.

In the posttest phase, describe any procedures that were implemented after the intervention. This includes any measurement instruments that were administered as a posttest or postintervention actions such as a follow-up meeting with the participants. These procedures can be similar to the pretest phase although sometimes researchers may implement additional measures that were not given during the pretest phase.

Here is an example of the description of the posttest phase (Nixon, 2004):

Each of the measurement instruments was administered two weeks after the completion of the intervention. On the reading comprehension measures, students were asked to independently read a different story than the one used on the pretest but at the same reading level (see Appendix C). Posttest administration procedures for all these measurements were the same as those used for the pretest.

Data Analysis

The eighth section is the *Data Analysis*. In this section, describe the procedures that were used to analyze the data from the study. The methods used to analyze the data depend on the research questions and the type of data that were collected. Just as there are numerous ways to collect data, there are also many different ways to analyze data. One suggestion that I give students is to analyze the data so that they can answer the research questions! For example, if one of the research questions asks whether the participants changed their behavior before and after the study, then one of the procedures for data analysis needs to be a comparison of the pre- and post-data.

Another factor in considering how to analyze the data is the type of data collected. For example, in a qualitative study where the data are mostly narrative, this would involve a coding process to organize and label the data into meaningful chunks. This is also necessary to interpret the data and draw out the major themes. Some qualitative data analysis also requires detailed descriptions or "pictures" of the research setting, participants, and activities. I will discuss this in more detail in Chapter 8.

Here is an example of data analysis adapted from a former student's master's thesis (Stephens, 2006):

> The collected data were transcribed and categorized in terms of research questions and emergent themes. Specific interview questions were matched to answer the five research questions. A coding method was used to organize interview data into a limited number of themes and issues around these questions. Quotations were then selected from the interviews that illuminated the themes and concepts. Specific survey questions were also matched to specific research study questions. Data from the survey were also compared with the data from the interview to see if they were in corroboration.

In quantitative studies where the data are numerical, data analysis typically involves either descriptive or inferential statistics. This includes identifying the indices that will be used to describe the data (e.g., mean, standard deviation) or any statistical tests (e.g., t test). In single subject design studies, the data can be analyzed by visually inspecting the graphed data. I will discuss quantitative data analysis in more detail in Chapter 8.

Here is an example of quantitative data analysis (Gomes, 2008):

> Two methods of quantitative data analysis were used in this study. The results of the reading comprehension tests were analyzed using descriptive statistics and inferential statistics. The participants' reading comprehension tests were divided into two subgroups for data analysis purposes: Group 1 was all of the students' mean test score after having read a graphic novel with illustrations, and Group 2 was all of the students' mean test score after having read a text-version of the stories. Statistical analysis using Statistical Package for the Social Sciences (SPSS) software was then conducted on these two subgroups to identify the range, mean, and standard deviation for each group. An independent samples t test was then conducted to compare the mean scores and to identify if there was a significant difference between the two subgroups' mean scores.
>
> The results from the reading motivation survey were analyzed descriptively. The use of zoomerang.com enabled the researcher to immediately view compiled results from the reading motivation survey. The results were reported in three ways: actual number of respondents, the percentages, and as bar graphs. The results were reviewed item-by-item by the researcher. The results could not be looked at by individual participants since zoomerang.com compiled all of the responses together as a group. Therefore, the researcher had to analyze the results by looking at the total number of responses to each individual question on the pre-survey and comparing them to the total number of responses to each individual question on the post-survey.

Although you are reporting the results in Chapter Four, it is important to describe the data analysis procedures in enough detail in Chapter Three so that the reported results will be meaningful. This means ensuring that for every data set collected, there is a description of how the data were analyzed. Many students struggle with this section because of their lack of familiarity with statistics or qualitative data analysis. If this is the case, your chairperson and committee members may offer recommendations; referring to a research methods textbook can also be extremely helpful. There are some textbooks listed in the *Resources*.

Summary

Chapter Three is a critical chapter in the thesis because it explains the methods that were used in conducting your study. Chapter Three is also one of the more enjoyable chapters to write because you are telling the story of how you conducted your research. However, the essential aspect of writing this chapter is to be as detailed and comprehensive in your descriptions as possible. In doing so, you build credibility for your study by giving the reader the opportunity to verify, interpret, and/or replicate the study. In addition, you lay the groundwork for the focus of the next two chapters in which you will report and interpret your findings. In the next chapter, I will discuss how to write Chapter Four, Results, for your thesis. Here is a summary of the most critical points from Chapter 7:

• The Methods chapter describes and explains the research design, that is, the setting/sample, measurement instruments, procedures, and analysis that were used to complete the study.

• The Methods chapter needs to be written with sufficient detail to provide a context for the results and for replicability purposes.

• While conducting the study, keep a log or journal of the dates and times that you collected data, materials or lessons that were used, individuals that you met with, and any problems, surprises, or changes that occurred throughout the study.

• The main sections are: (1) Introduction, (2) Setting, (3) Sample/Participants, (4) Intervention, (5) Materials, (6) Measurement Instruments, (7) Data Collection/Procedures, and (8) Data Analysis.

• You can have a random or nonrandom sample depending on the research design, questions, and accessibility of participants.

• In writing about the intervention, you should describe the independent and dependent variables.

• There are at least three kinds of measurement instruments that can be used to collect data: (1) standardized instrument, (2) researcher-made instrument, and (3) data that are normally collected or already exist.

• The measurement instruments should be valid and reliable.

- Data collection/procedures includes how the measurement instruments were administered, details of implementation for any intervention (e.g., length of treatment, time of day), and difference of conditions in treatment groups (if any).

- One way to analyze data is to organize the analysis around the research questions.

Resources

Common Obstacles and Practical Solutions

1. A common obstacle that students face in writing Chapter Three is failing to keep adequate records about their study. Words that come to mind are, "I can't remember everything I did!" Since it is very likely that you will need to go back to update/revise Chapter Three after the research has been conducted, it is important to keep track of all the research activities. When conducting the study, keep a log or journal of the research activities throughout the study. There is no set structure or format for the log, but you should write down information about the actual procedures that you used (especially details that you might forget about later). For example, write down the dates and times that you collected data, materials or lessons that were used, individuals who you met with, and any problems, surprises, or changes that occurred. This will help to ensure that you are implementing the research design and methods as you described in Chapter Three. Put dates and times on all field notes, observations, and transcripts. This will make the process of data analysis and writing Chapter Three more efficient and less frustrating. In addition to keeping a log, make sure to collect detailed information about the research site and the participants (e.g., demographic data). This will keep you from having to go back to the research site in order to retrieve this information. Remember to keep all collected data in labeled folders and in a safe place away from the research site (e.g., locked file cabinet in your home). You have confidential and personal information related to your participants, so you need to protect the data as much as possible. Finally, keep *printed* copies of any instructional materials, lessons, measurement instruments, audiovisual materials, field notes, and transcripts since you will need to refer back to them. In other words, do not throw any data away, ever, and always **back . . . up . . . your . . . work.** In this day and age where computers are prone to viruses and hard drives crash on a whim, you do not want your master's thesis to be the victim of a "fatal system error" (also known as the "Blue Screen of Death").

2. Another common obstacle faced by students is data overload. Often students will enjoy the data collection process (especially when interacting with participants), but when the study is over, they end up with piles and piles

of data. Words that come to mind are, "What am I going to do with all these data?" When conducting research, more data are not always better. What is most important is that you collect enough accurate data to answer the research questions. In fact, having an overabundance of data may diffuse your research, especially when the data are not related to the research problem or questions. One way to reduce this problem is to align the measurement instruments with the research questions from the very beginning. For example, if you are using an interview protocol, try to identify which items for the interview will help you answer specific research questions (of course you will always have initial buffer questions to build rapport that may not be related to the research questions). If you are using tests or surveys, make sure the items capture the essence of what is being asked in the research question.

Reflection/Discussion Questions

Before you conduct your study, it is important to identify the measurement instruments for data collection. Then, in order to write Chapter Three, you need to be able to "report" how the data were collected for replicability purposes. The following reflection/discussion questions will help guide you through these two processes.

1. What are the different kinds of measurement instruments that can be used to collect data? Give examples of measurement instruments that would be appropriate for quantitative or qualitative research designs. Then, pick a specific measurement instrument and discuss how you could use it in your study to collect data and how to make it valid and reliable.

2. Why is replicability important in research? Give examples of what information is critical to include in Chapter Three so that another researcher could replicate your study.

Try It Exercises

The following exercises are designed to help you write Chapter Three. In Activity One, you will outline the major sections of Chapter Three and begin to flesh out the components. In Activity Two, you will develop or find a measurement instrument that you could use for data collection.

1. Activity One: For this activity, focus on your research proposal.

  • Based on your research design, create an outline of the major sections that you will include in Chapter Three (e.g., setting, sample).
  • For each section, write at least three bullet points (they do not have to be complete sentences) about what you will include in the section (or information that you need to retrieve). For example,

what is your sampling plan? Who will be the participants in your study? What measurement instruments will you use? How will you collect data?

2. Activity Two: For this activity, focus on one measurement instrument that you will use to collect data.

- Develop or find a measurement instrument that you will use to collect data for your study.
- If you want to use a survey, develop or find a self-administered, paper and pencil instrument that you can give/send to a group of people to measure attitudes, perceptions, behavior, and so on.
- If you want to conduct an interview, create a list of questions to ask the research participant.
- If you want to do structured observations, create an observation checklist that you would use to observe, assess, tally, or otherwise document an event in a natural setting (e.g., behavior).
- If you want to use a cognitive test, create or find a written test that you would use to assess knowledge or skills in a subject area related to your research problem.
- Discuss the issues related to the measurement instrument's validity and reliability with your chairperson.

Key Terms

- convenience sample
- generalizability
- purposive sample
- random assignment
- random sample

- reliability
- replicability
- sampling
- validity

Suggested Readings

- Babbie, E. (2007). *The practice of social research* (11th ed.). Belmont, CA: Thompson.
- Creswell, J. W. (2007). *Qualitative inquiry and research design* (2nd ed.). Thousand Oaks, CA: Sage.
- Creswell, J. W. (2009). *Research design: Qualitative, quantitative, and mixed methods approaches* (3rd ed.). Thousand Oaks, CA: Sage.
- Law, M., Stewart, D., Letts, L., Pollock, N., Bosch, J., & Westmorland, M. (1998). *Guidelines for critical review form: Qualitative studies.* Available online: http://www-fhs.mcmaster.ca/rehab/ebp/pdf/qualguidelines.pdf
- McCotter, S. S. (2001, June). The journey of a beginning researcher. *The Qualitative Report, 6*(2). Available online: http://www.nova.edu/ssss/QR/QR6-2/mccotter.html

Web Links

- Basic Business Research Methods
  http://www.managementhelp.org/research/research.htm
- Qual Page: Resources for Qualitative Research
  http://www.qualitativeresearch.uga.edu/QualPage/index.htm
- Social Research Methods
  http://www.socialresearchmethods.net/

8

How to Write
Chapter Four, Results

Preparation and Organization   162

Chapter Four Sections   162

Quantitative Data   163

    Descriptive Statistics   164

        Measures of Central Tendency   164

        Measures of Variability   167

        Additional Ways to Report Data Descriptively   169

    Inferential Statistics   171

        Tests of Significance   172

        Independent-Samples *t* Test   172

        Independent-Samples *t* Test SPSS Output   174

        Paired-Samples *t* Test   176

        Paired-Samples *t* Test SPSS Output 177

Qualitative Data   180

    Major Themes and Patterns   180

    Research Questions   183

    Validity of Findings   185

Summary   186

Resources   187

(Continued)

(Continued)

Common Obstacles and Practical Solutions	187
Reflection/Discussion Questions	187
Try It Exercises	188
Key Terms	189
Suggested Readings	189
Web Links	190

However beautiful the strategy, you should occasionally look at the results.

—Sir Winston Churchill

If you have completed Chapter Three and are ready to write Chapter Four, this means that you have finished collecting all your research data—bravo! You are more than halfway finished with the thesis so keep the momentum going (and the coffee brewing). This chapter will focus on how to write Chapter Four, Results, of the thesis. In Chapter Four, you will report the study's findings; in doing so, you will apply what you have learned from your data collection and analysis. In essence, this is the meat of your thesis. After all the blood, sweat, tears, eye strain, and hair pulling—what did you find out?

Chapter Four, Results, is an essential component of the master's thesis because you will report the outcomes of the study. This means reporting the results of the data analysis for each variable and or measurement instrument that was used in the study. Therefore, you should have already consulted with your chairperson for the data analysis methodology. On occasion, you may need to make adjustments to the analysis or do additional analysis due to participants dropping out, and so on before reporting the results. Depending on the research questions and design, the presentation of the results can be in narrative, numerical, or tabular/graphic format. For example, if you collected quantitative (i.e., numerical) data, the results will be reported in statistical and or tabular/graphic format. These results are reported in a straightforward manner, the writing style is technical, and they can be monotonous. If you collected qualitative (i.e., nonnumerical) data, the results will be reported in narrative and sometimes tabular/graphic format. You will provide thick descriptions of the data to paint a narrative "picture" for the reader. Chapter Four needs to be written with sufficient detail for replicability purposes in case someone wants to verify the results.

In addition, how you report the results here will determine how you interpret and discuss them in Chapter Five.

Preparation and Organization

There are several tasks that need to be completed before you begin to write. First, since Chapter Four will be organized parallel to Chapter Three, I highly recommend that you make any final revisions to Chapter Three before starting Chapter Four. Second, make sure that all the data have been organized and analyzed. This will make the writing process go much faster. Typically, I advise students to analyze data collected from every measurement instrument (e.g., survey, test, interview, observation) to ensure nothing is overlooked. Depending on the data collected, this can involve simple scoring procedures and applying statistical tests or coding data and finding emerging themes. Third, if you are still struggling with data analysis, seek help from your chairperson. He or she can show you the best way to analyze the data or refer you to someone else. Your program or institution may also offer help with data analysis using a software program such as the Statistical Package for the Social Sciences (SPSS) for quantitative data or software computer programs to help code and analyze qualitative data.

Chapter Four Sections

Once you have analyzed all the data, you can start to write Chapter Four. Chapter Four starts on a new page in the thesis. Remember that writing a master's thesis is like telling the "story" of your research study. In Chapter Four, you are telling the main events (in this case main findings) of the research study. However, unlike the first three chapters, there are no predetermined sections except for a brief introduction. This is because the sections in Chapter Four are dependent on the research design and the specific data that were collected, and this varies from study to study. Although there are no predetermined sections, there are common organizational strategies that are used to report the results. Keep in mind that although the sections are written and discussed separately, they are intertwined, and collectively they form the results or outcomes of the study. Check with your chairperson for how he or she wants you to organize the sections in Chapter Four.

To guide you in writing Chapter Four, I will discuss how to report results for quantitative and qualitative data separately. The rationale for discussing them separately is that the data analysis and reporting procedures are very distinct. I will also provide examples of results from different types of studies adapted from former students' completed master's theses. You will notice that the examples are written in the past tense to indicate that the data have already been collected and analyzed.

Quantitative Data

If you collected quantitative data, I recommend that you organize Chapter Four by reporting the results from each measurement instrument independently. In other words, the results from each measurement instrument are organized into separate sections. For example, if you used two measurement instruments, such as a test and a survey, you would report the results for the test and survey in two separate sections with a subheading for each. You also want to report the results in the same order that the measurement instruments appeared in Chapter Three. Remember to use the three parallel ladders strategy from Chapter 7 (see Figure 8.1 for a depiction of the three parallel ladders strategy for Chapters Three and Four). For example, if you described the test first and the survey second in Chapter Three, then in Chapter Four you will report the results of the test first and the survey second. This will make it easier for you to write and less confusing for the reader.

When faced with a quantitative data set, researchers need a way to organize the data in order to interpret and explain the results to others. Otherwise, the process of reporting the raw data would be overwhelming.

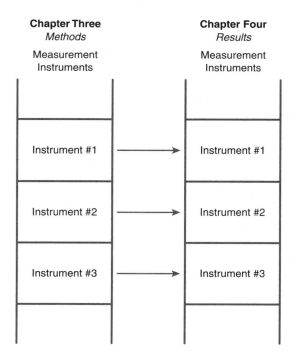

Figure 8.1   The three parallel ladders strategy for Chapters Three and Four.

There are two main ways to analyze and report quantitative data collected from a sample group—using descriptive or inferential statistics. Depending on the type of data collected and the research questions, this will determine how you should analyze and report the data from each measurement instrument. For example, if the data were collected from a survey, you would likely report the data using descriptive statistics. If the data were collected from an experimental study, you would likely report the data using descriptive and inferential statistics. As part of your master's program, I assume that you have already taken a research methods course with an introduction to statistics. This discussion will therefore be a review to focus on the statistical procedures that are commonly used in a master's thesis. I will discuss each type of statistical analysis and reporting separately and share some examples from students' completed theses.

Descriptive Statistics

Descriptive statistics refers to "a set of concepts and methods used in organizing, summarizing, tabulating, depicting, and describing collections of data" (Shavelson, 1996, p. 8). As the definition implies, researchers use this type of statistical analysis to *describe* the data set that was collected from the sample. Think of descriptive statistics as describing a picture of the quantitative results in a way that is comprehensible and meaningful for the reader.

Measures of central tendency. One major type of descriptive statistics is the measure of central tendency. The **measure of central tendency** is the "typical" or "average" score in a distribution. This is important because when you are looking at a large set of scores, there is too much information to digest. Knowing the typical or average score gives you a general sense of how the sample group fared. Usually when someone says "average," I tend to think of the arithmetic mean. The mean is one type of measure of central tendency. The mode and the median are also measures of central tendency.

To help clarify and apply these concepts, I will use a football example (baseball would work too, but my knowledge of baseball statistics is a little fuzzy). I will select my favorite team, the San Francisco 49ers, and my favorite wide receiver, Jerry Rice (when it is your turn, you can pick your own team and player). From 1985 to 2004, Jerry Rice was the wide receiver for the San Francisco 49ers, Oakland Raiders, and the Seattle Seahawks. During his career, he made 1,549 receptions for a total of 22,895 yards and scored 197 touchdowns ("Jerry Rice," n.d.). Knowing his total career statistics gives an overall picture of him as a wide receiver, but they do not show the pattern or trends of his 16 years with the San Francisco 49ers. Using Jerry Rice's football statistics on the chart as a sample group, I will apply some basic descriptive statistical measures, explain how to calculate them, and discuss what these measures tell us about the data set.

Year	Games	Receptions	Touchdowns
1985	16	49	3
1986	16	86	15
1987	12	65	22
1988	16	64	9
1989	16	82	17
1990	16	100	13
1991	16	80	14
1992	16	84	10
1993	16	98	15
1994	16	112	13
1995	16	122	15
1996	16	108	8
1997	2	7	1
1998	16	82	9
1999	16	67	5
2000	16	75	7

The first measure of central tendency I will address is the mode. The **mode** is the most common or most frequently occurring score in the distribution. In order to obtain the mode, find the score that occurred most frequently. For example, if I look at the number of receptions that Jerry Rice made from 1985 to 2000, 82 would be the mode because it appeared two times (1989 and 1998), whereas all the other numbers appeared only once. How would you find the mode for the number of touchdowns scored? Simply go through the column for the number of touchdowns and see which number appeared most frequently. Fifteen is the mode because it appeared three times; he scored 15 touchdowns in 1986, 1993, and 1995. Keep in mind that you can have more than one mode (bimodal), and the mode is not always the largest value.

Another measure of central tendency is the median. The **median** is the middle score in the distribution or the score that divides the distribution in half (50% above and 50% below). In order to obtain the median, I put the scores in order of magnitude from least to greatest. If there is an even number of scores, the median is the score value in the middle of the group. If there is an odd number of scores, the median is the score value halfway between the two middle scores. For example, I will find the median number of Jerry Rice's receptions. First, I need to put the number of receptions in order from least to greatest:

7, 49, 64, 65, 67, 75, 80, 82, 82, 84, 86, 98, 100, 108, 112, 122

There is an even number of scores, so next I have to find the two scores in the middle of the group. If I use the "magic finger trick," where I point two fingers at the outer ends and go in toward the center, the two middle numbers are 82, 82.

7, 49, 64, 65, 67, 75, 80, **82, 82,** 84, 86, 98, 100, 108, 112, 122

Normally, I would find the value that is halfway by adding the two middle numbers and dividing by two, but since they are the same, I know the median is 82. This means that 50% of the number of receptions that Jerry Rice made with the 49ers was above and below 82 (note that the mode and the median are the same for the number of receptions).

How would you find the median for the number of touchdowns Jerry Rice scored? First, put the number of touchdowns in order of magnitude from least to greatest. Then, since it is an even number of scores, use the magic finger trick to find the two scores in the middle of the group. Now, add those two scores together and divide them by two to get the halfway value. If you obtained a median value of 11.5 (10 + 13 divided by 2), you got it!

Finally, the most commonly used measure of central tendency is the mean. The **mean** is the arithmetic average and calculated by the sum of the scores divided by the number of scores in the distribution. For example, to find the mean number of Jerry Rice's receptions, first I add up all the receptions:

$$49 + 86 + 65 + 64 + 82 + 100 + 80$$
$$+ 84 + 98 + 112 + 122 + 108 + 7 + 82 + 67 + 75 = 1,281$$

Then I divide the sum by the number of scores in the set (1,281÷16 = 80.06). Now I know that throughout his career with the San Francisco 49ers, Jerry Rice had a mean of 80 annual receptions.

How would you find the mean number of touchdowns scored per season? First, add up all the number of touchdowns. Then, divide the sum by the number of scores. If you obtained a mean value of 11 touchdowns (176 divided by 16), bravo!

Now that you know how to calculate measures of central tendency to confirm what a spectacular wide receiver Jerry Rice was, how would you apply them to data from your master's thesis? Basically, when you have a set of scores, you should report a measure of central tendency as part of your results to inform the reader about the average score. The scores can be for any variable (e.g., height, weight, achievement level, self-esteem, heart rates) and from a variety of sources such as tests, surveys, observation checklists, and so on. Typically, for the master's thesis I recommend that students report the mean score because it is the most commonly used and takes into account every score in the data set. However, the mode and the median can also be appropriate (depending on the type of data that were collected).

Measures of variability. Knowing the measure of central tendency is important, but it does not give enough information about the data. For example, calculate the mean for each of the two groups of students' math test scores below.

Group A:	5	8	7	10	5
Group B:	8	1	5	14	7

The mean score for each group is 7. Based on this information, I could assume that the two groups of students did similarly well on the math test since they have the same mean score. Now, put the scores in order of magnitude:

Group A:	5	5	7	8	10
Group B:	1	5	7	8	14

If the maximum test score is 15, notice how the scores in Group A are closer together while the scores in Group B are more spread apart. There is not a huge difference in performance between the students in Group A and they cluster closer to the mean; however, for Group B, there was one student who received a score of one and one student who received almost a perfect test score. These scores are farther from the mean. With this information, I can see that the two groups are not very similar even though they have the same mean. Thus, knowing only the measure of central tendency (e.g., mean) is only part of the picture and can be misleading.

If you are describing a set of scores, you also need to report the measure of variability. A **measure of variability** indicates how close or spread apart (i.e., dispersed) the scores are in a distribution. In other words, how much do the scores differ from themselves and/or the mean of the distribution? If they differ quite a bit (scores are scattered), then there is a lot of variability. If they are pretty similar (scores are clustered), then there is less variability. There are many different kinds of measures of variability, but for the purpose of the thesis I will discuss only the range and standard deviation since they are the most relevant.

The range is one measure of variability that you are probably already familiar with. The **range** is the difference between the largest and smallest scores in a distribution. You can calculate the range by subtracting the smallest score from the largest score. For Group A, the range is $10 - 5 = 5$. What is the range for Group B? That's right. The range for Group B is $14 - 1 = 13$. In comparing the two groups, Group B has a larger range, and the scores are more spread apart than Group A's scores. However, the range is of limited use because it only looks at two scores, the largest and smallest scores, and does not take into consideration the other scores in the distribution.

A more commonly used measure of variability is the elusive standard deviation. The **standard deviation** indicates how much the scores vary from the mean in a distribution. The formula for the standard deviation is the square root of the variance, which is the average squared deviation of each number from its mean. Huh? Don't worry—it is not critical for you to calculate the standard deviation by hand because most computer programs or calculators will do it for you (although I think you would enjoy it). However, it is important to understand what it means in interpreting the results. Basically, if the standard deviation is small, then the scores are closer to the mean. If the standard deviation is large, then the scores are more spread apart from the mean. For example, look at the two normal distributions on the graph in Figure 8.2. They both have a mean of 50, but Distribution A is tall and skinny with a standard deviation of 5 whereas Distribution B is short and wide with a standard deviation of 10. This means that the scores in the Distribution A are closer to the mean, and the scores in the Distribution B are more spread apart from the mean. If I had graphed the two earlier datasets of Groups A and B, it would be a similar picture with Group A as Distribution A and Group B as Distribution B.

Since the standard deviation is in relation to the mean, it is critical to report them together (you should also include the sample size). Within APA format, this can be done in several ways ("Reporting Statistics," n.d.). If you want to use abbreviations, they would be within parentheses or at the end of the sentence. Here are the appropriate abbreviations to use: mean = M and standard deviation = SD. For example, "The 10 students in Group A had a higher mean score at the end of the intervention, $M = 18$, $SD = 2.3$." If there are two groups, then you can write, "The 10 students in Group A had a higher mean score ($M = 18$, $SD = 2.3$) than the 10 students in Group B ($M = 14$, $SD = 1.7$)." You can also write statistics spelled out as the subject

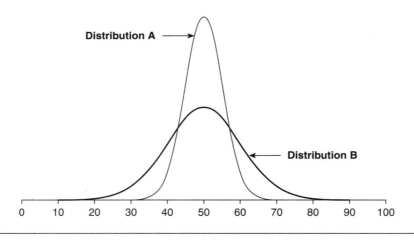

Figure 8.2   Normal distributions with different standard deviations.

SOURCE: Adapted from Lane, 2003.

of a sentence. For example, "The mean score on the math test for the 10 students in Group A was 18, and the standard deviation was 2.3." No matter which format you choose, remember to always report the sample size, mean score, and the standard deviation whenever possible.

Here is an example of results using descriptive statistics adapted from a former student's master's thesis (Henderson, 2007):

> The two measurement tools for social skill levels assessed students on their ability to perform 23 social skill tasks. These tasks ranged from making eye contact when speaking to someone to asking appropriately for help from an adult when needed. The first measurement tool was the teacher ranking survey in which the students' two teachers ranked the students individually on how well they were able to perform on each of the 23 social skill tasks. The only score generated from this survey was a total score. The range of scores for the teacher ranking survey was 36 (minimum 33, maximum 69). The mean total score of the teacher ranking survey was 52.29 points with a standard deviation of 10.13.
>
> The second measurement tool for social skill levels was the student self-rating questionnaire. Similar to the teacher ranking survey, the student self-rating questionnaire also assessed how well students could perform social skill tasks. However, the student self-rating questionnaire relied on the 14 students to rate their own ability to perform the tasks. The range of scores for the student self-rating questionnaire was 50 (minimum 64, maximum 114). The mean total score of the student self-rating questionnaire was 88.50 with a standard deviation of 13.24.

Additional ways to report data descriptively. In addition to measures of central tendency and variability, there are other ways to report quantitative data descriptively. This depends on the research questions/design as well as the intended message you want to convey to the reader. For example, you could report individual scores, percentages, frequency counts, and so on. I recommend that you include tables, charts, and figures as a graphical representation of the results to supplement the narrative explanation (see Chapter 10 for APA style).

If you have a study in which the sample group has only one participant, you would report the individual's scores. Here is an example of results for one participant adapted from a former student's master's thesis (Irey, 2008):

> Throughout the fluency intervention Amber steadily increased the number of correct words per minute (CWPM) from baseline to phase III. During the baseline phase, Amber read 55, 60, 65, 63, and 58 CWPM, respectively ($M = 60$) (see Figure 1). During phase I, Repeated Reading, she read 64, 84, 73, 89, 89, and 84 CWPM, respectively ($M = 81$) (see Figure 2). During phase II, Error Correction, she read 85, 82, 74, 85, 78, 84, and 83 CWPM, respectively ($M = 82$) (see Figure 3). During phase III, Corrective Feedback, she read 76, 82, 83, 90, 87, 88, and 85 CWPM, respectively ($M = 84$) (see Figure 4). As indicated by the CWPM, Amber's mean reading rate greatly increased when she began

Repeated Reading and increased slightly with the introduction of Error Correction and Corrective Feedback.

If you utilized a survey as a measurement instrument, you could report the frequency of responses in percentages across participants or for specific items. Here is an example of survey results adapted from a former student's master's thesis (Iniguez, 2007):

> The first survey item asked students about primary language instruction, *"Being taught in Spanish at school makes me feel good about myself."* On the pre-intervention survey, the mean was 4.09 (SD = 1.37). The frequency of the responses from the pre-intervention survey was: 9.1% chose *(4) A little like me,* and 63.6% chose *(5) Totally like me.* The post-intervention survey results had a mean of 4.81 (SD = 0.40). The frequency of the responses from the post-intervention survey included: 18.2% of the students chose *(4) A little like me,* and 81.8% of the students chose *(5) Totally like me.* The mean difference from pre- to post-intervention survey was 0.72 and the response of *(5) Totally like me* increased by 18.2 percentage points.
>
> Another item of the survey asked students to respond to, *"Being taught in Spanish will make it easier for me to speak English."* The pre-intervention survey results indicated the following scores: 36.4% of the students chose *(4) A little like me,* and 27.3% of the students chose *(5) Totally like me.* The pre-intervention survey results had a mean of 3.81 (SD = 0.98). The post-intervention survey results comprised the following scores: 18.2% of the students chose *(4) A little like me,* and 81.8% of the students chose *(5) Totally like me.* The post-intervention survey results had a mean of 4.81 (SD = 0.40). The mean difference from the pre- to post-intervention survey was 1.00 and the response of *(5) Totally like me* increased by 54.5 percentage points.

In this study, the student administered the survey before and after the intervention. Therefore, she also reported the change in responses from her participants.

If you observed participants' behaviors across multiple phases, you could report the individual or group data for each phase separately. Here is an example of frequency counts from a behavior intervention study adapted from a former student's master's thesis (Rau, 2006):

> Each type of off-task behavior was observed and recorded for the treatment phase. This information was used to determine whether there was an increase or decrease in behaviors from the baseline phase after the introduction of the Student Choice treatment.
>
> Incidents of *cross-talking* were observed and recorded for the treatment phase. Data indicated that there was a decrease in the range, total, and mean of cross-talking incidents from the baseline phase to the treatment phase. The range was 8 which was a decrease from 15. The total was 90 which was a decrease of 54 incidents. The mean number of incidents was 15 which was a decrease of 9 incidents.

Incidents of *out of seat behaviors* were observed and recorded for the treatment phase. Data indicated that the range of out of seat behaviors increased from 4 in the baseline phase to 5 in the treatment phase. The total number of out of seat behaviors was 34 which was a decrease of 16 incidents. Results also indicated that the mean out of seat behaviors was 5.67, a decrease of 2.6 incidents from the baseline phase to the treatment phase.

Incidents of students exhibiting *not working on assignment behaviors* were observed and recorded for the treatment phase. Data indicated a decrease between phases for the range, total, and mean observed incidents of not working on assignment behaviors. The range of incidents decreased from 13 in the baseline phase to 3 in the treatment phase. The total number of incidents decreased from 110 to 72. The mean number of incidents decreased from 18.3 to 12.

Total off-task behaviors was observed and recorded for the *direct instruction* portion of the treatment phase. Results indicated a decrease in the range, total, and mean incidents of total off-task behaviors observed in direct instruction between the baseline phase and the treatment phase. The range decreased from 12 incidents in the baseline phase to 10 incidents in the treatment phase. The total number of incidents decreased from 213 to 192. The mean number of incidents decreased from 35.5 to 32.

Total number of off-task behaviors was observed and recorded for the *independent work time* of the treatment phase. Data indicated a decrease in the range, total, and mean number of total off-task behaviors observed during independent work time between the baseline phase and the treatment phase. The range of observed off-task behaviors during independent work time decreased from 21 in the baseline phase to 7 in the treatment phase. The total number of incidents decreased from 204 to 117. The mean number of incidents decreased from 34 to 19.5.

In this study, the student had a baseline, treatment, and withdrawal phase. Therefore, he was able to compare the behaviors among the different phases and report changes in behaviors.

Descriptive statistics are very useful to summarize, simplify, and describe the data in a study. However, they are also limiting because you cannot make any conclusions beyond the present data. For that I need to journey into inferential statistics. This would be a good time for that coffee break.

Inferential Statistics

Inferential statistics refers to "a set of methods to draw inferences about a large group of people from data available on only a representative subset of the group" (Shavelson, 1996, p. 8). In other words, researchers use sample group data to make assumptions or conclusions about the general population. This is very useful because most of the time researchers do not have access or the resources to collect data from the population. For example, consider how statistics are reported on presidential elections—how do they know that 46% will vote for Candidate A, 44% will vote for Candidate B, and 10% are undecided? Obviously, pollsters cannot ask every single person whom he or she will vote for in the next election. Instead, they ask a *representative* sample, apply statistical tests, and then make inferences about the rest of the country (remember, there is always a margin of error). Keep in mind that the sample must be representative (best done through random sampling); otherwise, the conclusions may be skewed toward one segment of the population or another. Basically, it is more realistic and efficient to collect data from a representative sample of the population in order to make inferences about the population rather than include the entire population in the study.

Tests of significance. Inferential statistics are also used in experimental studies. In these studies, tests of significance are conducted to determine if observed mean differences between groups or conditions represent a real difference or are due to chance. There are many different kinds of tests of significance, but for the purposes of the master's thesis, you would most likely not be required to go beyond applying a *t* test. A **t test** is a statistical test that is used to determine whether the observed differences between *two* mean scores represent a true difference or are due to chance. There are two different types of *t* tests: (1) independent-samples *t* test, and (2) nonindependent-samples *t* test (also referred to as dependent-samples *t* test or paired-samples *t* test). I will discuss each one separately.

Independent-samples t *test.* In a basic experimental study where one independent variable (cause) is manipulated to see its effect on one dependent variable (effect), the **independent-samples *t* test** is used to determine whether the difference in means on the dependent variable between *two independent groups* is a real difference or one that is due to chance. In other words, is the mean difference for the dependent variable due to the independent variable or the result of some other chance factor such as sampling error? In order to use the independent-samples *t* test, the participants and their scores from the two groups must be completely independent and separate from each other. For example, a researcher wants to determine if a math intervention (independent variable) will improve students' performance on the statewide math assessment (dependent variable). If the new math intervention results in significantly higher scores on the statewide math assessment, she will make a recommendation to the state education board to adopt the new math curriculum, so there is a lot at stake. The researcher randomly assigns 60 students into two groups: Group A gets the new math curriculum, and Group B gets the traditional math curriculum. The students are exposed to the two treatments daily for eight weeks. At the end of the eight weeks, they all take the statewide assessment. The mean score on the statewide assessment for Group A was 90, and the mean score for Group B was 85. Since there is a five-point difference in favor of Group A, can the researcher make the recommendation to the state education board to adopt the new math curriculum? Not so fast. Unfortunately, researchers cannot simply eyeball the test scores and say, "Yes, five points seems like a big enough difference." You see, in statistics (and life in general), there is always room for error. Therefore, the researcher does not know whether the five-point difference represents a real difference (due to the new math treatment) or one that is due to chance. This is where the independent-samples t test comes in handy.

With this test, the researcher can determine the *probability* of whether the observed five-point mean difference between the two groups is statistically significant (i.e., represents a real difference). First, she needs to set up a null hypothesis (sorry, I was hoping to avoid this). The **null hypothesis**, H_0, represents the "chance" theory, meaning any observed differences are due to chance, and the treatment has no significant effect on the dependent variable. For example, the null hypothesis for the study would be

H_0: There is **no** significant difference on the statewide math assessment between students who received the new math curriculum and the students who received the traditional math curriculum.

She can either reject or retain the H_0; typically, researchers want to reject the H_0 in order to "support" their new intervention. However, retaining the H_0 may be as valuable to the research literature as rejecting it (you may have discovered what treatment is not effective!). Remember that as the researcher you are committed to reporting the findings objectively and accurately whether or not the data support your hypothesis.

Next, in order to determine whether or not to reject or retain the H_0, the researcher needs to set the probability or significance level (referred to as alpha, or α). The setting of the probability level is a bit like gambling, where the researcher gets to decide how much risk of making an error she is willing to accept. In social science studies, most researchers set the significance level at .05 ($\alpha = .05$), which means they are willing to take a 5% chance of making a Type I error. A **Type I error** is when you reject the H_0 when it is true. In other words, there is a 5% probability that the researcher concludes that the mean difference was due to the treatment when it was really due to chance. The good news is that she has a 95% of being correct (rejecting the H_0 when it is false)! After setting the significance level, the researcher conducts the independent-samples t test and compares the probability value (p value) with the preset significance level. If the probability value is less than or equal to the significance level, then she can reject the H_0. By rejecting the H_0, she can conclude that the treatment did have a significant effect on the dependent variable, and the mean difference was statistically significant and not due to chance. In the math example, this means that the five-point difference between the two groups was due to the treatment. The researcher could then make the recommendation to the state education board to adopt the new math curriculum. If the probability value is greater than the significance level, then she retains the H_0. By retaining the H_0, she concludes that the treatment did not have a significant effect on the dependent variable, and the five-point mean difference was due to chance. The researcher should not recommend the new math curriculum to the state education board.

While it is not important for you to be able to conduct the independent-samples *t* test by hand (and this is not a statistics book), it is critical for you to understand its importance in determining cause-effect relationships in research studies and how to report these findings. Since it is highly likely that you or your chairperson will use a computer software program such as SPSS to conduct the independent-samples *t* test, I will briefly discuss how to read/interpret the output and report the results in APA format. If you would like more information about the independent-samples *t* test or other significance tests, I highly recommend taking an introductory statistics course or perusing a statistics textbook.

Independent-samples t *test SPSS output.* When you conduct an independent-samples *t* test on SPSS, the first output screen you will see is the *Group Statistics* (see Figure 8.3 for group statistics output for independent-samples *t* test). These are the descriptive statistics for the total data set. There are several items to note in Figure 8.3. On the far left-hand side above the first arrow, you see *Statewide Math Test Scores.* This indicates the dependent variable. Moving to the next arrow between the first set of brackets is the two levels of the independent variable—*Group A New Math* and *Group B Traditional Math.* Above the next arrow is *N,* or the sample size, which is 30 in each group. The next two arrows between the second set of brackets indicate the mean scores and standard deviations for each group. Group A's mean is 90 (*SD* = 4.92), and Group B's mean is 85 (*SD* = 4.41).

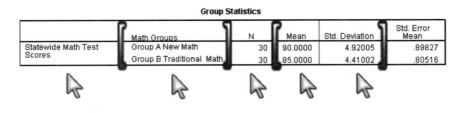

Figure 8.3   Group statistics from SPSS output for independent-samples *t* test.

The next output screen you see is the *Independent Samples Test* (see Figure 8.4 for independent-samples *t* test SPSS output). These are the inferential statistics for the test. There are several statistics here, but I will only comment on the ones in the brackets since these are the items you will need to interpret and report in the results section of the thesis. Figure 8.5 is an enlarged section of the independent-samples *t* test SPSS output that I will focus on. On the left-hand side above the first arrow, you see the *t.* This indicates the value of the *t* test. In Figure 8.5, *t* = 4.145. Alone, this does not tell us whether or not to reject or retain the H_0. Moving to the next arrow, you see *df*. This stands for degrees of freedom. For the independent-samples *t* test, the **degrees of freedom** is calculated by adding the sample sizes of the two groups together minus two ($n1 + n2 - 2$). In Figure 8.5, *df* = 30 + 30 − 2 = 58. Finally, in between the next set of brackets you see *Sig. (2-tailed)*. This is very critical and indicates the probability (*p* value). Remember the significance level of .05 that was set before the test was conducted? I need to compare the set significance level (.05) with the probability value to determine if there is a statistically significant difference between the two groups. If the probability value is equal to or less than .05 ($p \leq .05$), then I can reject the H_0 and conclude that there is a significant difference between the two groups. If the probability value is greater than .05 ($p > .05$), then I retain the H_0 and conclude that there is not a significant difference between the two groups. In Figure 8.5, the probability is .000, which is definitely less than .05. YIPPEE! Typically for researchers, getting a probability value less than .05 feels like winning the lottery (well, almost). In our study example, this means that the researcher can reject the H_0 and conclude that the new math treatment had an effect on the statewide math assessment scores. There was a statistically significant (real) difference in the mean scores between the new and traditional math groups that was not due to chance. She can make her recommendation to the education board.

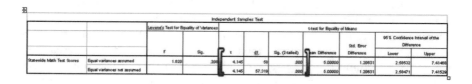

Figure 8.4   Independent-samples *t* test SPSS output.

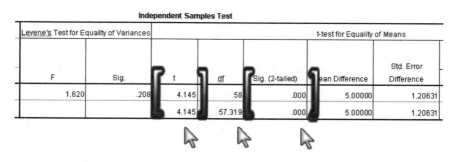

Figure 8.5   Enlarged image of the independent-samples *t* test SPSS output.

There are several variations of how you can report the results of an independent-samples t test in APA format. Be sure to include the two mean scores with standard deviations, t value with degrees of freedom, and the probability value. Here is one example:

> The results indicated that there was a significant difference in math statewide assessment scores between the two groups, t (58) = 4.145, p < .001. The students in the new math group had a significantly greater mean score ($M = 90$, $SD = 4.92$) than the traditional math group ($M = 85$, $SD = 4.41$).

The independent-samples t test is the most common and simplest test to use when comparing mean differences between two independent groups. However, for a master's level research study it may be difficult to have access to a large sample with two separate and independent groups. More commonly, you may only have access to one group. For this type of research design, you need to utilize the nonindependent-samples t test. I will refer to this as the paired-samples t test since this is what is used in the SPSS computer software program.

Paired-samples t *test.* In a basic experimental study where one independent variable (cause) is manipulated to see its effect on one dependent variable (effect), the **paired-samples t test** is used to determine whether the difference in means on the dependent variable between *two sets of related scores* is a real difference or one that is due to chance. This analysis is similar to the independent-samples t test except that with the paired-samples t test, there is no control group and the scores are systematically related to each other. There are different ways for scores to be related, but typically the two sets of scores are from one group of participants. For example, a researcher wants to determine if a new reading intervention that utilizes high school English learners' primary language will enhance their vocabulary performance. He randomly selects one class of 30 high school students who are English learners. The students are given a pretest to measure their vocabulary level before the intervention begins. Then, they receive the new reading intervention daily for 10 weeks. At the end of the 10 weeks, he administers the same test to measure their vocabulary level as a posttest. The mean pretest score on the vocabulary measure was 86 ($SD = 3.86$), and the mean posttest score on the vocabulary measure was 88 ($SD = 3.04$). Since the two sets of scores (pretest and posttest) are from the same set of students, they are in fact related.

In this scenario, the researcher needs to determine whether the two-point mean difference between the pretest and posttest indicates a statistically significant difference (related to the vocabulary intervention) or one that is due to chance. The null hypothesis for the study would be

H_0: There is **no** significant difference between the high school English learners' pretest and posttest vocabulary scores.

In order to determine whether to reject or retain the H_0, he must set the significance level ($\alpha = .05$) and conduct a paired-samples t test. Since it is highly likely that you or your chairperson will use SPSS to conduct the test, I will briefly discuss how to read/interpret the output and report the results in APA format.

Paired-samples t *test SPSS output.* When you conduct a paired-samples t test on SPSS, the first output screen is the *Paired Samples Statistics* (see Figure 8.6 for paired-samples statistics output for paired-samples t test). These are the descriptive statistics for the total data set. There are several items to note in Figure 8.6. On the far left-hand side above the first arrow, you see *Pair 1*. This indicates the pair of scores that were compared—the vocabulary pretest and posttest scores. Moving to the next arrow between the first set of brackets are the mean scores for the pretest and posttest. The pretest mean score is 86.07, and the posttest mean score is 88.23. Above the next arrow is *N*, which is the sample size in each set of scores (note that the 30 for each group represents 30 scores for the pretest and 30 scores for the posttest and not 60 participants). The next arrow between the second set of brackets indicates the standard deviations for each set of scores, which are 3.86 and 3.04, respectively. The *Paired Samples Statistics* indicates that there is a two-point difference between the pretest and posttest score mean; however, we do not know whether this is a statistically significant difference or one due to chance.

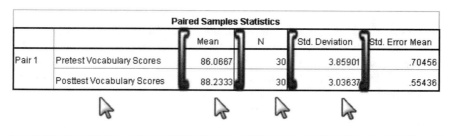

Paired Samples Statistics

		Mean	N	Std. Deviation	Std. Error Mean
Pair 1	Pretest Vocabulary Scores	86.0667	30	3.85901	.70456
	Posttest Vocabulary Scores	88.2333	30	3.03637	.55436

Figure 8.6   Paired-samples statistics SPSS output for paired-samples t test.

The next output screen is the *Paired Samples Correlations*. These statistics tell you the correlation or the relationship between the two sets of scores (see Figure 8.7 for paired-samples t test correlations output). Above the first arrow in Figure 8.7, the *Correlation* column tells you the strength and direction of the relationship. The symbol to represent the correlation is r. Above the second arrow, the *Sig.* column tells you whether the relationship is statistically significant. In our example, the correlation between the two sets of scores is positive and significant since r is a positive number and p is less than .05 ($r = .623$, $p < .001$). This means that the students who scored high on the vocabulary pretest before the intervention also tended to score high on the vocabulary posttest after the intervention.

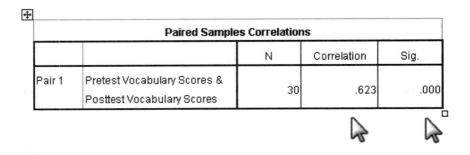

Figure 8.7   Paired-samples *t* test correlations SPSS output.

The next output screen you will see is the *Paired Samples Test* (see Figure 8.8 for paired-samples *t* test output). These are the inferential statistics for the test and similar to the ones for the independent-samples *t* test. There are several statistics here, but I will only comment on the ones on the right side in between the brackets since these are the items you will need to interpret and report in the results section. Figure 8.9 is an enlarged section of the paired-samples *t* test output that I will focus on. Above the first arrow between the first set of brackets is the *t*. This indicates the value of the *t* score. In our example, *t* = −3.846. Notice that this time the *t* is a negative value. This indicates that the mean of the first set of scores (pretest) was less than the mean of the second set of scores (posttest). Moving to the second arrow, you see *df*, degrees of freedom. For the **paired-samples *t* test,** the degrees of freedom are calculated by the sample size minus one (*N* − 1). In Figure 8.9, *df* = 30 − 1 = 29. Finally, in between the next set of brackets above the third arrow is *Sig. (2-tailed)*. This indicates the probability of whether or not there is a statistically significant difference between the two sets of scores. Remember that I need to compare this to the set significance level of .05. Therefore, if the probability is equal to or less than .05 (*p* ≤ .05), I can reject the H_0 and conclude that there is a significant difference between the pretest and posttest. If the probability is greater than .05 (*p* > .05), then I retain the H_0 and conclude that there is not a significant difference. In Figure 8.9, the probability is .001, which is less than .05. YIPPEE! This means that I can reject the H_0 and conclude that the vocabulary intervention did result in a statistically significant

					Paired Samples Test				
					Paired Differences				
					95% Confidence Interval of the Difference				
		Mean	Std. Deviation	Std. Error Mean	Lower	Upper	t	df	Sig. (2-tailed)
Pair 1	Pretest Vocabulary Scores - Posttest Vocabulary Scores	-2.16667	3.08593	.56341	-3.31897	-1.01436	-3.846	29	.001

Figure 8.8   Paired-samples *t* test SPSS output.

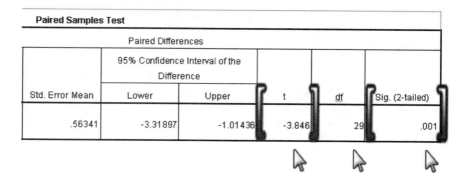

Paired Samples Test						
	Paired Differences					
		95% Confidence Interval of the Difference				
	Std. Error Mean	Lower	Upper	t	df	Sig. (2-tailed)
	.56341	-3.31897	-1.01436	-3.846	29	.001

Figure 8.9   Enlarged paired-samples *t* test SPSS output.

(real) difference in the mean scores between the pretest and posttest vocabulary scores, and it was not due to chance.

To report this in APA format, be sure to include the two mean scores with standard deviations, *t* value with degrees of freedom, and the probability value. Here is one example:

> The results indicated that there was a significant difference between the pretest and posttest vocabulary scores, *t* (29) = −3.846, *p* = .001. The high school English learners scored significantly greater on the posttest vocabulary test (*M* = 88.23, *SD* = 3.03) than on the pretest vocabulary test (*M* = 86.07, *SD* = 3.86).

Here is an example of the results of a paired-samples *t* test adapted from a former student's master's thesis (Williams, 2006):

> To analyze the results of the Arc's Self-Determination Scale (ASDS), first descriptive statistics were calculated for the pretest and posttest scores for each subgroup of the ASDS domains. The pretest means and standard deviations for each subgroup of the ASDS domains were as follows: Autonomy (*M* = .51, *SD* = .20), Psychological Empowerment (*M* = .73, *SD* = .15), Self-Realization (*M* = .75, *SD* = .16), and Self-Determination Total (*M* = .57, *SD* = .15). The posttest means and standard deviations for each subgroup of the ASDS domains were as follows: Autonomy (*M* = .63, *SD* = .18), Psychological Empowerment (*M* = .88, *SD* = .10), Self-Realization (*M* = .81, *SD* = .18), and Self-Determination Total (*M* = .68, *SD* = .14). There were mean gains of .12 in Autonomy, .15 in Psychological Empowerment, .06 in Self-Realization, and .11 in the Self-Determination Total from pretest to posttest results.
>
> Next a paired-samples *t* test was conducted to determine if there was a significant difference between the mean pretest and posttest scores for each domain. There was a significant difference between the Psychological Empowerment pretest mean of .73 (*SD* = .15) and posttest mean of .88 (*SD* =.10), *t* (10) = −3.16, *p* = .01, in favor of the posttest. There were no significant differences between the pretest and posttest mean scores for the other domains or total score.

In summary, the *t* tests for independent-samples and paired-samples are essential statistical tests to conduct when trying to determine whether the difference between two mean scores is statistically significant. They are easy to conduct using SPSS (or even by hand) and the output is straightforward for interpreting and reporting the results in APA format. In addition to the narrative explanation, it is also helpful to include tables or figures as part of the results. Now that I have discussed how to report the results of quantitative data, for you adventurous types, I will trek into our discussion on how to report qualitative data.

Qualitative Data

There is often a misconception among graduate students that interpreting and reporting data from qualitative studies is "easier" or "faster" than quantitative studies since there are no scary statistics involved. However, this is typically not the case. At the end of a qualitative study, a researcher may be faced with piles of data in the form of field notes from observations, transcripts from interviews, documents, audio files, and so on. Therefore, there needs to be a way to organize and analyze the raw data to answer the research questions and provide a deeper understanding of the phenomenon being studied that is meaningful to the reader. This process often includes countless hours to clean and prepare field notes, transcribe data, code data, categorize data, and identify supporting data. As mentioned, there are many different types of qualitative research designs and ways to analyze and report the narrative data. However, from my experience advising graduate students, the two most commonly used data collection methods are interviews and observations. Therefore, I will focus my discussion on how to report these types of narrative data according to (1) major themes and patterns, and (2) research questions. I will also discuss how to enhance the validity of the findings. For more detailed information on qualitative data analysis and reporting, I strongly recommend taking a course in qualitative research or examining textbooks on this topic.

Major Themes and Patterns

One of the ways to report results or findings from narrative data is to organize them around the major themes and patterns. Where do these major themes and patterns come from? Unlike quantitative studies where the researcher has a preset hypothesis that he or she tests, in qualitative research you do not start with preset themes and patterns. Instead, the major themes and patterns *emerge* during data analysis. For you chefs out there, think of this process as "reducing" sauces where you are producing a thicker, more flavorful, and concentrated sauce. Let us use the example of a case study where a researcher wants to examine business managers' communication styles. She spends six weeks taking field notes as a nonparticipant observing the communication interactions between managers and their employees during weekly two-hour staff meetings. First, the researcher codes the data from her field notes by labeling different topics. She puts a code "interaction" every time there was a communicative interaction between the manager and the employee. Next, she categorizes or groups the "interaction" codes into larger meaningful chunks with a new label. For example, perhaps there was a clear distinction in managers who used verbal versus nonverbal interactions or collaborative versus coercive interactions. These larger chunks indicate a potential theme or pattern in the findings. Thus, by coding and recoding the data, the major themes or patterns will emerge depending on the findings in the data. An average of five to six major themes is reasonable. However, the major themes and patterns should also be related to the research questions or purpose of the study. Remember that it is critical to leave your desires and expectations outside of the analysis and reporting process. Although it is inevitable that some personal bias will slip through, you want to minimize this as much as possible.

After the major themes or patterns are identified, each one represents a separate heading and section in the results chapter. Then for each theme, it is critical to paint a "picture" of the findings for the reader by providing a rich and thick description. A **thick description** is an explanation that includes both the behavior and the context in which the behavior was displayed. The concept of thick description was originally derived from the writings of British philosopher Gilbert Ryle and anthropologist Clifford Geertz (Ponterotto & Grieger, 2007). Then sociologist Norman Denzin expanded the definition of thick description in his work:

> Thick description evokes emotionality and self-feelings. It inserts history into experience. It establishes the significance of an experience, or the sequence of events, for the person or persons in question. In thick description, the voices, feelings, actions, and meanings of interacting individuals are heard. (Denzin, 1989, p. 83, as cited in Ponterotto & Grieger, 2007)

As part of the thick description, key pieces of evidence from multiple sources that support the major theme should be included. One major piece of support is in the form of the participants' quotations. This brings the participants' perspective into the study (Creswell, 2007). Keep in mind that you do not want to include everything that was said; instead, quotations should be selected carefully to represent the major theme. This will require you to interpret or infer the participants' true meaning while trying to stay as unbiased as possible. The descriptions could also involve the setting and participants, and the use of visuals in the form of tables or figures should be used to supplement the narrative description.

Here is an example of findings reported around major themes adapted from a former student's master's thesis (Mireles, 2004):

> The informal group discussion provided a wealth of knowledge to the researcher with regards to the elementary students' perceptions around their disabilities. During the discussion, the researcher read from the pre-selected text. At the end of each subtopic, the following questions were addressed: Can you relate to anything in the passage or can you make a personal connection? The discussions were then left purposely unstructured to allow the students to speak freely and openly but with the guarantee of confidentiality. Four patterns of responses emerged from the discussion group: feelings about learning, disappointing others, how learning disabilities make you feel, and types of learning problems.
>
> *Feelings about learning.* The students were asked if they could relate to the statement: For some kids, school is not fun because they have trouble succeeding, and they just do not feel good about learning. All six students were able to verbalize that they do not always feel good about learning. Some students gave concrete examples such as Cesar saying, "I don't feel good when I can't do my work in class."
>
> *Disappointing others.* The students were asked to make a personal connection to the provided statement: Some kids feel like they let down their loved ones. All six students stated that they could relate to disappointing their parents, teachers, and/or themselves. Cesar stated, "I disappoint my parents and teachers every day when I don't do my work and I act out in class." At first Jessica and Charlie were both reluctant to state that they disappointed anyone. Then Jessica said,
>
>> I know that my parents don't get mad when I do things wrong. But I know that I disappoint myself because there are things that I can't do. I try and try but I can't. Someone always tells me that I am wrong. This is why I sometimes don't want to come to school.
>
> Charlie stated that he knows he disappoints his teachers because, "I just don't get things, especially math. Even when things are explained over and over, I still have trouble."
>
> *How learning disabilities make you feel.* This section provided a lot of opportunity for discussion. When the students heard the word "dumb" in the text, some students verbalized that they felt dumb at times. However, Jessica was also able to express that having a type of learning disability does not mean that you are dumb. She made the personal connection that her father also had a learning disability, and he too had difficulty in school.
>
> *Types of learning problems.* In this section, the students had the opportunity to relate to the difficulties faced by students with learning disabilities. The text discussed difficulties such as memory, concentration, and the ability to make

friends, etc. Kenny, Cesar, and Jessica could all relate to the difficulty with concentration. In response to memory problems, Sam stated, "I just get so frustrated because I don't know my multiplication facts. I try and I try but I just don't know. I am never going to learn them so I just have to add." There were not many students who reported difficulty making friends or maintaining friendships, which appeared to be a sensitive topic.

Research Questions

Another way to organize the narrative findings is around the research questions. Here, the researcher is also reporting the major themes and patterns that emerge from the data. However, in this type of organizational format, the research question(s) are directly connected to the items in the data collection instruments. The data collection instruments could be observation protocols, interview protocols, open-ended questionnaires, documents, and so on. For example, a researcher wants to explore the leadership styles of school administrators at high-performing schools. The research questions are

1. What are the leadership characteristics of administrators at high-performing schools?

2. How do these administrators overcome barriers to success?

She conducts one-hour interviews with four administrators from high-performing schools. There are four main questions that she asks at each interview:

(1) What is your leadership style?

(2) What makes you an effective leader?

(3) What are the barriers that you face as a school administrator?

(4) How do you get faculty and staff to support your leadership style?

In this study, the four interview questions are directly tied to the research questions; interview questions one and two help to answer the first research question, and interview questions three and four help to answer the second research question. By connecting the interview questions to the research questions, the researcher increases the likelihood that the data will help to answer the research questions. This also makes it easier to report the findings because you can focus on smaller sections of the data at one time.

Once it is clear which interview questions are connected to corresponding research questions, the researcher must still follow a process for data analysis. After conducting the interviews, she first transcribes all of the interview data. Next, she codes the data from the transcripts by labeling different topics. Then, she categorizes or groups the codes into larger meaningful chunks with a new label. However, the key difference with this organizational format is that she pulls out major themes only from interview questions one and two to answer the first research question. For example, perhaps there was a clear pattern that leaders believed collaboration was a key component of their effective leadership style. Then she pulls out major themes from interview questions three and four to answer the second research question. After the major themes are identified, then rich, thick descriptions with supporting evidence and quotations are reported.

Here is an example of findings reported around research questions adapted from a former student's master's thesis (Kendall, 2006):

> An analysis of the data yielded from the student and staff questionnaires revealed findings within the areas of the research questions. Student and staff participants' responses to the questionnaires were grouped to correspond to the research questions and then categorized for major themes or patterns.
>
> Research question one asked what factors of communication (whether verbal or nonverbal) triggered negative behavioral outbursts or promoted positive and effective communication in classrooms serving students with emotional disturbances (ED) and learning disabilities (LD). The data revealed that the verbal factors of communication that triggered students' behavioral outbursts were yelling, especially once the student was already upset. Other factors included students feeling like they were not being understood or listened to, not getting help with their assignments, and negative peer interactions in the classroom. The nonverbal factors of communication that triggered students' negative behavioral outbursts were slamming books down and making angry faces. The data revealed various verbal factors that promoted positive behavior and effective communication in classrooms serving students with ED and LD. Some of these factors were taking the time to discuss classroom issues with the students in a calm voice, giving the students some extra chances, the implementation of classroom reward systems, explaining the lessons thoroughly when needed, and positive peer interactions. The nonverbal factors that promoted positive behavior and effective communication were allowing the students space when their behaviors were escalating.
>
> The questions on the students' questionnaires that corresponded to this research question were questions 1, 4, 7, 8, and 10.
>
> Question #1 asked what the staff should or should not do to help when the students were having a particularly rough day. Most students responded that yelling would only escalate their behavior, and that the teachers should either speak to them about whatever the problem was in a calm voice or give them some extra chances. For example, one male Caucasian student in the 11th grade said, "They should tell me to cool down or give me a break outside. They shouldn't get on my back when I am mad." A few students felt the need to be left alone when they were having rough days. For example, one female

African American student in the 12th grade said, "[If I am having a bad day,] they shouldn't do anything because I will still get mad."

Question #4 asked for the reasons behind the students' best and worst behaviors. Most students attributed their best behavior to factors outside of the classroom such as having a good night sleep, a good breakfast, good weather, or positive experiences with friends prior to class. For example, one male Caucasian student in the 11th grade said, "I woke up on the right side of the bed, and played with my brother. That made me happy." Other participants reported that on days when their behaviors were at their best, they were connected to factors inside the classroom such as classroom rewards, having lessons explained to them well, or positive student interactions. For example, one male African American student in the 9th grade said, "[The day my behavior was at its best] was the day I hit level 5." With regards to negative behavior, a few students attributed the behavior to factors outside of the classroom such as showing up in a bad mood. Most attributed their negative behavior to factors inside the classroom such as the teacher yelling at them, not being understood or listened to, not getting help with assignments, or negative peer interactions. For example, one male Caucasian student in the 11th grade responded, " . . . when my teacher always yells and gets in my face and I get mad and punch the walls." Another male Latino student in the 11th grade reported, "They don't even listen to me, and they act like I wasn't even there. That's why I had the worst behavior in Mrs. C.'s class because I don't get any help with my work."

Validity of Findings

Regardless of the format that is chosen to report findings, an important component of reporting nonnumerical data is to ensure their validity. Validity in this context is about the quality of the findings, which is different than the validity with regard to quantitative measures that was mentioned in Chapter 7. For qualitative studies, validity refers to the accuracy and credibility of the findings (Creswell, 2003). In other words, are the findings trustworthy? There are several ways to increase the validity of qualitative findings throughout the study such as keeping detailed records, checking back with participants (i.e., member checking), and providing thick descriptions to ensure accuracy and quality. A commonly used method to increase validity when reporting findings is triangulation. Triangulation is "the combination of methodologies in the study of the same phenomenon" (Denzin, 1978, p. 291, as cited by Onwuegbuzie, 2002). **Data triangulation** is one form of triangulation where multiple methods of data collection are used to study one phenomenon. For example, a researcher could use multiple data sources such as observations and interviews to answer the research question. The point is not to combine the data but rather to find the intersections or connections between them. In doing so, the researcher is able to confirm and corroborate findings between data sources and have a holistic picture of the phenomenon.

Summary

Chapter Four is a significant chapter in the thesis because it reports the major findings of the study to the reader. Chapter Four may also be one of the most satisfying chapters to write because after all the months of data collection and data analysis, you finally get to share all that was discovered. Whether you are reporting quantitative or qualitative data, it is critical to be as detailed and comprehensive in your descriptions as possible. This will enhance the validity, quality, generalizability, or transferability of the results. In this chapter, you are also laying the foundation for the final discussion and conclusions, which are the focus of Chapter Five, Discussion, of your thesis. This will be the topic of the next chapter of the book. Here is a summary of the most critical points from Chapter 8:

- Depending on the research questions and design, the presentation of the results can be in narrative, numerical, or tabular/graphic format.

- Before reporting the results, make sure that all your data have been organized and analyzed.

- In descriptive statistics, measures of central tendency, such as the mean, median, and mode, tell you the "average" score in a distribution.

- Measures of variability, such as the range or standard deviation, tell you how close or spread apart (i.e., dispersed) the scores are in a distribution.

- Inferential statistics use sample group data to make assumptions about the general population.

- In experimental studies, tests of significance are used to determine if observed mean differences between groups or conditions represent a real difference or were due to chance.

- The null hypothesis, H_0, represents the "chance" theory, meaning any observed differences are due to chance, and the treatment has no significant effect on the dependent variable.

- One of the ways to report findings from narrative data is to organize them around the major themes and patterns that *emerge* during data analysis.

- Another way to organize the narrative findings is around the research questions where items from the data collection instruments are directly connected to the research question(s).

- There are several ways to increase the validity of qualitative findings throughout the study, such as keeping detailed records, member checking, providing thick descriptions, and data triangulation, to ensure accuracy and quality.

Resources

 ### Common Obstacles and Practical Solutions

1. A common obstacle that students face in writing Chapter Four is being overwhelmed with the amount of results to report. Words that come to mind are, "How do I make sense of all these data?" If you have quantitative data, the best way to overcome this obstacle is to report the results in chunks. First, look at the total data set. Then, examine the data to see which method would make the most sense to report in terms of organization (usually by each measurement instrument). Next, decide whether you should report the data with descriptive statistics, inferential statistics, or with visual representation such as figures and graphs. Definitely get help from your chairperson if you do not understand the results from the data analysis. Then, report the results from one measurement instrument and have your chairperson review it before you go on to do the rest.

2. Another common obstacle faced by students is finding the major themes and patterns in the qualitative data. Although the major themes and patterns do emerge from the data, sometimes it is not obvious as to what they are. Words that come to mind are, "How do I tie all these together?" After coding the data for specific topics, you need to step back and look at the data from a broader perspective. Sometimes, you have to recode the data into larger categories. Using multiple highlighting colors to code or physically cutting and grouping "like data" together may also help to find the themes and patterns. One thing to always keep in mind is the purpose of the study and the research questions. If you use these as your guiding principles, this will help to make sure you do not get lost in all the trees.

Reflection/Discussion Questions

When you report your data in Chapter Four, it is important to understand the differences in how to organize the results (depending on the type of data collected) so that it is meaningful to the reader. This is also important for replicability purposes in case someone is interested in confirming or corroborating the results. The following reflection/discussion questions will help guide you through the reporting process.

1. What is the difference between descriptive and inferential statistics? Give examples of measures of central tendency and variability. Give examples of when you would use an independent-samples t test versus a paired-samples t test. Then, pick one specific measurement instrument that you used in data collection and discuss what type of statistics you would use to report the results.

2. What is the definition of a "thick description?" Why is having a thick description important in reporting nonnumerical data? Give examples of what information you could provide in the thick description to give the findings validity.

Try It Exercises

The following exercises are designed to help you write Chapter Four. In Activity One, you will calculate the descriptive statistics for a given data set. In Activity Two, you will identify the inferential statistics that will be used to report the data. In Activity Three, you will report the findings from one measurement instrument that you used to collect data.

1. Activity One: For this activity, utilize your knowledge of descriptive statistics.

A researcher conducted a study on the effects of an online course to teach nursing students how to provide proper drug dosage calculations for their critical care patients. The students were randomly assigned into two groups: online course (Group A) or traditional course with instructor (Group B). The following data set represents their posttest scores on a drug dosage calculation test. With a partner, identify the descriptive statistics for each set of scores.

Group A:	3	4	4	9	1	15
Group B:	3	17	12	4	3	3

- What are the mode scores for Groups A and B?
- What are the median scores for Groups A and B?
- What are the mean scores for Groups A and B?
- What are the range scores for Groups A and B?
- Which group do you think has a larger standard deviation?
- Report the findings for each group in APA format.

2. Activity Two: For this activity, utilize your knowledge of inferential statistics.

Now the researcher wants to know if there was a statistically significant mean difference between the two groups. With a partner, identify the inferential statistics using the scores from Activity One.

- What test of significance should the researcher use to analyze the mean difference?
- Write a null hypothesis for the research study.
- What should the researcher set the significance (alpha) level at and what does this mean?
- What would be the degrees of freedom for the test?

- If the *t* score is 4.52 and the probability value is .03, should the researcher reject or retain the null hypothesis?
  - What is the researcher's final conclusion about the online course?
  - Report the findings in APA format.

3. Activity Three: For this activity, focus on the data from one measurement instrument that was used during the study.

- Pick one measurement instrument that you used to collect data such as a test, survey, interview questions, and so on.
- Decide the best way to report the data. If you collected numerical data, decide whether to report descriptive or inferential statistics. If you collected nonnumerical data, decide whether you want to report the major themes/patterns from the entire data set or want to connect specific items to corresponding research questions.
- Prepare a draft report of the results and have a partner or your chairperson review it before proceeding with the other data.

Key Terms

- data triangulation
- degrees of freedom
- descriptive statistics
- independent-samples *t* test
- inferential statistics
- mean
- measure of central tendency
- measure of variability
- median

- mode
- null hypothesis
- paired-samples *t* test
- range
- standard deviation
- thick description
- *t* test
- Type I error

Suggested Readings

- Angrosino, M. V. (2005). Recontextualizing observation. In N. K. Denzin & Y. S. Lincoln (Eds.), *The SAGE handbook of qualitative research* (3rd ed., pp. 729–745). Thousand Oaks, CA: Sage.

- Elliot, R., Fischer, C. T., & Rennie, D. L. (1999). Evolving guidelines for publication of qualitative research studies in psychology and related fields. *British Journal of Clinical Psychology, 38,* 215–229.

- Fischer, C. T. (1999). Designing qualitative research reports for publication. In M. Kopala & L. A. Suzuki (Eds.), *Using qualitative methods in psychology* (pp. 105–119). Thousand Oaks, CA: Sage.

- Fontana, A., & Frey, J. H. (2005). The interview: From neutral stance to political involvement. In N. K. Denzin & Y. S. Lincoln (Eds.), *The SAGE handbook of qualitative research* (3rd ed., pp. 695–728). Thousand Oaks, CA: Sage.

- Little, L. (2005). *Reporting results of common statistical tests in APA format.* Available online: http://depts.washington.edu/psywc/handouts/pdf /stats.pdf

- Morrow, S. L. (2005). Quality and trustworthiness in qualitative research in counseling psychology. *Journal of Counseling Psychology, 52,* 250–260.

- Ponterotto, J. G., & Grieger, I. (2007). Effectively communicating qualitative research. *The Counseling Psychologist, 35*(3), 404–430.

- Sands, R. G., & Roer-Strier, D. (2006). Using data triangulation of mother and daughter interviews to enhance research about families. *Qualitative Social Work, 5*(2), 237–260. doi: 10.1177/1473325006064260

Web Links

- Psychological Statistics

  http://www.uwsp.edu/PSYCH/stat/5/CT-Var.htm#II

- Reporting Statistics in APA Style: A Short Guide to Handling Numbers and Statistics in APA Format.

  http://www.ilstu.edu/~mshesso/apa_stats_format.html

- Reporting Statistics in APA Style

  http://www.ilstu.edu/~jhkahn/apastats.html

- Using SPSS to Understand Research and Data Analysis

  http://wwwstage.valpo.edu/other/dabook/home.htm

9

How to Write
Chapter Five, Discussion

Preparation and Organization	192
Chapter Five Sections	193
Introduction	193
Discussion	194
Limitations	197
Recommendations for Future Research	199
Conclusion	200
Summary	204
Resources	205
Common Obstacles and Practical Solutions	205
Reflection/Discussion Questions	205
Try It Exercises	206
Suggested Readings	207
Web Links	207

Say not, 'I have found the truth,' but rather, 'I have found a truth.'

—Kahlil Gibran

If you have completed Chapter Four and are ready to write Chapter Five, this means that you have finished reporting all your research data and findings—fantastic! Conducting research and writing the master's thesis has been like running a marathon. You now realize how much work is involved in conducting research and how tedious it can be at times. In addition, you have learned about the ethics involved throughout the research process. Chapter Five is the last chapter of the thesis. Like the last 6.2 miles of a marathon, it may be the most difficult chapter to write. Chapter Five requires you to think differently about your study than in previous chapters. You are called upon to use all of your research skills and, in addition, you need to utilize the skills of reflection and interpretation. Sometimes readers will read Chapter One and then skip to Chapter Five for a quick check on what you have learned. Thus, you will need to demonstrate what you have learned as a researcher as well as what you learned in your research.

This chapter will focus on how to write the Discussion chapter of the thesis. Chapter Five is a vital component of the master's thesis. This is where you will make the final interpretation of the results that were reported in the previous chapter. However, this is more complex than writing a summary. This chapter needs to be written so that the results are interpreted in a meaningful way, and the implications are made clear to the reader. As you prepare to write Chapter Five, ask yourself, "So what? What do these findings really mean and how do they help me understand the research problem?" Remember that in conducting your research, the end goal was not to collect data and report the results. Rather, the goal was to identify a research problem (reflecting personal interests) and explore solutions and in the process to increase understanding of a particular phenomenon. Keep in mind that your readers share your interest in the research questions.

Preparation and Organization

There are several tasks that need to be completed before you begin to write. First, make sure that all the results have been edited and clearly reported in Chapter Four. This will make the writing process go much faster since you will be following the organizational structure of Chapter Four. Once all the results are in final form, make an appointment with your chairperson. Although you have already discussed the findings, you will need another meeting to help you with the interpretation and conclusions of the findings. Aside from yourself (and some unsuspecting friend or partner), your chairperson is the person most familiar with your research study. With this knowledge, he or she will be able to ask you guiding questions to "draw out" the interpretations and conclusions related to the results. Think of it as a friendly Vulcan "mind-meld." However, before meeting with your chairperson, review Chapter Four and frame in your mind what you believe to be the key findings.

Chapter Five Sections

Once you have met with your chairperson and discussed the final interpretations, you can start to write Chapter Five. Chapter Five starts on a new page in the thesis. Chapter Five is divided into five main sections: (1) *Introduction*, (2) *Discussion*, (3) *Limitations*, (4) *Recommendations for Future Research*, and (5) *Conclusions*. Check with your chairperson before you start writing for how he or she wants you to organize the sections in Chapter Five. If you remember the research synthesis structure from the literature review, the sections in Chapter Five are very similar to the discussion section of a research article. Although they are written and discussed separately, the sections may be intertwined. Collectively, they form the discussion of the study. If writing a master's thesis is like telling the "story" of your research study, this is the resolution or conclusion of the story. As most narrative stories go, there are usually "lessons learned" embedded in the conclusions. To guide you in writing Chapter Five, I will first discuss how to write each section in general. Then I will provide examples of written work adapted from former students' completed master's theses.

Introduction

Like every chapter of the thesis, this one begins with an introduction (this section usually does not have a level heading). In the introduction, remember to use purposeful redundancy to connect this chapter seamlessly to the previous ones. The introduction should include a broad statement of the general problem. This is similar to a recap of the issues raised in Chapter One of the thesis. Then include a reminder of the purpose and design of the study. The introduction should be concise and can be short.

Here is an example introduction adapted from a former student's master's thesis (Gomes, 2008):

> Students with Asperger Syndrome (AS) typically have challenges that primarily affect reading comprehension. Children with AS tend to exhibit high vocabulary and decoding skills, but have low reading comprehension (Gillberg, 1991). This challenge, coupled with an increased emphasis on standardized testing, has put pressure on educators to identify strategies to aid in the development of reading comprehension for students with AS.
>
> Various studies have sought to identify the causes behind this reading comprehension deficit. As previously discussed, students with AS often have high vocabulary and decoding skills, meaning these factors may not be contributing to their poor reading comprehension. One theory is that children with AS have

difficulty creating gestalt imagery when they are reading (Bell, 1991). Research has also shown that a correlation may exist between reading comprehension and one's motivation to read. Since children with AS tend to have circumscribed interests surrounding one or two topics, they are less likely to be motivated to read outside of their limited interests. This could also possibly contribute to their lower reading comprehension skills.

The purpose of this quantitative study was to extend the research on reading comprehension and visualization for students with AS by introducing students with AS to graphic novels, which incorporated both words and images, in order to see if reading comprehension improved as a result of the images. This investigation also sought to determine whether the students' motivation to read was influenced by reading the graphic novels. Previous research using graphic novels with students with AS is very limited; therefore, the intent of this study was to fill a gap and offer further research in this area.

Discussion

The second section in Chapter Five is the discussion (this section usually does not have a level heading). One way to organize this section is to use the three parallel ladders strategy and write the discussion of the results in the same order they were reported in Chapter Four. For example, if you reported quantitative data for various measurement instruments in Chapter Four, then the discussion for each measurement instrument would be written as a subsection in Chapter Five (see Figure 9.1 for the three parallel ladders strategy for Chapters Three, Four, and Five). Similarly, if you reported qualitative data by major themes or patterns, then the discussion for each major theme or pattern would be a subsection in Chapter Five. Finally, if you reported qualitative data by research questions, then the discussion for each research question would be a subsection in Chapter Five.

In the discussion for each subsection, include a summary of the major findings and a brief interpretation of the findings. This section is usually difficult for students because for the last four chapters, you were asked to minimize your personal interpretations of the findings. I usually receive first drafts of this section that look exactly like what was reported in Chapter Four because students do not feel like they have anything "new" or "enlightening" to say. Remember, you have already reported the results in Chapter Four, so you do not need to repeat that information here. Instead, report a summary or synthesis of the major results. The summary should help to answer the research questions. If appropriate, you can include the research questions here as a reminder for yourself and the reader.

After the summary of the major results, provide a brief interpretation of the results. For this process, ask yourself, "What factors from the study could have contributed or influenced these results?" This is where the "interpretation" part comes in except that the "interpretation" is not based on pure conjecture. Instead, it is based on your knowledge of what occurred during the research study. As the primary researcher, you have more information

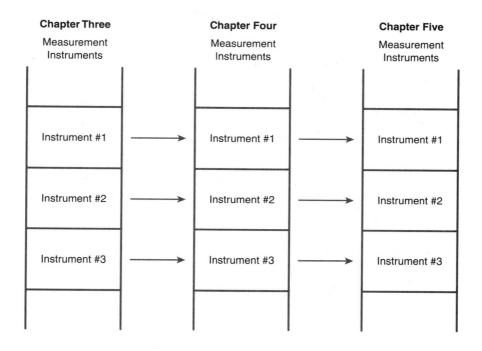

Figure 9.1 The three parallel ladders strategy for Chapters Three, Four, and Five.

about the study than anyone else because you have spent a considerable amount of time and energy at the research site interacting with or observing the participants. Therefore, your interpretations should help to explain, increase understanding, or add a different perspective to the results. However, since they are still considered personal interpretations of the results, be careful not to use strong or definitive language such as "A was a direct cause of B"; instead, use softer forms such as "A may have been related to B" or "A could have been a result of B." In addition, providing "evidence" from the study can support the interpretation that was made.

For example, in a study with a quantitative math intervention the results indicated that there was no significant difference between the pretest and posttest mean scores (this would be a major result to include in the discussion section). However, the lack of significant differences could have been due to certain aspects related to the intervention that only the researcher knew about. Perhaps there were certain parts of the intervention that were not sensitive to the measurement instrument. The interpretation can also provide an explanation of positive results. Perhaps there were certain parts of the intervention that were engaging and motivating to the participants that increased their math scores, but unfortunately this was a small part of the intervention. By providing additional information about the study, you are providing a context for the reader that will help him or her understand and interpret the results. However, be sure that the interpretations are supported by data from the study.

Here is an example of the discussion from a quantitative study from a former student's master's thesis (Hess, 2008):

> The Teaching Each other About Meaning (TEAM) intervention was designed partially to assess the effects of peer-mediated instruction on the inferential reading comprehension of elementary school students with emotional disturbance who are performing at a variety of reading levels. While the students were chronologically in the third through seventh grades, they were performing approximately at the first and second grade reading levels (except for one student who was reading at about the fifth grade level). After working together in their peer-mediated-instruction teams, students demonstrated some improvements in the areas of Basic Skills and Reading Comprehension skills on the Woodcock Reading Mastery Tests-Revised (WRMT-R).
>
> The Basic Skills cluster measured the students' decoding ability. Mean gains in grade equivalency and percentile rank were statistically significant from pretest to posttest. The gain in standard scores was not statistically significant. Through the TEAM intervention, students were exposed to interesting and varied grade-level passages, articles, and stories. Since the text was above some students' grade level, the text was read aloud initially by the researcher to the students while they followed along. Students then had to refer back to the text to extract information for the various skills taught to them during Collaborative Strategic Reading (CSR). Documenting this information on the CSR learning logs may have helped them to learn and remember new words. However, as the intervention took about three months to complete (and was not focused on decoding), it is difficult to determine whether the gain on the Basic Skills subtest was due to the intervention or to the increased language arts instruction that was conducted over the intervention period.
>
> On the Reading Comprehension subtest, four of seven students made gains in grade equivalency, percentile rank, and standard scores for reading comprehension. The CSR skills taught during the TEAM intervention may have had a direct impact on these improvements in the four students' reading comprehension scores. The Preview task not only helped the students generate interest in the text but also allowed them to connect to their previous knowledge about the subject matter. The Click and Clunk task helped the students break down and interpret the meaning of unfamiliar words they encountered. The Get the Gist task helped the students determine the main idea of what they read. All of these tasks were designed to help students understand the text better. However, there were no statistically significant results for grade equivalencies, percentile ranks, and standard scores for the reading comprehension cluster. Although the four students did show improvement, the WRMT-R questions may not have assessed the specific types of reading comprehension skills taught through CSR. In addition, the reading comprehension subtests required that the students read the information independently (as opposed to having it read to them). They may have been difficult for the students since the items were read aloud to them during the TEAM intervention.

Here is an example of the discussion of major themes from a qualitative study from a former student's master's thesis (Kendall, 2006):

> The major communicative factors that triggered negative behaviors were peer "put downs" and "horse play." Based on the observations, the "put downs" and "horse play" started off as playful and friendly. However, they may have been the antecedent behavior to verbal and physical altercations between students. For example, two African American male students, both in the 9th grade, were observed using verbal put downs and laughing until one student said something about the other student's mother. That was when one of the students stood up and began posturing at the other, threatening the student with bodily harm. In another instance, two African American male students, one in the 9th grade and the other in the 11th, were observed "horse playing." Another student who was observing (a female African American student in the 12th grade) began laughing and said to the 11th grade student, "He just dipped you!" The 11th grade student then began to get rough with the 9th grade student, and as the situation escalated, the two students needed to be separated from each other.
>
> The communicative factors that promoted positive behavior and effective communication were using clear language, helping students with their work, and one-on-one interaction. This could possibly be due to an increase in clarity of expectations. Clear communication and direct instruction may have been more successful in promoting positive behavior than ambiguous or negatively affective language because students were observed engaging in more positive behaviors during structured/supervised times. For example, the psychologist never reported having behavior problems when conducting assessments with students in a one-on-one situation. Furthermore, negative behaviors were not observed when the students were given clear instructions during the one-on-one interviews for the data collection of this study. Conversely, when the class was observed returning from lunch, only two out of five students were given an assignment. The three students who did not receive an assignment, began to engage in verbal put downs, and the two students who did receive assignments stopped working after five minutes and began to observe the other three students.

Limitations

The third section is *Limitations* (this section typically has a level heading). In this section, you will discuss the limitations and weaknesses of the study. In Chapter One, there was a section on limitations; however, those were the limitations based on the design of the study. Now that you have completed the study, you are aware of additional limitations that occurred during the study. Remember that all research studies have limitations or weaknesses; as you become a more experienced researcher, you will find ways to reduce the limitations, but you can never get rid of them altogether. Thus, having limitations or weaknesses does not mean that you did a "bad job" on your study. This just means that in research you are rarely able to control all the variables. What you are unable to control becomes the focus of your limitations. The best way to handle limitations and weaknesses in a study are to be honest and up-front about them. Concealing, falsely reporting, or not reporting the limitations would be considered unethical.

There are several benefits to discussing the limitations of the study. First, you can learn from your mistakes. One way to prepare for this section is to ask, "If I had to do the study again, what would I do differently?" This could be a variety of things including changing the sampling plan, adapting the measurement instruments, using different materials, changing the timeline, taking more detailed notes, having more or fewer research sites, asking different questions, and so on. By reflecting on the things that you would do differently, this helps you grow as a researcher and ensures you will not make the same mistakes on your next study! This also helps you to become a "critical consumer" of the research literature as you begin to identify similar limitations/weaknesses in other studies.

Another benefit of the limitations section is that other researchers will learn from your mistakes. By sharing the "do's and don'ts," this will allow the next researcher to modify his or her study before it is conducted to correct for these limitations. For example, perhaps for a quantitative study the next researcher should plan for a longer intervention period. Perhaps for a qualitative study the next researcher should allow for more time and fewer interview questions to obtain more in-depth responses from the participants.

In addition, the limitations may also help to provide possible explanations for disappointing or unexpected results. For example, perhaps many students were unexpectedly absent or pulled out of class during an intervention, or there were substantial behavioral problems that interfered with the teaching. Perhaps there were an inordinate amount of weather-related issues that interfered with data collection (this has actually happened to me!). These would be limitations that could affect the study's results. However, do not use the limitations section as a justification or excuse for conducting unethical or low-quality research. There is no tolerance for "blaming" participants or "covering up" unwanted results.

Finally, when describing the limitations of the study it is not sufficient to list them. The purpose of the limitations section is to allow the reader to make a judgment on how the limitations impacted the research. Thus, you need to explain what the limitation was and *why* it was a limitation. In other words, how did the limitations affect the validity of the results? Remember that there are many different kinds of validity; there is the validity or trustworthiness of the results for qualitative studies and internal validity (variables within the study) and external validity (applicability outside the study) for quantitative studies. Consider limitations as little caution signs for the reader when extrapolating from the results.

Here is an example from the limitations section of a former student's master's thesis (Hess, 2008):

> Although the TEAM intervention helped the students improve their inferential reading comprehension skills and their social skills, there were several limitations to the study. The first limitation was related to the sample and sample size. The sample size was very small—the self-contained classroom in the non-public school consisted of 10 students at the beginning of the intervention. During the study, three students were discharged from the school due to extreme behaviors. A second limitation was that the students were generally placed at this school because they were unsuccessful in public school. The students were all diagnosed with emotional disturbance (ED) but some had dual diagnoses of learning disability or mild mental retardation, while others had minimal issues with learning. Therefore, both of these limitations have an impact on external validity and make the results difficult to generalize to other students with disabilities in special education settings.
>
> Other limitations were related to the implementation of the intervention. First there were problems with the scheduling. There were typically only two sessions per week; therefore, there was a lot of time between lessons, and the students may not have been able to retain information during the gaps in lessons. Furthermore some of the students with ED displayed extreme behaviors such as disruptions, tantrums, and crises during several of the lessons which caused some students to be removed from the classroom by staff escort. This also meant less staff was present in the classroom to monitor and assist the peer tutoring teams. In addition, due to behavioral issues such as extreme tantrums, pull-outs due to therapy sessions, or classroom disruptions, the researcher was not able to maintain the same student teams throughout the program. Therefore, partners were reassigned on a regular basis. The above limitations affect the internal validity of the results—with a greater number of sessions in a more condensed time frame, consistency of partners within a team, and the appropriate number of staff present, the results may have more accurately reflected the impact of the intervention.

Recommendations for Future Research

The fourth section is the *Recommendations for Future Research* (this section typically has a level heading). There are several methods that you can use to write this section. First, you can tie the recommendations for future research to the issues that were identified in the limitations section. In other words, which procedures should be changed by the next researcher? With this method, the recommendations are based on the weaknesses from your study. For example, perhaps you would recommend adding another measurement instrument such as an observation protocol for data triangulation. This will help the next researcher modify his or her study to strengthen it. Another method to consider is to suggest recommendations on how your study could be continued or expanded. In other words, what are the next steps in order to extend the findings that were produced in the study? This will help the next researcher identify gaps that still exist in the literature. For example, perhaps you would recommend implementing the intervention with a different sample group such as adults or a more diverse sample. By including these two types of recommendations, you are making a major contribution to your field in terms of moving the research base forward and launching the next line of studies.

Here is an example of recommendations for future research from a former student's master's thesis (Rau, 2006):

> Based on the results of the study, there are several recommendations for future research. First some of the limitations outlined in this study may be minimized or eliminated in a revised implementation of the Student Choice treatment. In order to improve or verify the accuracy of the data collection, inter-rater reliability could be used to cross check the number of off-task behaviors exhibited and verify the portion of the instruction in which they occurred. Second in order to identify which of the components of the Student Choice treatment had the largest impact on the decrease or increase of off-task behaviors, each of the components could be introduced separately. In addition to determine whether the number of exhibited off-task behaviors remains consistent for longer than three weeks, the treatment phase should be extended. Third, this study did not measure student satisfaction and perceptions toward the increase in choices and decision-making opportunities. Future studies should employ a student survey or interviewing procedure to measure student perceptions toward the Student Choice treatment. Finally this study only measured the impact of the Student Choice treatment on the off-task behavior of students with learning disabilities. Future studies could implement the treatment and measure the impact on students with other disabilities such as emotional/behavioral disorders or attention deficit disorders.

Conclusion

The last section of the chapter is the *Conclusion* (this section typically has a level heading). In this section, you will identify at least three critical conclusions based on the results of the study. One way to think about this is to ask, "What are the three main lessons learned from the study?" Your conclusions are like a synthesis of the major findings. For example, perhaps one of the major conclusions from a survey study on marital satisfaction was that the participants' level of marital happiness was related more to time spent with his or her spouse than the spouse's level of income. The conclusions may also include unintended but significant discoveries that were made as a result of the study. However, base the conclusions on the findings of the study, and avoid overstating or overgeneralizing the findings (i.e., do not claim that you discovered the fountain of youth). If appropriate, you may also reference previous research that either substantiates or contradicts your conclusions.

After you have identified each major conclusion, discuss the implications of the conclusion. The implications are recommendations for how to bridge the "research to practice" and can be in the form of actions, policies, or procedures. For example, one implication from the study above would be for individuals to set aside a period of "sacred" time during the week to spend with his or her spouse even if it means not bringing work home or refusing to work overtime. These implications are critical because the reader has some guidance for how to actualize and benefit from the conclusions.

Here are four different examples of conclusion sections from various students' master's theses. For each example, there is an advance organizer, which states the major conclusions, and then a discussion around one of the conclusions with implications.

Three major conclusions can be made from this study [Gomes, 2008]. The first conclusion is that using the graphic novels may have improved the reading comprehension of some students with Aspergers (AS), because providing the students with visual images may have been responsible for the increase in reading comprehension. The second conclusion is that using graphic novels with students who have very low levels of reading comprehension may not be effective in improving their reading comprehension. The third conclusion is that the students' motivation and amount of time spent reading was increased after reading the graphic novels, possibly translating to increased reading comprehension.

The first conclusion is that reading graphic novels improved the reading comprehension of some students who had low reading comprehension and high decoding skills. Other studies have noted the correlation between reading comprehension and decoding, but have not yet identified the root cause of poor reading comprehension skills for students who have high decoding skills. In schools with students with AS and other autism spectrum disorders, using graphic novels may help bridge the gap between high decoding and low reading comprehension, allowing these students to be successful in an academic environment. On a broader scale, similar results may be found for students exhibiting like characteristics in a general education setting.

If this gap exists because these students are not creating visual images when reading, one method to bridge this gap is to provide students with the visualizations needed to comprehend the text. Although the study did not show significant results to conclude that the visual imagery provided by the graphic novels increased their reading comprehension, the visual images did seem to help four of the students comprehend the stories. Though this may not be universally effective for all students with AS, using graphic novels in a Language Arts class could be a strategy that teachers can use to help some students with AS. Teachers may also want to consider incorporating visual images into other aspects of teaching outside of Language Arts. Using visual images to correspond with written directions may help with a student's comprehension of the directions. Additionally, visual images could be used to illustrate historical events or to explain a scientific process rather than just relying on text.

The results of this intervention led to four major conclusions [Irey, 2008]. The first is related to the effect of the various fluency strategies on reading rate and errors. The data suggest that repeated reading was an effective strategy in terms of improving reading pace although not for decreasing errors for students with learning disabilities (LD) or who are English learners (EL). Error correction with corrective feedback was effective in decreasing errors although its effect on reading pace was minimal, and prosody instruction appears to have had a minimal effect on rate and a moderate effect on decreasing errors. The second conclusion is that the intervention was successful in increasing the reading comprehension of participants as measured at pre- and posttest which suggests that fluency instruction can lead to improved comprehension for this student population. The third conclusion is that the prosody skill level of this student population was improved through fluency instruction. The fourth conclusion is that students' attitudes toward reading improved from pre- to posttest which suggests that the components of this intervention were effective in improving students' opinions towards reading.

Several fluency strategies were utilized in this study. Each appears to have strengths and weaknesses in terms of student achievement. Repeated readings were found to have a significant effect on reading rate which suggests this strategy would be beneficial for students who need assistance increasing their reading rate. This strategy did not greatly decrease the number of errors made, so it would not be appropriate for use with a student who needs error correction. However, error correction and corrective feedback can be added to repeated readings to address the needs of such a student. The addition of prosodic instruction did not greatly affect reading rate, but it did serve to decrease the number of errors made.

Students will be well served by teachers who select the most appropriate strategy for the needs of each student. The time and effort required by implementing error correction and corrective feedback would not serve the needs of a student who makes minimal errors but needs to increase his rate of reading. Conversely, a student who reads at an appropriate pace but makes multiple errors would not benefit from an intervention of only repeated reading. By determining the appropriate strategy to address each individual's needs, educators will be able to provide all students the opportunity to reach his or her full academic potential.

Several conclusions can be made based on the results of this study [Hess, 2008]. One of the conclusions is that students with emotional disturbance (ED) benefit from direct instruction in social skills. Another conclusion is that peer-mediated instruction is an engaging and effective method for delivering reading comprehension instruction. A third conclusion is that students with ED appeared to perform better in the program when staff was facilitating the team's activities.

The results of this study indicated that students with ED benefited from explicit instruction and modeling of social skills. When a new social skill was introduced through the TEAM intervention, the students listened to an explanation of the skill and how to use it, discussed the skill and how it was relevant to them, watched and participated in teacher modeling of examples (and non-examples) of the skill, practiced with a peer, and then implemented the skill in the program. The researcher found that many programs designed to incorporate cooperative learning relating to reading skills did not have a sufficient emphasis on the social skills involved in working together as a team. As students with ED often have difficulty with peer interactions, it would have been difficult to ask them to engage in peer-mediated instruction without explicit instruction in how to teach, learn from, and cooperate with their peers. The results of this study indicated that student behaviors did improve as a result of the intervention. Therefore, whether educators are implementing peer-mediated instruction or grouping students together during lessons or learning activities, students with ED would benefit from direct instruction in social skills prior to (and during) being asked to work together in pairs or groups. Utilizing more social skills instruction in the classroom could help educators minimize disruptive behaviors and foster more positive communication between peers.

The present study illuminated some salient findings within the area of effective communication in classrooms serving students with emotional disturbance (ED) and learning disabilities (LD) [Kendall, 2006]. First, the power of verbal and nonverbal communication in a classroom setting to influence behavior either positively or negatively by specific means was revealed. The greater implication of this finding is that classrooms serving students with ED/LD, often placed the fault and blame of students' negative behaviors upon the student, rather than considering factors such as tone of voice, levels of ambiguity, body tension, and other forms of communicative intent of the educators. On the other hand, the root of all conflicts cannot rightfully be placed upon the communication styles of the educator. A deeper awareness of the way educators come across within a cultural framework of the population they serve could only benefit in preventing the conflicts and misunderstandings between both educators and students, which often invariably lead to negative behavior blowouts. Teachers and educators may consider getting additional training in cultural sensitivity to avoid these misunderstandings with the populations that they serve.

Second, it was revealed by the student and staff participants in the study that students with ED and LD wanted more individualized assistance with academic tasks, and furthermore, students' behavior was positively impacted by prolonged, individualized help. Currently in high school special education classrooms for students with ED teachers may often focus more on students' behavior than academics. This may not be that irrational being that recurring negative behavior can be a major impediment to student learning. However, it could be argued that when students do not receive academic instruction at their instructional level, combined with individualized help, this could be a causal factor for frustration, acting out, and incomplete assignments. The greater implication for this finding was that behavior needed to be analyzed on a deeper level than prevalence. Understanding the causal factors of negative behaviors may be a more effective tool for analysis than simply recording the occurrence of negative behaviors. Therefore, when students act inappropriately, teachers should be aware of the antecedent events and consider a causal framework for the negative behavior.

After you have completed the conclusion section, it is typical to have one last closing paragraph. You are probably thinking, "She's not seriously expecting me to write one more sentence? What more could I possibly say?" The closing paragraph is typically your final thoughts and reflection on the entire study. As these will be the last sentences in the thesis, they should leave a lasting and profound impression on the reader.

Summary

Chapter Five is perhaps the most significant chapter in the thesis because it provides interpretations and conclusions of the major findings from the study. Chapter Five may also be one of the most difficult chapters to write because it involves synthesizing the results to draw out the "lessons learned." In this chapter, you are also providing the implications or applications of the findings for the reader. In the next chapter I will discuss the APA editorial style and other formatting issues to help you complete the master's thesis and get it ready for printing and binding. Here is a summary of the most critical points from Chapter 9:

- Chapter Five can be divided into five main sections: (1) Introduction, (2) Discussion of Major Findings, (3) Limitations, (4) Recommendations for Future Research, and (5) Conclusions.

- One way to organize the discussion section is to use the three parallel ladders strategy and write the discussion of the results in the same order they were reported in Chapter Four.

- The interpretations of the results should help to explain, increase understanding, or add a different perspective to the results.

- All research studies have limitations or weaknesses. As you become a more experienced researcher, you will find ways to reduce the limitations, but you can never get rid of them altogether.

- There are several benefits to discussing the limitations of the study: (1) learn from your mistakes, (2) help other researchers learn from your mistakes, and (3) provide possible explanations for disappointing or unexpected results.

- When describing the limitations of the study, you need to explain what the limitation was and *why* it was a limitation.

- One method to write the recommendations for future research section is to connect the recommendations to the issues that were identified in the limitations section.

• Another method to write the recommendations for future research section is to offer suggestions on how your study could be continued or expanded.

• Base the conclusions on the findings in the study; avoid overstating or overgeneralizing the findings.

• The implications of the conclusions are recommendations for how to bridge the "research to practice" and can be in the form of actions, policies, or procedures.

Resources

Common Obstacles and Practical Solutions

1. A common obstacle that students face in writing Chapter Five is interpreting the findings. Words that come to mind are, "What does this really mean?" The best way to overcome this obstacle is to review your journal notes (I hope you kept those updated!). The notes will remind you of the procedures that were used during the study and perhaps shed light on situations or events that were irregular or unexpected. In addition, definitely meet with your chairperson. You have been so immersed in reporting the minute results that sometimes it is difficult to tie them back to the research questions. Speaking with your chairperson or someone familiar with your study will help you make these connections.

2. Another common obstacle faced by students is finding the major conclusions from the study. Although you have reported a summary of the major findings and interpretations, sometimes the overall conclusions are not so obvious. Words that come to mind are, "What is the bigger lesson here?" One thing to always keep in mind is the original purpose of the study and the research questions—did you find what you were looking for? The major conclusions could be related to one of the research questions or focus of the study. However, sometimes a major conclusion could be something that you found but were not looking for at all. These unanticipated conclusions are sometimes even more beneficial than confirming preset hypotheses because they expand your perspective and knowledge about the research topic beyond what was expected or indicated in the research literature.

Reflection/Discussion Questions

When you discuss your study's findings in Chapter Five, it is important to understand the differences in reporting results versus making interpretations about the results. The following reflection/discussion questions will help guide you through the discussion process.

1. What are different kinds of limitations and weaknesses that could exist in a study? Give examples of limitations that may have occurred in your study. Discuss how these limitations affect the internal/external validity or quality of the results.

2. What are the differences among making interpretations, conclusions, and implications about a study's findings? Give one example of each and discuss how they are interrelated.

 Try It Exercises

The following exercises are designed to help you write Chapter Five. In Activity One, you will outline the first four major sections of Chapter Five and begin to flesh out the components. In Activity Two, you will write an outline of the conclusions section.

1. Activity One: For this activity, focus on the results that were reported in Chapter Four.

- Based on your research design, you will create an outline of three major sections in Chapter Five (e.g., discussion, limitations, and recommendations).
- For each section, write at least three bullet points (they do not have to be complete sentences) of what you will include to answer these questions:
  A. Summarize the major findings. What interpretations could be made around these findings?
  B. What were some of the limitations? How do the limitations affect the internal/external validity or quality of the findings?
  C. What recommendations do you have for future research?

- Meet with your chairperson to discuss the bullet points before writing each section.

2. Activity Two: For this activity, focus on the synthesis of the major findings.

- Write one conclusion (one paragraph) based on a synthesis of the major findings.
- Write one implication of the conclusion (one paragraph).
- Meet with your chairperson to discuss the conclusion and implication before moving on to the next two conclusions.

Suggested Readings

- American Educational Research Association. (n.d.). *Standards for reporting empirical social science research in AERA publications.* Available online: http://www.aera.net/uploadedFiles/Opportunities/StandardsforReporting EmpiricalSocialScience_PDF.pdf

- Guttmacher Institute. (2006). *Interpreting research studies.* Available online: http://www.guttmacher.org/pubs/2006/07/27/IB_Interpreting.pdf

- Richardson, L., & Adams St. Pierre, E. (2005). Writing: A method of inquiry. In N. K. Denzin & Y. S. Lincoln (Eds.), *The SAGE handbook of qualitative research* (3rd ed., pp. 959–978). Thousand Oaks, CA: Sage.

Web Links

- Academic Grammar for Students of the Arts and Social Sciences

  http://ec.hku.hk/acadgrammar/

- Free Management Library: Analyzing, Interpreting and Reporting Basic Research Results

  http://www.managementhelp.org/research/analyze.htm

10

Final Formatting, APA Style

Preparation and Organization	**211**
APA Style	**211**
Levels of Heading	**212**
Citations in Text	**216**
Direct Quotes and Paraphrasing	**216**
One Work, One Author	**216**
One Work, Multiple Authors	**217**
One Work, Group Author	**218**
Two or More Works	**218**
Web Sites and Web Pages	**219**
Personal Communications	**219**
Secondary Sources	**219**
Reference List	**220**
Order and Format	**220**
Periodicals	**222**
Books and Book Chapters	**222**
Electronic Sources	**223**
Online Journals and Electronic Versions	**225**
Online Documents	**226**
Web Sites and Web Pages	**227**
Tables	**228**
Tables in Text	**230**
	(Continued)

(Continued)

Placement and Spacing	230
Title	230
Headings and Body	230
Notes	232
Figures	233
Figures in Text	233
Placement, Size, and Font	234
Captions and Labels	234
Graphs	235
Appendixes	235
Appendixes in Text	236
Placement and Cover Pages	236
Front Pages	237
Title Page	237
Signature Page	237
Acknowledgments	238
Abstract	238
Table of Contents	240
Lists of Tables and Figures	240
Copying and Binding	241
Final Tips and Checklist	242
Summary	243
Resources	243
Common Obstacles and Practical Solutions	243
Reflection/Discussion Questions	244
Try It Exercises	244
Key Terms	245
Suggested Readings	245
Web Links	246

There are three rules for writing the novel. Unfortunately, no
one knows what they are.

—W. Somerset Maugham

A hearty congratulations for completing the text of your master's thesis!
You should feel really proud of yourself. Now that you have completed
the bulk of the work, we will focus on putting on the final touches. Yes,
every muscle and joint in your back aches from all the sitting, and you have
blisters on your fingertips from all the typing. Your vision is fuzzy, and you
feel lightheaded from staring at the computer screen. But wait! What is that
sound you hear? No, those are not voices in your head; those are the screams
from your loved ones on the sidelines cheering you on! In fact, if you wipe
away the sweat, you can actually see the finish line! Now is not the time to
slow down but rather to regroup and reenergize for the last leg of the race.
Depending on how much formatting you have completed up to this point,
this may take a bit of time, so keep the momentum going knowing there are
loved ones waiting for you on the other side of the finish line!

This chapter will focus on the style form of the thesis using the fifth edition of the *Publication Manual of the American Psychological Association*
(APA, 2001). As mentioned, the APA style is commonly used in various
social science disciplines such as education, psychology, sociology, business,
economics, nursing, and social work. The American Psychological Association
uses the APA style to publish all of its books and journals. Two other common style forms are the Modern Language Association (MLA) style and the
University of Chicago style. Check with your institution to find out which
style form is required for your thesis. Typically, the style form requirements
are included in documents made available from the graduate school or your
department. However, confirm with your chairperson that you are following the correct form.

When referring to a particular style such as APA, publishers are focusing on
the *editorial* style in addition to the writing style. This includes rules and guidelines on how to format level headings, citations, references, tables, figures, statistics, and so on. By following a particular style, the publisher ensures that the
printed material is consistent and uniform (think of it like a common language). While this common language is important to publishers, it is of equal
importance to academic disciplines and institutions of higher education for
many of the same reasons. Keep in mind that style forms do change. When this
occurs, the changes are published through revisions or addendums of the APA
manual (check to make sure you are using the most current version). Updates
also posted on the Web site (http://apastyle.apa.org).

There is quite a bit of information in the publication manual, which can
be overwhelming at first glance. However, much of it may not apply to the
master's thesis. Therefore, in this chapter I will focus on only those sections

that are most relevant to the "typical" thesis. Depending on your discipline, you may have some rather unique formatting needs and will need to refer to the APA manual for specific queries. In this chapter, I will also make suggestions on other formatting issues that are not in the APA manual that I have found to be useful for the master's thesis.

Preparation and Organization

There are several tasks that need to be completed in preparation for the final formatting process. First, make sure you have all the sources that were cited in the text (we will discuss how to format the citations and references later) or know where to find them. This is often the task that requires the most work if you have not been keeping track of the sources throughout the writing process. Second, make sure that you have all the data available in an easy-to-read format. These will be needed to prepare tables and figures. Third, make sure that all the text has been edited in Chapters One through Five. Since you will be developing a table of contents based on the existing document, the text needs to be in its final draft to determine the appropriate level headings and page numbers. Finally, prepare clean blank photocopies of all the materials and measurement instruments that were used including the Institutional Review Board (IRB) cover letter, consent forms, intervention materials, surveys, tests, interview questions, observation protocols, and so on. These will be included as the appendixes. Doing these preparation and organizational tasks first will make the formatting process much quicker and less stressful for you in the end.

APA Style

Once you have completed all the necessary preparation tasks, you can start the final editorial process in APA style. I highly recommend that you have a copy of the APA publication manual handy at all times. The manual has over 400 pages of rules, guidelines, and examples. However, I do not recommend reading the manual from cover to cover (unless you are having trouble sleeping). Instead, it is a great tool that you can refer to for specific style elements. The manual is divided into nine chapters. Chapters 1 and 2 focus on the "writing style" aspects such as the content and language. I will not focus on these two chapters, but I do recommend that you read them as there are some very good writing strategies and examples for language usage and grammar (see Appendix D in this volume for additional writing tips). Chapters 3 and 4 of the APA manual focus on the "editorial style" aspects such as headings, citations, references, and tables. Chapter 6 is a short chapter dedicated to students writing non-journal manuscripts such as theses, dissertations, and papers; I also recommend reading this one as it provides a general overview. The rest of the chapters are specific for submitting journal manuscripts for publication, so these may not be relevant for you in the preparation of your thesis for submission to your department (unless your program requires you to publish your thesis in an academic journal). On the other hand, you should visit with your chairperson on the merits of your study for publication purposes.

In this chapter, I will focus on specific "editorial style" sections in Chapters 3 and 4 of the APA manual. I will discuss how to format the following elements since these are most relevant to the master's thesis and often confusing to students: (1) headings, (2) citations, (3) references, (4) tables, and (5) figures. Since presenting statistics was covered in Chapter 8 of this volume, I will not review that information here. To guide you in this process, I will first discuss the APA style rules in general. Then I will provide examples of general templates and specific examples. I have also listed numerous resources at the end of the chapter to assist you with applying APA style.

In addition to covering APA style, I will discuss how to format sections of the master's thesis that I have used with my graduate students. These are not necessarily in APA style. These include the appendixes and a section that I call the "front pages." The front pages include the title and signature pages, acknowledgments, abstract, table of contents, and lists of tables and figures. Check with your chairperson to see if there are formatting rules and guidelines for the appendixes and "front pages."

Levels of Heading

One element of APA style is determining the levels of heading to use in the thesis. This is like solving a Rubik's cube: very difficult to solve initially, but once you are proficient, it becomes routine. The **levels of heading** refer to the organizational structure or hierarchy of the sections. They inform the reader of the "importance" of the sections and whether they are main sections or subsections. Sections that are of equal importance are on the same number level heading while subsections would be on a different number level heading. A good way to determine how many levels will be required in your thesis is to look at your initial outline. How many sections and subsections are there in each chapter? Are there larger sections that could be divided into smaller subsections? While changing the number of levels is not terribly cumbersome, it is better to know at the beginning how many levels of heading will be required.

In APA style, there are five levels of heading (see Figure 10.1). Keep in mind that the number of level headings is different from the number level heading. Huh? The *number of* level headings refers to the quantity of level headings you use. The maximum number of level headings is five. The *number level* heading refers to a specific heading location. There are five different locations, and the headings can be at Level 1, 2, 3, 4, or 5. Note in Figure 10.1 that the number level headings are not in chronological order; the top level heading is Level 5, and the descending level headings from there are 1, 2, 3, and 4.

In Figure 10.2, there is an example with five levels of heading from Chapter One of a sample thesis. As you read down the levels, each descending level acts as a subheading for the previous level (i.e., Level 1 is a subheading for Level 5, Level 2 is a subheading for Level 1, and so on). Note that even though the Level 4 heading ends with a period, the heading does not have to be a complete sentence. When you have multiple levels of heading, you can have as many of the same number level headings as necessary. These show that the sections are of equal importance. For example, you can have three Level 4 headings as subheadings to one Level 3 heading. In Figure 10.3, there is an example with five levels of heading from Chapter One of a sample thesis that also has multiple subheadings at the same number level. Note how the Level 3 heading, *Students With Disabilities,* has two subheadings at Level 4, and the same is true for the Level 3 heading, *English Learners.* In this figure, I have also indicated where you would start to write the text. Obviously, you would not include the labels of each level in your thesis— those are included here to help you see the different levels and how they relate to one other.

It is rare that you would need five levels of headings in a master's thesis; three or four levels are more common. In Figure 10.4, there is an example with three levels of heading. With three headings, the Levels are 1, 3, and 4, and the Level 2 heading is omitted. In Figure 10.5, there is an example with three levels of heading from Chapter One of a sample thesis. Note that there are multiple Level 4 subheadings that have equal importance.

CENTERED UPPERCASE HEADING **(Level 5)**

Centered Uppercase and Lowercase Heading **(Level 1)**

Centered, Italicized, Uppercase and Lowercase Heading **(Level 2)**

Flush Left, Italicized, Uppercase and Lowercase Side Heading **(Level 3)**

Indented, italicized, lowercase paragraph heading ending with a period. **(Level 4)**

Figure 10.1   Five levels of heading in APA style.

CHAPTER ONE **(Level 5)**

Introduction **(Level 1)**

Statement of the Problem **(Level 2)**

Students With Disabilities **(Level 3)**

Students with learning disabilities. **(Level 4)**

Figure 10.2   Five levels of heading from sample Chapter One.

CHAPTER ONE **(Level 5)**

Introduction **(Level 1)**

You would indent and start writing the text here.

Statement of the Problem **(Level 2)**
You would indent and start writing the text here.

Students With Disabilities **(Level 3)**
You would indent and start writing the text here.

Students with learning disabilities. **(Level 4)** You would start writing the text here after the period and keep wrapping around underneath the subheading like this.

Students with autism. **(Level 4)** You would start writing the text here after the period and keep wrapping around underneath the subheading like this.

English Learners **(Level 3)**
You would indent and start writing the text here.

Spanish-speaking English learners. **(Level 4)** You would start writing the text here after the period and keep wrapping around underneath the subheading like this.

Other-language English learners. **(Level 4)** You would start writing the text here after the period and keep wrapping around underneath the subheading like this.

Figure 10.3   Five levels of heading from Chapter One with multiple subheadings.

For the master's thesis, I typically advise students to use four levels of heading because large sections can be divided into smaller subsections, which makes the text more reader-friendly. In addition, with four levels you can use the three parallel ladders strategy. For example, the number of the Chapter is at Level 1 (e.g., Chapter One, Chapter Two), the title of the chapter is at Level 2 (e.g., Introduction, Literature Review), the main sections in the chapter are at Level 3 (e.g., *Statement of the Problem, Purpose of the Study, Procedures*), and the subsections for each main section are at Level 4 (e.g., *Problem area number one*). In Figure 10.6, there is an example with four levels of heading. With four headings, the Levels are 1, 2, 3, and 4. In Figure 10.7, there is an example with four levels of heading from Chapter One of a sample thesis. Note that both the *Statement of the Problem* and *Background and Need* sections have multiple Level 4 subheadings. These would be the three subsections from the three parallel ladders strategy.

Centered Uppercase and Lowercase Heading **(Level 1)**

Flush Left, Italicized, Uppercase and Lowercase Side Heading **(Level 3)**

    Indented, italicized, lowercase paragraph heading ending with a period. **(Level 4)**

Figure 10.4   Three levels of heading in APA style.

Chapter One **(Level 1)**

Statement of the Problem **(Level 3)**

    Reading difficulties. **(Level 4)**

    Math difficulties. **(Level 4)**

    Behavioral difficulties. **(Level 4)**

Figure 10.5   Three levels of heading from sample Chapter One.

Centered Uppercase and Lowercase Heading **(Level 1)**

Centered, Italicized, Uppercase and Lowercase Heading **(Level 2)**

Flush Left, Italicized, Uppercase and Lowercase Side Heading **(Level 3)**

    Indented, italicized, lowercase paragraph heading ending with a period. **(Level 4)**

Figure 10.6   Four levels of heading in APA style.

Chapter One **(Level 1)**

Introduction **(Level 2)**

Statement of the Problem **(Level 3)**

    Reading difficulties. **(Level 4)**

    Math difficulties. **(Level 4)**

    Behavioral difficulties. **(Level 4)**

Background and Need **(Level 3)**

    Reading strategies. **(Level 4)**

    Math strategies. **(Level 4)**

    Social skills training. **(Level 4)**

Figure 10.7   Four levels of heading in sample Chapter One.

Citations in Text

The next element in APA style is how to cite sources (referred to as works) in the text of the thesis. This is extremely important for several reasons. First, readers may want to read the source document, and they will need an accurate citation. Second, including citations from the research literature adds credibility to support your claims. Finally, if you do not give appropriate credit to the original work, this is considered a form of plagiarism, which is a very serious offense akin to stealing. Citations of works are necessary when you use a direct quote or paraphrase someone else's words, ideas, or research findings. Be very careful when paraphrasing, as simply changing the order of the words or substituting a few words can still be considered plagiarism (see the Web site on plagiarism, http://www.plagiarism.org/index.html). Academic institutions typically have a zero tolerance for any form of plagiarism, and this can result in not receiving your degree or having it revoked (not to mention any legal and/or monetary penalties).

Direct quotes and paraphrasing. One of the items that you must cite is a direct quote. However, I would recommend using direct quotes sparingly and only if paraphrasing the original work would not capture the essence of the message. If you cite a direct quote, put the words in quotation marks and write the author's last name, year of publication, and page number of where the quote is located in parentheses at the end of the quote. Here is an example:

> "I am using this direct quote only because I could not paraphrase it" (Bui, 2008, p. 14).

Since a page number is required for direct quotes, it is always preferable to have a PDF reproduction of the written material if possible. If you are quoting a lengthy passage (e.g., more than 500 words) from copyrighted material, you may need to get permission from the copyright holder.

Another case in which items must be cited in the text is when you paraphrase ideas, words, or findings. There are multiple ways to do this, depending on the number of authors, type of author, number of works, source of the material, and so on. I will give examples of how to reference a citation in the text for different numbers of authors, group as author, multiple works, Web sites and Web pages, personal communications, and secondary sources. For specific queries or unusual circumstances, please refer to the APA manual or Web site.

One work, one author. A common citation is one work by one author. This consists of the author's last name and the year of publication. There are two different formats. The first format is when the author is the subject of the sentence. When this is the case, the year of publication is put in parentheses.

Note that the verb "argued" is in the past tense to indicate that the research has already been conducted. Here is an example:

> Bui (2008) argued that having a Chihuahua as a companion extended people's life span.

The second format is used when the citation is at the end of the paraphrased sentence or paragraph. When this is the case, the author's last name and year of publication are separated by a comma and put in parentheses. If the same author (and work) is cited more than once within the same paragraph, you list the author but do not need to include the year again. Here is an example of the second format:

> Having a Chihuahua as a companion may extend a person's life span (Bui, 2008).

One work, multiple authors. If there are multiple authors (between two and five) for one work, they are listed similarly with their last names and year of publication. If the authors are listed as subjects in the sentence, separate the names with commas and spell out the word "and" between the second to last and last author. The year of publication is in parentheses after the listing of the authors. If the citation is at the end of the sentence, put the authors' names in parentheses, separate them with commas, and use an ampersand (&) between the second to last and last author. After the last author, put a comma and the year of publication. Here are three examples of multiple authors in both formats:

> Bui and Meyen (2008) argued that having a Chihuahua as a companion extended people's life spans; Having a Chihuahua as a companion may extend a person's life span (Bui & Meyen, 2008). [**two authors**]

> Bui, Meyen, and Nguyen (2008) argued that having a Chihuahua as a companion extended people's life spans; Having a Chihuahua as a companion may extend a person's life span (Bui, Meyen, & Nguyen, 2008). [**three authors**]

> Bui, Meyen, Nguyen, and Lee (2008) argued that having a Chihuahua as a companion extended people's life spans; Having a Chihuahua as a companion may extend a person's life span (Bui, Meyen, Nguyen, & Lee, 2008). [**four authors**]

Keep the listing of the authors in their original order from the article even if it is not in alphabetical order. This is critical as authors are usually listed in a particular order based on their contribution to the manuscript. If there are more than three authors, you can shorten the citation to reduce space (after the first full citation) by using "et al." (which means "and others") after the first author's last name and then the publication date. If there are six or more authors for one work, you would automatically use the "et al." format. For example,

Bui et al. (2008) argued that having a Chihuahua as a companion extended people's life spans; Having a Chihuahua as a companion may extend a person's life span (Bui et al., 2008).

One work, group author. Sometimes the author of a work is not an individual but rather an organization or a group. The name of the group is spelled out entirely followed by the year of the publication. For example,

> Having a Chihuahua as a companion may extend a person's life span (University of San Francisco, 2008).

However, if it is a name that is commonly referred to in abbreviated form, you can list the entire name the first time and then use the abbreviated form in subsequent citations. Here is an example for the first citation:

> Having a Chihuahua as a companion may extend a person's life span (U.S. Department of Education [USDE], 2002).

Then for the subsequent citations you would use the abbreviated form: (USDE, 2002).

Two or more works. Finally, there will be times when you need to cite two or more works with a variety of single or multiple authorships for the same idea. In this case, you would keep the individual authors in the order that they appear in the work and then list the works in alphabetical order by the first author's last name. The works are separated with semicolons. Here is an example:

> Several studies have indicated that having a Chihuahua as a companion may extend the life span (Bui, 2008; Meyen & Lee, 2005; Nguyen, Edwards, Hawk, & Bobbett, 2007).

Note how the works are listed in alphabetical order but within each work the authors are listed as they would appear in a separate citation.

Web sites and Web pages. For periodicals and documents from Web sites and Web pages, treat them like regular citations when the author's last name and year of publication are provided. You can also refer to an entire Web site by providing the Internet address in the text. The Internet address is known as the uniform resource locator, or URL. Here is an example URL address:

> http://www.apastyle.org/elecref.html

Here is an example of how you would cite the Web site in the text:

> There is information on APA style on their Web site (http://www.apastyle.org).

Citations of Web sites would not be included in the reference list.

Citing works on Web sites and Web pages can be tricky because often the author or date is unknown or there are no page numbers. Here is what you should do when this information is missing. First, if you are quoting a work from a Web site or Web page that does not have page numbers, list the paragraph number using the paragraph symbol "¶" or section heading and paragraph number instead. Here are two examples:

"I am using this direct quote because I could not paraphrase it" (Bui, 2004, ¶ 5).

"I am using this direct quote because I could not paraphrase it" (Bui, 2004, Conclusion section, ¶ 1).

Second, when no author is listed, abbreviate the title with one to two words with heading capitalization. **Heading capitalization** is when all the major words are capitalized like in the title of a movie. Then put the title in quotation marks and list the publication year. Here is an example:

The senior participants all stated that they felt healthier and less stressed because of their new furry companions ("Chihuahua Love," 2006).

Third, if no date is given, use the abbreviation "n.d." to signify "no date." Here is an example:

The participants all stated that they felt healthier and less stressed because of their new furry companions ("Chihuahua Love," n.d.).

By following these three rules, you are giving appropriate credit to the source and helping the reader find the correct citation in the reference list.

Personal communications. In addition to printed or electronic works, a source can also be a personal communication. A **personal communication** is a source of information in the form of a letter, e-mail, interview, phone conversation, and so on. These are only cited in the text and not included in the reference list. In order to cite a personal communication, provide the source's initials and last name followed by the exact date on which the information was obtained. Here are two examples:

Y. N. Bui confirmed that Munsterlander dogs have wonderful dispositions (personal communication, March 9, 2008).

Munsterlander dogs have wonderful dispositions (Y. N. Bui, personal communication, March 9, 2008).

Secondary sources. Finally, there may be times when you want to cite a work that was mentioned in another work. This is referred to as a secondary source because the information was not obtained from the original work. For example, you read an article by Bobbett (2008) who included a quote by

Hawk (1990), and you want to use the quote by Hawk. In this case, you would cite both authors in the text. Here is an example:

> "The temperament of English Setters is hard not to love" (Hawk, 1990, p. 68, as cited by Bobbett, 2008).

In the reference list, you would only list the secondary source, Bobbett (the one you actually read), and not the original work, Hawk (the one you did not read). However, you may find that by reviewing the original source you will gain more accurate information. That way you can cite the original source rather than a secondary source in the reference list. I will discuss how to format the reference list in the next section.

Reference List

All of the works that are cited in the text (excluding the few exceptions) will be included in the reference list at the end of the thesis. Therefore, it is imperative that they match! In other words, if the work is cited in the text, it must be in the reference list and vice versa. In addition, the citation in the text (e.g., spelling and order of the authors, year of publication) will be exactly the same as the citation in the reference list. Thus, be very careful not to miss any references in either location, and you should also compare them to make sure they are identical.

The different ways to list references are so numerous that Chapter 4 (more than 60 pages!) in the APA manual is devoted to this cause. Thus, it would be impractical to discuss every possible configuration you might encounter. Therefore, I will focus on only the most common and relevant references for the thesis. These include typical references for periodicals, books and book chapters, and electronic sources. For the print references, you will need to locate the author's last name and initials, year of publication, title, and publishing data such as journal title, volume, issue, page numbers, and location. The electronic sources require the same information as the print references as well as the retrieval date and Internet address. Basically, the references listed must be thorough and specific enough so that another person could find it in his or her literature search. Thus, it is recommended to have access to the original documents and/or a search engine/electronic database while formatting the reference list.

Order and format. APA has strict rules about how to order and format the reference list. The references are listed in alphabetical order by the last name of the first author, name of the group, or title of the work when there is no author provided. In general, the listing follows typical rules for alphabetical order (see APA manual for exceptional cases). For example, the author/group/title starting with "A" would precede those starting with "B" and so on. The APA manual recommends double spacing in the reference list for a journal manuscript, but single spacing is allowed within references (use a double space between references) for the thesis. Check with your chairperson to see if single or double spacing is preferred for your thesis. For the purposes of this chapter, I will use single spaces within references to make them easier to read.

There are a few general formatting rules. First, list each reference using a hanging indent. A **hanging indent** is when the first line is flushed all the way to the left margin and the rest of the lines in the reference are indented one-half inch. This makes it easier to read down the list to find specific references and helps to separate the references from each other. Second, in addition to listing the last name, always include the first and middle initials (if given) of the author's full name. This helps to distinguish between authors with the same last name. Third, list the publication year in parentheses or "n.d." if no date is provided. Finally, use sentence capitalization to write the title of the work. **Sentence capitalization** is when only the first word of the title and proper nouns are capitalized (like in a regular sentence). Unlike the citations in the text, the titles do not have quotation marks around them in the reference list. In Figure 10.8, there is a sample reference list. Note how there are many different types of references, including a journal article, book, book chapter, and electronic sources. I will next discuss how to reference each specific type of material.

References

Becker, L. B., Vlad, T., Huh, J., & Prine, J. (2001). Annual enrollment report: Number of students studying journalism and mass communication at all-time high [Electronic version]. *Journalism & Mass Communication Educator, 56*(3), 28–60.

Creswell, J. W. (2008). *Educational research: Planning, conducting, and evaluating quantitative and qualitative research* (3rd ed.). Boston: Pearson Allyn & Bacon.

Criminological transition in Russia. (n.d.). Retrieved January 11, 2008, from Indiana University Web site: http://newsinfo.iu.edu/news/page/normal/3876.html

Gay, L. R., Mills, G. E., & Airasian, P. (2006). *Educational research: Competencies for analysis and applications* (8th ed.). Upper Saddle River, NJ: Merrill Prentice Hall.

Johnson, P. J. (2003). Immigration. In J. J. Ponzetti (Ed.), *International encyclopedia of marriage and family* (2nd ed., Vol. 2, pp. 859–864). New York: Macmillan Reference USA. Retrieved December 18, 2007, from Gale Virtual Reference Library via Gale: http://0-go.galegroup.com.ignacio.usfca.edu/ps/start.do?p=GVRL&u=usfca_gleeson

Niolin, R. (2001). *Families and substance abuse.* Retrieved January 11, 2008, from http://www.psychpage.com/family/library/familysubstanceabuse.htm

U.S. Department of Health and Human Services. (1979). *The Belmont report.* Retrieved January 5, 2008, from http://www.hhs.gov/ohrp/humansubjects/guidance/belmont.htm

---

Figure 10.8 Condensed sample reference list.

Periodicals. The first common type of reference is a periodical. A **periodical** refers to items that are published on a regular basis such as articles in journals, magazines, newsletters, or newspapers. For the purpose of the thesis, it is most likely that you will find articles for your literature review in journals. In order to reference a journal article, write the author(s) by last name, first and middle initials, and publication year in parentheses. If there are more than six authors, list only the first six authors and write "et al." at the end of the sixth author. Next, write the title of the article using sentence capitalization with a period at the end. Then, write the title of the journal in italics using heading capitalization. Finally, write the volume number (italicized) and issue number (in parentheses) of the journal, beginning and ending page numbers separated by en dash, and end with a period. Here is an example of a general template:

> Author's last name, A. B. (year). Title of article in sentence capitalization. *Title of Journal in Heading Capitalization and Italicized, Volume*(Issue), #–##.

In Figure 10.9, there are different examples of journal articles from a reference list. Notice how they are listed in alphabetical order by the author's last name.

Books and book chapters. The next common types of reference are books and book chapters. In order to reference a book, write the author's last name, first and middle initials, and publication year in parentheses. Sometimes you will encounter an edited book. An **edited book** is a book

---

Hallinger, P., & Snidvongs, K. (2008). Educating leaders: Is there anything to learn from business management? *Educational Management, Administration, & Leadership, 36*(1), 9–31. **[two authors]**

Owen, S., & Standen, P. (2007). Attracting and retaining learning disability student nurses. *British Journal of Learning Disabilities, 35*(4), 261–268. **[two authors]**

Proctor, E. K. (2008). Notation of depression in case records of older adults in community. *Social Work, 53*(3), 243–253. **[one author]**

Richeson, N. E., White, P., Nadeau, K. K., Chessa, F., Dreher, G. K., & Frost, C., et al. (1998). Geriatric, ethics, and palliative care: Tending to the mind & spirit. *Educational Gerontology, 34*(7), 627–643. **[more than six authors]**

Smith, L., Foley, P. F., & Chaney, M. P. (2008). Addressing classism, ableism, and heterosexism in counselor education. *Journal of Counseling & Development, 86*(3), 303–309. **[three authors]**

Figure 10.9   Examples of journal articles in reference list.

where the individual chapters are written by different authors. There can be one or multiple editors. If the book is an edited book, write (Ed.) if there is one editor or (Eds.) if there are multiple editors before the publication year. If there are more than six authors, only list the first six authors and write "et al." at the end of the sixth author. The author of a book can also be an association. In this case, write the entire name of the association followed by a period before the publication year. Next, write the title of the book using sentence capitalization in italics with a period at the end. Sometimes you will encounter a book that has been revised or is a new edition. In this case, write the abbreviations (Rev. ed.) to indicate a revised edition or (3rd ed.) to indicate the number of the edition (use ordinal numbers 2nd, 3rd, 4th, etc.) after the title of the book. Finally, write the location of where the book was published and the name of the publisher. If the city is a common one, such as San Francisco or New York, you do not have to list the state. If the city is uncommon, then list the city, comma, and the abbreviation of the state. After the location, put a colon and write the name of the publisher ending with a period. Here is an example of a general template:

> Author's last name, A. B. (Ed. if editor). (year). *Title of book in sentence capitalization and italicized* (# ed. if a new edition). City, State abbreviation: Name of Publisher.

Book chapter references from edited books are similar to book references. The difference is that the author of the chapter is the listed author in the reference. The first and middle initials and last name of the editor(s) of the book are written with the title of the book followed by the beginning and ending page numbers of the chapter. Here is an example of a general template:

> Author's last name, A. B. (year). In C. D. Editor's last name (Ed.), *Title of book in sentence capitalization and italicized* (# ed. if a new edition, pp. #–##). City, State abbreviation: Name of Publisher.

In Figure 10.10, there are different examples of books and book chapters from a reference list in alphabetical order.

Electronic sources. The next set of common references is electronic sources. These are a bit more complicated as there is a large variety of electronic sources including online periodicals, documents, and Web sites or Web pages. In the next few sections, I will review only these three electronic sources since they are most common to the thesis. For other specific queries, please refer to the APA manual or Web site.

Remember that the reference list is intended to give credit to the source and allow readers to retrieve the sources that were cited in your thesis. For electronic sources, this means providing additional information beyond what is required for printed material. You want to give as much specific

American Psychiatric Association. (1994). *Diagnostic and statistical manual of mental disorders* (4th ed.). Washington, DC: Author. **[association as author]**

Brownell, M., League, M. A., & Seo, S. (2007). In E. L. Meyen & Y. N. Bui (Eds.), *Exceptional children in today's schools: What teachers need to know* (4th ed., pp. 83–102). Denver, CO: Love Publishing. **[book chapter in edited book]**

Hall, H. R. (2006). *Mentoring young men of color: Meeting the needs of African American and Latino students.* Lanham, MD: Rowman & Littlefield Education. **[one author]**

Merrell, K. W. (2008). *Helping students overcome depression and anxiety: A practical guide* (2nd ed.). New York: Guilford Publications. **[one author, second edition]**

Morrison, G. R., Ross, S. M., & Kemp, J. E. (2006). *Designing effective instruction* (5th ed.). Indianapolis, IN: Jossey-Bass. **[multiple authors, fifth edition]**

Taylor, B. M., & Ysseldyke, J. E. (Eds.). *Effective instruction for struggling readers, K–6.* New York: Teachers College Press. **[edited book]**

Figure 10.10   Examples of books and book chapters in a reference list.

information as possible about the author, title, retrieval date, and location. The retrieval date refers to the actual date that the information was obtained. For example, you would write, "Retrieved March 9, 2008, from . . ." This is very critical with electronic sources such as Web pages because the content is frequently changed or updated and the retrieval date gives a general impression of when the information was accurate. The location of the electronic source is the URL Internet address. Referencing the location of electronic sources can be tricky because URLs can change, move, or be deleted altogether. Thus, you need to be very careful when copying the URL; the best way is to copy and paste it directly from the computer rather than type in the individual letters. Do not underline the URL in the reference list; sometimes your computer will automatically do this, so make sure you undo the line. In addition, be careful not to add any spaces or punctuation marks to the end of the URL as this may make it unreadable. If the URL is very long and you need to continue the address on the next line, do not put in a hyphen and separate before a punctuation mark such as a slash or period. Here is an example:

http://library.nmu.edu/guides/userguides
/style_apa.htm#

After you have listed the URL in the reference list, test it to make sure that it works!

Online journals and electronic versions. One common type of electronic source for articles is online journals (i.e., these journals do not come in print form). References for online journal articles look very similar to regular journal citations with the author's last name and initials, publication year, title of article, title of periodical, volume (issue) number, and page numbers (if paginated). However, additional information of retrieval date and URL location are required for an online journal article.

One method that some publishers have recently introduced to avoid the problem of nonworking URLs is to assign each journal article or document a **Digital Object Identifier (DOI)**. The DOI is a unique code of letters and numbers that provide a link to the article's location on the Internet (think of it as a tracking device). Typically, the DOI can be found on the first page of the article and should be copied exactly as it is written. Here is an example DOI listed from an online article:

DOI: 10.1371/journal.pone.0002593

If you have access to both the DOI and the URL, list only the DOI as it is the preferable locator. If there is no DOI and a subscription is necessary for the journal, list the journal's home page URL. If there is no DOI but the article is given freely by the publisher, list the URL that leads directly to the article. Here are two examples of general templates:

Author's last name, A. B. (year). Title of article in sentence capitalization. *Title of Journal in Heading Capitalization and Italicized, Volume*(Issue), #–##. doi: 912384y2938/03895–2903

Author's last name, A. B. (year). Title of article in sentence capitalization. *Title of Journal in Heading Capitalization and Italicized, Volume*(Issue), #–##. Retrieved month day, year, from URL address to journal home page or directly to article.

Because of the ease of finding full-text articles online, most articles found on the Internet are actually the electronic version of a printed article. An electronic version is an exact duplication of the printed version (usually in PDF format). In this case, write [Electronic version] at the end of the title to indicate that you did not read the print version and use the regular journal reference. Here is an example of a general template:

Author's last name, A. B. (year). Title of article in sentence capitalization [Electronic version]. *Title of Journal in Heading Capitalization and Italicized, Volume*(Issue), #–##.

In Figure 10.11, there are examples of online journal articles and an electronic version of a print article from a reference list in alphabetical order.

Fuchs, D., Compton, D. L., & Fuchs, L. S. (2008). Making "secondary intervention" work in a three-tier responsiveness-to-intervention model: Findings from the first-grade longitudinal reading study of the National Research Center on Learning Disabilities [Electronic version]. *Reading and Writing: An Interdisciplinary Journal, 21*(4), 413–436. doi: 10.1007/s11145-007-9083-9 **[electronic version, DOI as locator]**

Gudino, O. G., Lau, A. S., & Hough, R. L. (2008). Immigrant status, mental health need, and mental health service utilization among high-risk Hispanic and Asian Pacific Islander youth [Electronic version]. *Child & Youth Care Forum, 37*(3), 139–152. **[electronic version of print article]**

Sleeter, C. (2008). An invitation to support diverse students through teacher education. *Journal of Teacher Education, 59*, 212–219. Retrieved September 19, 2007, from http://jte.sagepub .com/ **[URL to journal home page as locator]**

Stewart, A., Livingston, M., & Dennison, S. (2008). Transitions and turning points: Examining the links between child maltreatment and juvenile offending. *Child Abuse & Neglect: The International Journal, 32*(1), 51–66. Retrieved October 31, 2007, from http://www.aic.gov .au/publications/tandi/ti241.pdf **[URL directly to article as locator]**

Figure 10.11   Examples of online journal articles and electronic versions in reference list.

Online documents. In addition to journal articles, you may also need to cite different types of online documents such as reference materials (e.g., encyclopedia, dictionary), research reports, and government documents. There are a variety of different types of online documents, so I will provide some general tips here. Please refer to the APA manual for specific queries.

References to online documents are fairly similar to those for online journal articles with the author's name, title, retrieval date, and location. In the case of a document from an organization, there will often not be a single author listed. In this case, write the name of the organization in heading capitalization ending with a period before the publication date. If there is no organization or author identified, write the title of the document in sentence capitalization before the publication date. If there is no date provided, use (n.d.) to indicate "no date." For documents with multiple pages and/or reference materials, write the URL address of the source's home page rather than a direct link to the document. For documents from university or government agency Web sites, write the name of the host organization before the URL. Here are four examples of general templates:

Organization as Author in Heading Capitalization. (year). Retrieved month day, year, from Title of Agency Department or University Web site: URL direct address to document or source's home page depending on type of document.

Author's last name, A. B. (Ed.). (year). *Title of reference material in sentence capitalization and italicized* (# ed. if a new edition, # vols.). City, State abbreviation: Name of Publisher. Retrieved month day, year, from URL address to reference home page.

Author's last name, A. B. (year). Title of work in sentence capitalization. In A. B. Editor's last name (Ed.), *Title of reference material in sentence capitalization and italicized* (# ed. if a new edition, Vol. #, pp. #–##). City, State abbreviation: Name of Publisher. Retrieved month day, year, from URL address to reference home page.

Title of document in sentence capitalization. (n.d. if no date). In *Title of reference material in sentence capitalization and italicized*. Retrieved month day, year, from URL to reference home page.

In Figure 10.12, there are examples of different online documents from a reference list in alphabetical order.

Web sites and Web pages. Finally, a common electronic source is a Web site or Web page. When listing a source from a Web site or Web page, treat it

---

Borgatta, E. F., & Montgomery, R. (Eds.). (2001). *Encyclopedia of sociology* (2nd ed., 5 vols.). New York: Macmillan Reference USA. Retrieved January 7, 2008, from Gale Virtual Reference Library via Gale at http://0go.galegroup.com.ignacio.usfca.edu /ps/start.do?p=GVRL&u=usfca_gleeson **[online reference material]**

Institutional Review Board for the Protection of Human Subjects manual. (2001). Retrieved January 5, 2008, from University of San Francisco Web site: http://www.usfca.edu /humansubjects/ **[no author, document on university Web site]**

Johnson, P. J. (2003). Immigration. In J. J. Ponzetti (Ed.), *International encyclopedia of marriage and family* (2nd ed., Vol. 2, pp. 859–864). New York: Macmillan Reference USA. Retrieved December 18, 2007, from Gale Virtual Reference Library via Gale at http://0-go.galegroup.com.ignacio.usfca.edu/ps/start.do?p=GVRL&u=usfca_gleeson **[article in online reference material]**

Neighborhood. (n.d.). *In Merriam-Webster online dictionary*. Retrieved September 14, 2007, from http://www.merriam-webster.com/ **[online reference material, no author, no date, URL to source's home page]**

U.S. Department of Health and Human Services. (1979). *The Belmont report*. Retrieved January 5, 2008, from http://www.hhs.gov/ohrp/humansubjects/guidance/belmont.htm **[government report, organization as author, URL directly to report]**

Figure 10.12   Examples of different online documents in a reference list.

similarly to a regular citation and list the author's last name and initials, publication date, title, retrieval date, and URL directly to the work. If the work is from a university program/department or government agency Web site, list the host name before the URL address. One of the difficulties in referencing material from Web sites and Web pages is that the information provided varies. Often the author is unknown. In this case, the title of the Web page is listed in sentence capitalization with a period at the end before the publication date. If the publication date is unknown, use "n.d." Then list the retrieval date and URL directly to the Web page. Here are three examples of general templates:

Author's last name, A. N. (year). Retrieved month day, year, from URL direct address to Web page.

Organization as Author in Heading Capitalization. (year). Retrieved month day, year, from Title of Agency Department or University Web site: URL direct address to Web page.

Title of document in sentence capitalization. (n.d. if no date). Retrieved month day, year, from URL direct address to Web page.

In Figure 10.13, there are examples of different Web sites and Web pages from a reference list in alphabetical order.

Criminological transition in Russia. (n.d.). Retrieved January 11, 2008, from Indiana University Web site: http://newsinfo.iu.edu/news/page/normal/3876.html **[Web page on university Web site, author unknown, no date]**

Master's degree. (n.d.). Retrieved September 9, 2007, from http://www.answers.com **[Web page, unknown author, no date]**

Niolin, R. (2001). *Families and substance abuse*. Retrieved January 11, 2008, from http://www.psychpage.com/family/library/familysubstanceabuse.htm **[Web page, author and date provided]**

U.S. Department of Health and Human Services. (n.d.). *U.S. public health service syphilis study at Tuskegee*. Retrieved January 5, 2008, from Centers for Disease Control and Prevention Web site at http://www.cdc.gov/tuskegee/timeline.htm **[Web page on government agency Web site, organization as author, no date]**

Figure 10.13   Examples of Web sites and Web pages in reference list.

Tables

Tables are another element of APA style that students often have difficulty with in the thesis. Since there are 30 pages devoted to how to format tables in the APA manual, I can definitely sympathize! A table is an alternative method to communicate ideas, words, or findings in the thesis. Number tables are typically used to portray data from a quantitative study (e.g., results in Chapter Four), and word tables are sometimes necessary for findings from a qualitative study. Researchers will also sometimes include a table to describe participants' demographic data (e.g., methods in Chapter Three). When considering whether or not to include a table in the thesis, you should first decide if it is necessary. Sometimes it is more effective to present information in text format (and will save you a lot of time and effort). However, there are a few occasions when it is recommended to use a table. First, the table should increase efficiency for the reader. Sometimes presenting information in the text, especially when there are a lot of data, can be dense or rambling, and the reader can get lost in all the words. A table is a great way to convey information in a more efficient manner. Second, the table should supplement the text rather than duplicate it. In other words, the information in the table should extend or enhance the information that is in the text. If the table matches exactly what is in the text, then decide which is more efficient and select only one approach. Third, the table should allow for easy comparison between groups or participants. For example, in quantitative studies, sometimes you will have pre-/posttest scores or scores from different groups. In qualitative studies, you might have different responses to the same interview question. Presenting this information in text might be too cumbersome and confusing for readers to keep track of which group performed better or who said what, so a table is a great way to show comparative data between participants and groups.

If you have decided to include a table, follows the three "C" rules for design: comprehensibility, clarity, and consistency. The first rule is comprehensibility. Since a table is a communicative tool, the reader should be able to understand it instantly. In other words, the table should be able to "stand on its own." The reader should not have to guess what table headings or data in the body represent or refer back to the text to understand the table. The second rule is clarity. In order for the table to "stand on its own," it is critical that the title, headings (e.g., for rows and columns), and data clearly convey the information. All uncommon abbreviations should be spelled out in the title or explained in the notes. The table should be easy to read and not distracting with superfluous information. Finally, the last rule is consistency. The presentation of the table needs to be consistent within and between tables. This means using similar formatting for titles and headings, being consistent with terminology, and expressing values in the same manner (e.g., decimal points, unit of measurement).

Formatting a table in APA style is like measuring happiness: There are many different ways to do it, and it depends on the "message" that you want to convey. There is no one "best" way, but if you follow the three C's you will create a table that is organized and efficient for the reader. In the next few sections, I will provide a few general tips on how to refer to and format a table. For queries on specific types of tables, please refer to the APA manual.

Tables in text. When discussing a table in the text, number the table in the order that it appears. For example, the first table that you refer to in the text would be Table 1, then Table 2, and so on. Then give a brief description of what the table entails. Here are two examples:

> The participants in the study were very diverse. Table 1 displays the participants' demographic data.

> The participants in the study were very diverse (see Table 1 for participants' demographic data).

You can also highlight some of the major findings of the table, but remember that the text and table should not be redundant.

Placement and spacing. APA has recommendations for where to place tables and what type of spacing to use in the body of tables. In a manuscript for publication for a journal, the table is placed at the end of the manuscript text. However, for student theses and dissertations, APA allows the table to be included within the text close to where it was first mentioned. A short table can share the page where it was mentioned, while a long table would be on the next page by itself. I prefer and advise students to put tables at the end of the thesis for readability purposes; check with your chairperson to see where you should place the tables.

In terms of spacing, for a manuscript for publication, everything in the table is double-spaced. Again APA makes some adjustments for student papers and allows single-spacing for table titles and headings. I prefer students to use double spacing as it makes the table easier to read. I also want students to use the regular APA rules so that they will be prepared to publish their work! Ask your chairperson if you should use single or double spacing in tables.

Title. In terms of selecting a title, it should be evident from the title what data are being presented in the table; this follows the rule of comprehensibility. However, the title should not be too vague or detailed. For example, the title "Participants' Responses" is too vague because it does not tell the reader what the responses were from. The title, "Participants' Responses to the Online Zoomerang Survey to Measure Employees' Satisfaction With Changes in their Health Plan, Manager's Leadership Style, and Growth Opportunities" is too long and detailed. The title, "Participants' Responses to Satisfaction Survey" is just right. The title of a table is italicized with heading capitalization and flushed left (on the left side margin of the table). Underneath the title is a line that spans across the entire table. Here is an example:

Table 1

Participants' Responses to Satisfaction Survey

Headings and body. The way to format headings within a table is probably the most difficult part to master; these follow the rule of clarity. Remember to organize the table to minimize distractions and maximize comprehension. In addition, if the purpose of the table is to compare data, align the two sets of data closely together. In a table, there are columns and rows. The column is vertical (up and down), and the row is horizontal (left to right). However, there are no visible vertical lines in the table. Every column and row must have a heading, and they are written in sentence capitalization. While it is not important for you to memorize APA's names of headings, it is important to understand how the headings help to organize the table and facilitate comprehension. Table 2 presents an example of an APA table.

The first column on the left side of the table is called the **stub column.** The stub column's heading is called the **stub head.** The stub head, in this case "Ethnicity," identifies the major category for the items listed in the stub column. Underneath the stub head are the stubs. The **stubs** are the row

Table 2

Students' Mean Scores by Ethnicity on the Arc's Self-Determination Scale

Ethnicity	Autonomy		Self-Regulation		Psych. Empowerment	
	Pretest	Posttest	Pretest	Posttest	Pretest	Posttest
African American	59	59	29	62	62	75
Boys	49	59	40	60	58	77
Girls	69	73	29	75*	65	79
American Indian	40	30	43	43	75	75
Boys	49	59	40	60	58	77
Girls						
Asian American	50	66	33	33	75	81
Boys	49	59	40	60	—	—
Girls	69	73	24	75*	65	79
Caucasian	46	67	95	71	94	94
Boys	49	59	40	60	58	77
Girls	69	73	29	75	65	79
Latino/Hispanic	92	83	52	81*	88	88
Boys	49	59	40	60	58	77
Girls	69	73	34	75*	40[a]	79*

Note. Psych. = Psychological. Maximum score = 100. A dash indicates that the score was not available. From "Transition from School to Work," by Y. N. Bui, 2006, *Journal for Educators, 84,* p. 81. Copyright 2006 by the American Association of Educators. Adapted with permission.

[a] Three students did not complete the entire subscale.

p < .05

headings, which are the major independent variables related to the stub head. In this table, the stubs are African American, American Indian, Asian American, Caucasian, and Latino/Hispanic. This is not surprising since the stub head was "Ethnicity." You can also have a subordinated stub (a subgroup of the independent variable). To add a subordinated stub, add more row headings that are slightly indented underneath the stub. For example, perhaps I wanted to further divide each group by gender. In the table, the scores for each ethnic group are further divided into stubs for boys and girls.

In addition to the stub column, the other columns in the table also have headings. The headings identify the items that are listed vertically in each column. The headings can be column spanners or column heads. A **column spanner** is a broad heading that covers two or more columns (kind of like an umbrella heading). In this example, the column spanners are "Autonomy," "Self-Regulation," and "Psychological Empowerment," which are the subscales within the Arc's Self-determination Scale (Wehmeyer & Kelchner, 1995). Underneath the column spanners are the column heads. The **column head** identifies the items in just one column. In the table example, the column heads are "Pretest" and "Posttest." Note that the column heads are the same for all three column spanners. In addition, note that the pretest and posttest scores are placed next to each other for easy comparison.

There are several rules to follow when inputting items into the body of the table. The key rule is consistency. However you decide to display the data, it should be consistent within the columns. For example, if you round a score in one item to two decimal points (which is usually recommended), then all the scores in that column should be rounded to two decimal points. In addition you cannot change the unit of measurement within a column. If there is a cell (intersection between row and column) where the data are not applicable, then leave the cell blank. For example, the cells for American Indian girls for the "Autonomy Pretest and Posttest Scores" are left blank because there were only American Indian boys in the study. If there is a cell where the data were not obtained or reported, then insert a dash in the cell and write an explanation in the notes. For example, this table has dashes in the cells for the "Psychological Empowerment Pretest and Posttest Scores" for Asian American boys because they did not complete that particular subscale.

Notes. APA allows you to write notes to explain certain items within the table. There are three kinds of notes, and they are listed in this order at the bottom of the table: (1) general, (2) specific, and (3) probability. **General notes** are those that explain information relating to the entire table such as abbreviations or symbols. To include a general note, write the word *"Note."* at the bottom of the table and write the notes. The notes are written in a slightly smaller font size than the rest of the table, and do not have to be in complete sentences. If the table was adapted or reprinted from another source, this also needs to be indicated in the general notes. If you are reprinting a table or adapting parts of a table from a copyrighted source, you must first obtain permission from the copyright holder. The original source is then cited in the general note. Use the two example templates if the table was reprinted or adapted from a table in a journal article or book (APA, 2001, p. 175):

> *Note.* From "Title of Article in Heading Capitalization," by A. B. Author, Year, *Title of Journal Italicized, Volume #,* p. #. Copyright Year by the Name of the Copyright Holder in Heading Capitalization. Reprinted with permission *or* Adapted with permission.

> *Note.* From Title of Book in Heading Capitalization (p. #), by A. B. Author, Year, Place of Publication: Publisher. Copyright Year by the Name of the Copyright Holder in Heading Capitalization. Reprinted with permission *or* Adapted with permission.

After the general notes, you can list specific notes. **Specific notes** are those pertaining to an individual column, row, or item. These are labeled with a lowercase letter superscript in the cell and explained in the specific notes (after the general notes).

Finally, **probability notes** indicate whether results were statistically significant (meaning that the null hypothesis was rejected). An asterisk (*) is placed in the cell, and $*p < .05$ or $**p < .01$ is written in the probability note to identify the alpha level. The probability notes are listed after the specific notes. In Table 2, there are examples of the three different kinds of notes at the bottom of the table although it is not required to have all types of notes in one table.

Figures

In addition to tables, it is sometimes helpful to include figures in the thesis. A figure can be a "chart, graph, photograph, drawing, or other depiction" (APA, 2001, p. 176). Figures are a great way to show nonlinear relations, patterns of results, concepts, or ideas that are difficult for the reader to "see" from text descriptions. As mentioned, there are many different kinds of figures, and each one serves a different purpose. However, before including a figure, make sure that it is necessary. The decision rules for whether or not to include a figure are similar to those for a table in terms of efficiency over text format and text enhancement. If you decide to include a figure in the thesis, be sure to follow the three C's of comprehensibility, clarity, and consistency. The figure should be easy to understand (stand on its own), easy to read, and consistent in appearance. Since there are many different types of figures you could include, I will provide a few general rules. They are very similar to those for tables. For queries on specific types of figures, please refer to the APA manual.

Figures in text. When discussing a figure in the text, number the figure in the order that it appears. For example, the first figure you refer to in the text would be Figure 1, then Figure 2, and so on. Then give a brief description of what the figure entails. Here are two examples:

> Figure 1 displays the pattern of students' off-task behaviors in minutes during the two-week program.

> The students' off-task behaviors steadily decreased over the two-week program (see Figure 1).

You can also refer to some of the major highlights in the figure, but remember that the text and figure should not be redundant.

Placement, size, and font. In a manuscript for publication, the figures are placed at the end of the manuscript after the tables with a separate page listing the captions. However, for student theses and dissertations, APA allows the figure to be included on the next page after it was first mentioned in the text. The figure caption is then typed below the figure. I prefer and advise students to put figures at the end of the thesis; however, check with your chairperson to see where you should place the figures.

In terms of size and font, all of the elements of the figure must be legible. The smallest font size is 8 point, and the largest is 14 point. The figure should also fit on the page (landscape or portrait) although APA has dimension rules for publication purposes. APA also recommends a sans serif font. Sans serif means "without serifs." Serifs are the small features added to strokes (which can clutter up the figure). Here is an example of a Microsoft sans serif font in Microsoft Word:

> This is a Microsoft sans serif font. Arial looks like this and is an acceptable sans serif font.

Another thing to consider is the shapes that are used in the figure. APA recommends using circles and triangles (open and solid) because other combinations of shapes, such as squares and diamonds, can look too similar. If there is a legend to help explain the lines and points in a graph, this must be included within the margins of the graph.

Captions and labels. For a thesis, the figure caption, or title, is placed below the figure itself. The caption is labeled *Figure 1.* (or whatever number figure it is), italicized with a period, and flushed to the left margin. The description of the figure follows this label using sentence capitalization. The caption should be detailed enough (but not overly detailed) so that the reader can understand the figure without having to refer to the text. The caption does not have to be a complete sentence although it ends with a period. Following the description, you can add any necessary notes such as explaining symbols, abbreviations, and reprints from other sources. Use the same notes format APA recommends for tables.

Graphs. One common type of figure used in the master's thesis is graphs. Graphs are typically used to show relationships between two variables, comparisons of data, percentages/proportions, or patterns over time. There are many different types of graphs including scatter plots, line graphs, bar graphs, pictorial graphs, and circle (pie) graphs. In many graphs, there is an *x* axis (horizontal line) and a *y* axis (vertical line). The independent variable is represented on the *x* axis, and the dependent variable is represented on the *y* axis. These both need to have labels in heading capitalization that are parallel to the axes. This means that the label on the *y* axis (vertical) must be placed so that when you turn the graph 90 degrees clockwise, you can read it. To do this in Microsoft Word, select the object (usually in a text box) or table cell. Then click in the Format menu on the top tool bar, and click Text Direction. Then select which direction you want the text to face. In addition, the units of measure must be specified with tick marks (at equal distances) on the axes. In Figure 10.14, there is an example of a graph in APA style.

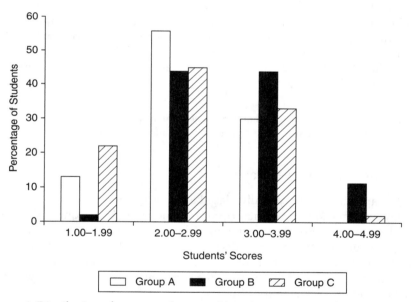

Figure 1. Distribution of scores on the statewide writing assessment by groups.

Figure 10.14   Example graph in APA style.

Appendixes

Appendixes are a critical part of the thesis because they allow you to include detailed information about the study and procedures that would not be appropriate to include in the five chapters. Some items that I require students to include in the appendixes are the IRB (Institutional Review Board) cover letter and blank consent form(s), sample lessons/intervention materials, and measurement instruments. I require these items because they are critical to understanding the design and results of the thesis. An advantage of putting these items in the appendix is that they do not have to be computer-generated by you. For instance, if you used a commercial assessment tool or instructional materials, you could photocopy parts of these (with permission from the copyright holder) as examples.

APA does have rules to follow for appendixes in a manuscript for publication, but I do not follow all of them because I want to allow for greater flexibility in the thesis. Check with your chairperson for how he or she wants you to include appendixes in the thesis.

Appendixes in Text

The APA rule for referring to appendixes in the text is similar to tables and figures. When mentioning an appendix in the text, label the appendix in the order that it appears; however, use capital letters instead of numbers. For example, the first appendix you refer to would be Appendix A, then Appendix B, and so on. Then give a brief description of what the appendix entails. Here is an example:

> The researcher obtained parental consent prior to contacting the students for participation in the study (see Appendix A for informed parent consent forms).

Placement and Cover Pages

The appendixes are typically placed at the very end of the thesis after the tables and figures. For a manuscript for publication, APA requires that page numbers extend into the appendixes. I do not require students to continue the page numbers for the appendixes in the thesis. This allows for flexibility in photocopying items from other sources. However, since the individual items do not have page numbers, make sure that each item has an appropriate heading for easy identification.

In order to identify and label the appendixes, each one begins with a cover page on a separate page. The cover page lists the title of the appendix and the items within the appendix (i.e., you can have more than one item in a single appendix). On the cover page, use a larger font for the title of the appendix and then list the items in a smaller font. The title is centered near the top of the page and the items are below the title, flushed left with bullet points. In Figure 10.15, there is an example of a cover page. Note that there are four different measurement instruments included in this

---

Appendix B: Measurement Instruments

- Student satisfaction survey
- Student observation protocol
- Teacher interview protocol
- Caregiver interview protocol

Figure 10.15   Sample cover page for appendix.

appendix. These items would be inserted after the cover page in the order that they are listed.

Front Pages

Remember when I promised in Chapter 1 that I would pull you through the finish line if I had to? Well look at where you are today! If you are ready to prepare the front pages of the thesis, this is like the last 385 yards of the marathon. You can almost touch the finish line, and your loved ones are on the other side taking pictures and chanting your name! Savor this moment. As soon as you complete the front pages, you are truly done. I promise. The front pages include the title and signature pages, acknowledgments, abstract, and table of contents. These are not in APA style, so check with your chairperson for how he or she wants you to proceed with these items.

Title Page

The title page is the cover page for the entire thesis. On this page, you need to identify the title of the thesis, institution, name of the degree, your name, and date. The title of your thesis should be between 10 and 12 words and encompass the essence of your study. There is a sample title page in Figure 10.16 (adjust the spacing on your page to make it look aesthetically pleasing).

Signature Page

The next page is the signature page; this is where your chairperson and committee members will sign the thesis. Remember, the thesis is not "official" until it has been approved and signed by your chairperson and committee members. On this page, leave space and lines for your chairperson and committee members to sign (add more lines if necessary). There is a sample signature page in Figure 10.17 (adjust the spacing on your page to make it look aesthetically pleasing).

Title in Heading Capitalization [Centered and Bold]

A Thesis Presented to the Faculty of the School of Education [Name of School]

University of San Francisco [Name of University]

In Partial Fulfillment of the Requirements of the Degree of

MASTER OF ARTS [DEGREE TITLE]

in

LEARNING & INSTRUCTION [DEGREE AREA]

by

Yvonne N. Bui [Your Name]

May 15, 2009 [Date thesis will be signed]

Figure 10.16   Sample title page for thesis.

Title in Heading Capitalization

In Partial Fulfillment of the Requirements of the

MASTER OF ARTS

in

LEARNING AND INSTRUCTION

by

Yvonne N. Bui

UNIVERSITY OF SAN FRANCISCO

May 15, 2009

Under the guidance and approval of the committee, and approved by all its members, this thesis has been accepted in partial fulfillment of the requirements for the degree.

Approved:

_____   _____
Chairperson   Date

_____   _____
Committee Member   Date

Figure 10.17   Sample signature page for thesis.

Acknowledgments

The next page is the Acknowledgments. This is really the best page in the entire thesis because you get to acknowledge and thank every person who supported you along the way. Do not forget to acknowledge your chairperson and committee members, family, friends, pets, the local coffee barista, me, and so on. The title of this page is "Acknowledgments" (in British spelling, it is "Acknowledgements"), and it is centered at the top of the page. This page is also where you begin the page numbers in roman numerals (e.g., i, ii, iii, iv). I prefer page numbers at the bottom of the page in the center. However, APA style is upper right-hand corner for manuscripts, so check with your chairperson to see if he or she has a preference.

Abstract

The next page is the abstract. The abstract is a brief (no more than 120 words) summary of the thesis. While it is brief, the abstract should also be comprehensive in describing the purpose, participants, methods, and major results/conclusions. The title "Abstract" is centered, but the text is flushed to the left margin. There is an example of an abstract in Figure 10.18.

Table of Contents

The next few pages are the table of contents. The table of contents is extremely critical because it is a road map to the entire thesis. Therefore,

---

Abstract

The purpose of the study was to measure the effects of a comprehensive writing program for students with and without learning disabilities (LD) in inclusive general education classrooms. The program included prewriting, narrative text structure, writing strategies, and process writing. The study was conducted in five 5th-grade classrooms with 113 students (14 students with LD). A quasi-experimental comparison-group design was utilized; three experimental classes received the intervention, and two comparison classes received traditional writing instruction. Measures included writing indicators as well as state writing competency test scores. The students in the experimental group made significant gains from pretest to posttest on most writing measures. Students in the comparison group made gains on some measures, but the effect sizes were smaller.

Figure 10.18   Sample abstract that summarizes the study.

make sure the page numbers and headings match exactly what is in the text of the thesis. I typically advise students to create the table of contents at the end after all the final, final, final edits are completed (in case things shift around). The title of your thesis is at the top center and every letter should be capitalized. Then the front pages are listed on separate lines starting with the Acknowledgments, Abstract, and Table of Contents.

Lists of Tables and Figures

The next items in the table of contents are "List of Tables," "List of Figures," and "List of Appendixes." These are recommended if you have more than one table, figure, or appendix, as it makes it easier for the reader to find the information embedded in the text or at the end of the thesis. The "List of Tables" and "List of Figures" are lists of the titles and page numbers of individual tables and figures. The "List of Appendixes" lists the titles of the appendixes but there are no page numbers. Here is an example:

List of Tables

Table 1: *Pretest and Posttest Scores for Geometry Assessment*   73

Table 2: *Pretest and Posttest Scores for Students' Self-Perceptions* 74

The next page is the first page of Chapter One. This page starts the Arabic numerals (1, 2, 3, etc.) that extend into the references, tables, and figures. After each chapter heading, list all the Level 2 and Level 3 headings with their corresponding page numbers. Slightly indent each subheading within the chapter. Do not list Level 4 headings. After the chapters, the last item on the table of contents is "References" with the corresponding page. Figure 10.19 is a sample of a condensed Table of Contents.

Copying and Binding

After you are done with the front pages, thesis text, references, tables, figures, and appendixes, you can bring it all to get copied and bound (see Final Tips and Checklist below). Check with your chairperson for the guidelines for copying and binding. At my institution, we require students to make at least three copies: the chairperson keeps one, the department keeps one, and the student keeps one. However, you should be able to make as many copies as you want (they make great gifts)! Make sure you choose a reliable place for photocopying, and tell them it is for a master's thesis. I ask students to

TITLE [ALL LETTERS ARE CAPITALIZED]

Acknowledgments	i
Abstract	ii
Table of Contents	iii
List of Tables	v
List of Figures	vi
List of Appendixes	vii
Chapter One	1
Introduction	1
Statement of the Problem	3
Background and Need	10
Purpose of the Study	13
Research Questions	13
Educational Significance	14
Definition of Terms	14
Limitations	17
Ethical Considerations	17
Chapter Two	19
Literature Review	19
References	66

Figure 10.19   Sample condensed table of contents.

have the thesis bound with a Velobind strip. These are the hard plastic strips with little tines/holes that squeeze the papers and hold them together tightly. I prefer this to coil bind, which may tear easily. I also have students copy the thesis onto high-quality heavy white paper. This ensures that the print does not fade over the years. Finally, the front cover is a sheet of clear plastic, and the back cover is a black plastic sheet. You may choose to have hardbound copies although this will be more expensive. If you choose a professional copy center, you should not have problems. However, ask them whether they want the original in print or electronic format. In addition, allow the center a few days to have the copies made, since they are usually very busy at the beginning and end of semesters. After you have the bounded copies signed by your chairperson and committee members, you are truly done.

CONGRATULATIONS!!! Bravo! Hooray! Yippee! Yahoo! I don't have the words to express how happy I am for you and how relieved you must be. Thank you for taking this journey with me. Now sprint across the finish line with your head held high, arms waving in the air. Then reward yourself with a nice long vacation.

Final Tips and Checklist

The final tips and checklist is to ensure that everything is in place before you copy and bind the thesis forever. They are not in any particular order. Some of them may not apply to your situation, so when in doubt, check with your chairperson.

- Do a final grammar and spell check for all chapters
- Match citations in text with reference list
- Set left hand margin at 1.5 (4 cm) for binding purposes
- Copy thesis on heavyweight high-quality white paper
- Start each chapter on a new page
- Use Roman numerals (i, ii, iii) for the front pages (e.g., Acknowledgments, Abstract)
- Use Arabic numerals (1, 2, 3) on the first page of Chapter One and continue into the references, tables, and figures
- Keep at least one signed copy for yourself (your chairperson and institution/program usually also get a copy)
- All text, references, and tables should be double spaced (unless your chairperson says otherwise)
- Check the levels of heading to make sure they are correct
- Spell out all abbreviations at first mention and put in notes in the tables and figures
- Check that all table columns have headings
- Obtain written permission for all copyrighted material for quotes, tables, and figures from the copyright holder
- Cite all direct quotations with page numbers
- List a retrieval date and location for electronic sources
- Check all URLs to ensure they work

Summary

In this chapter, I discussed the editorial style rules and guidelines established by APA (2001) for citations, references, tables, figures, and other issues to help you format the master's thesis. I hope they helped you complete the final product. Congratulations again on completing your master's thesis, a major feat! Here is a summary of the most critical points from Chapter 10:

- The APA editorial style is commonly used in various social science disciplines such as education, psychology, sociology, business, economics, nursing, and social work.

- The *number* of level headings refers to the quantity of headings you use. The total maximum number of level headings is five. The *number level* heading refers to a specific heading location.

- Citations of works are necessary when you use a direct quote (which needs a page number) or paraphrase someone else's words, ideas, or research findings.

- Keep the listing of the authors in their original order from the source even if it is not in alphabetical order.

- If the work is cited in the text, it must be in the reference list and vice versa. In addition, the citation in the text (e.g., spelling and order of the authors, year of publication) must be exactly the same as the citation in the reference list.

- For electronic sources, provide the retrieval date and location in addition to information required for printed material.

- Follow the three "C" rules for table and figure design: comprehensibility, clarity, and consistency.

- Figures are a great way to show nonlinear relations, patterns of results, concepts, or ideas that are difficult for the reader to "see" from text descriptions.

- Items that may be included in the appendixes are the IRB cover letter and blank consent form(s), sample lessons/intervention materials, and measurement instruments.

- The front pages include the title and signature pages, acknowledgements, abstract, and table of contents.

Resources

Common Obstacles and Practical Solutions

1. A common obstacle that students face in final editing is keeping track of the citations and references. Words that come to mind are, "Where do I

find all these references?" The best way to overcome this obstacle is to cite and reference as you write (rather than wait until the very end). Put the citation in the text immediately when you paraphrase or quote with the year and page numbers. Then keep a list of all the sources, even if it is not in the correct APA format. You can format the references at the end, but this will save you time searching for the references.

2. Another common obstacle is preparing tables. Words that come to mind are, "Do I really need this table?" First, you should decide if the table really is necessary. If it is, then keep it as simple as possible. Have a few columns (no more than three) and rows. Since printing cost and spacing is not as much of an issue in the thesis (like it is for manuscripts for publication), you can spread out your data over several tables. This will help you in terms of formatting and may make it easier for your reader to decipher the tables.

Reflection/Discussion Questions

When you are doing the final formatting for the thesis, it is important to understand the APA style editorial rules and guidelines. The following reflection/discussion questions will help guide you through the editorial process.

1. What is a level of heading? What is the difference between the number of level headings and a number level heading? What does it mean when headings are at the same or different levels? Give examples of how you would use different levels of heading in your thesis.

2. Why is it important to provide citations and references for the sources that you use? What are the different types of sources? What is the difference between a print and an electronic source? List the information that is needed to reference print and electronic sources.

Try It Exercises

The following exercises are designed to help you edit and format the thesis. In Activity One, you will create a reference list for various sources. In Activity Two, you will create a table using demographic data from the participants in your study.

1. Activity One: For this activity, create a reference list from the entries listed below. Be sure to identify the type of work and then include all necessary information in your reference. Have a partner check them to make sure they are correct!

- Title: Researching Pupils, Schools and Oneself. Teachers as Integrators of Theory and Practice in Initial Teacher Education

  Author(s): Maaranen, Katriina; Krokfors, Leena

  Source: Journal of Education for Teaching: International Research and Pedagogy, v34 n3 p207–222 Aug 2008. 16 pp. (Peer Reviewed Journal)

- Title: *Counseling* methods.

  Author(s): Krumboltz, John D., (Ed); Thoresen, Carl E., (Ed)
  Source: Oxford, England: Holt, Rinehart & Winston, 1976. xvi, 576 pp.

- Title: Criminology jobs

  Retrieval date: September 1, 2008
  http://www.unixl.com/dir/law_and_legal_studies/criminology_jobs/

2. Activity Two: For this activity, create a table based on your participants' demographic data. Have a partner check it to make sure it is comprehensible, clear, and consistent.

- Create a table for your participants' demographic data.
- Include the stub column, one column spanner, and two column headers.
- Include at least one stub (row header).
- Insert data for at least five participants.

Key Terms

- column head
- column spanner
- Digital Object Identifier (DOI)
- edited book
- general notes
- hanging indent
- heading capitalization
- levels of heading

- periodical
- personal communication
- probability notes
- sentence capitalization
- specific notes
- stub column
- stub head
- stubs

Suggested Readings

- American Psychological Association. (2001). *Publication manual of the American Psychological Association* (5th ed.). Washington, DC: American Psychological Association.

- American Psychological Association. (2007). *APA style guide to electronic references* (PDF format). Order online: http://books.apa.org/books.cfm?id=4210509

- Gelfand, H., & Walker, C. J. (2001). *Mastering APA style: Student's workbook and training guide* (5th ed.). Washington, DC: American Psychological Association.

- Szuchman, L. T. (2008). *Writing with style: APA style made easy* (4th ed.). Belmont, CA: Wadsworth.

- The Writing Center. (2006). *APA overview.* The University of Wisconsin–Madison Writing Center. Available online: http://www.wisc.edu/writing/Handbook/American_Psychological_Association_(APA)_Documentation_M.pdf

Web Links

- APA Online
  http://www.apastyle.org/

- APA Online: APA Style Helper (software)
  http://www.apa.org/software/

- APA Reference Style: Tightening Up Your Citations
  http://linguistics.byu.edu/faculty/henrichsenl/APA/APA01.html

- APA Research Style Crib Sheet
  http://www.psychwww.com/resource/APA%20Research%20Style%20Crib%20Sheet.htm

- APA Style Resources
  http://www.psychwww.com/resource/apacrib.htm

- Formatting Tables & Presenting Figures
  http://www.docstyles.com/apa15.htm

- A Guide for Writing Research Papers Based on Styles Recommended by The American Psychological Association
  http://webster.commnet.edu/apa/

- Guide to Grammar and Writing
  http://grammar.ccc.commnet.edu/grammar/

- NoodleTools: Software Tools
  http://www.noodletools.com/tools/freetools.php

- North Michigan University Lydia M. Olson Library: APA Reference Style Guide
  http://library.nmu.edu/guides/userguides/style_apa.htm

- The OWL at Purdue: APA Formatting and Style Guide
  http://owl.english.purdue.edu/owl/resource/560/01/

- Plagiarism.Org: Learning Center
  http://www.plagiarism.org/learning_center/what_is_plagiarism.html

- Psychology With Style: A Hypertext Writing Guide (for the fifth edition of the APA Manual)
  http://www.uwsp.edu/PSYCH/apa4b.htm

- ScholarWord: Paper Formatting Software
  http://scholarword.com/

- The Write Direction: Dr. Paper (Software)
  http://thewritedirection.net/drpaper/

Appendix A

Sample Institutional Review Board Initial Application

Project Title: Bridging Cultural Themes in Educational Practices: Increasing Students' Math Performance

(1) Background and Rationale

With today's changes in demographics, there is evidence to suggest that the United States is becoming *more* culturally and linguistically diverse. Unlike 50 years ago when schools and classrooms were primarily composed of a homogeneous student population, today's schools and teachers are increasingly challenged with educating students from diverse cultural, linguistic, and economic backgrounds. By the year 2020, it is estimated that nearly 50% of school-age students in the United States will represent African American, Asian, Hispanic, or some other non-European ethnic group (Woolfolk, 2001).

The recent demographic changes have serious implications for the nation's public education system. In addition to adjusting to differences in cultural values and behaviors, classroom educators are faced with the additional challenge of teaching students who may come from cultural and linguistic backgrounds that differ from their own. Moreover, as the student population in the United States continues to become more heterogeneous, the demographics of school staff have become more homogenous (Taylor, 2000). In other words, although most teachers are middle class, monocultural, and many are also monolingual, depending on the geographic region and type of district (e.g., rural, urban, suburban) they teach in, the students they serve may be from diverse cultural, economic, and linguistic backgrounds. Thus, teachers are less likely than in the 1950s to be from the same cultural and language backgrounds as their students (Santos, Fowler, Corso, & Bruns, 2000). This is even more apparent in states and regions where students from different cultures and languages are disproportionately represented in certain disability categories (Meese, 2001). For example, African American, Hispanic, and Native American students tend to be over-identified with emotional disturbances, learning disabilities, and speech/language impairments and under-identified for gifted and talented placements (Artiles & Trent, 1994; Artiles & Zamora-Duran, 1997; Gollnick & Chinn, 1990).

Students of color also tend to perform lower on national and state standardized assessments than White students. For example, on the National Assessment of Educational Performance math tests, at both Grades 4 and 8, White and Asian/Pacific Islander students scored higher, on average, than Black, Hispanic, and American Indian/Alaska Native students. Black students scored lower than both Hispanic and American Indian/Alaska Native students (NAEP, 2006). On average, students with disabilities scored 23 points lower at Grade 4 and 40 points lower at Grade 8 than students without disabilities.

Considering the disproportionate rates with which minority students are placed in special education and identified with learning disabilities (LD), there is a tiny database of empirical articles on ethnic minority students in special education journals (Artiles, Trent, & Kuan, 1997). The lack of empirical research on math instruction for minority students with disabilities over the past two decades has serious implications for researchers and educators. By not providing special educators with information and training in effective math practices for minority students with LD that are empirically supported, we are only increasing the probability of cultural dissonance and academic frustration and failure for these students. Thus, the purpose of this study is to increase the mathematics performance of students with disabilities from culturally and linguistically diverse backgrounds. This will be accomplished by integrating African American cultural themes of *communalism, movement,* and *orality* into the math instruction as a means to align the students' home and school cultures.

(2) Description of Sample

The research study will examine and measure the effectiveness of an intervention, Bridging Cultural Themes in Educational Practices, in an elementary classroom in an urban school district. The research will be conducted at one public elementary school in (name of city) in the (name of district) School District. This district was targeted because of its urban climate and high proportion of low-income students with disabilities representing culturally diverse populations. One 4th- through 6th-grade class (special education day class) in a school where the principal and teacher have shown significant interest and support for the project will be selected

for participation. The class is made up of 12 boys with emotional disturbance and/or learning disabilities. Ten of the students are African American
and two are Latino. Two of the students are 4th graders, six of the students
are 5th graders, and four of the students are 6th graders.

(3) Recruitment Procedure

Once the district and principal have given their permission to conduct the
study, the researcher will then ask the classroom teacher to send home consent forms to the students' parents, informing them about the study, the benefits that the knowledge obtained might have for the students, and requesting
that their children participate. The classroom teacher will also make follow-
up phone calls to the students' parents to answer any questions that they
might have. The students' parents will be informed that their consent to participate in the study is voluntary and may be rescinded at any time.

(4) Subject Consent Process

In order to obtain consent from the subjects, the researcher (through
the classroom teacher) will send the students' parents a consent form that
describes the study, procedures, and expected outcomes. In the consent
form, the parents will be assured that their child's identity will remain confidential, including test scores and responses to any measurement instruments. The consent form will also inform parents that whether or not they
give consent, the quality of their child's education will not be affected. The
researcher will send home three separate consent forms through the classroom teacher. If consent is not achieved after three attempts, the researcher
will no longer pursue the student for participation.

(5) Procedures

The intervention, Bridging Cultural Themes in Educational Practices
(BCTEP), integrates the African American cultural themes of communalism,
movement, and orality (Boykin, 1983) with standards-based mathematics
instruction for students with disabilities. For example, students will work in
interdependent groups (i.e., communalism) to solve math problems together.
Movement during math instruction will be integrated through dance, rhythm,
and music. Orality will provide the opportunity for students to participate in
the mathematics instruction through various forms of spoken language (e.g.,
call and response). The study goes beyond addressing superficial cultural differences and the need to be *culturally sensitive* toward minority groups.
Instead, the premise of the study is based on the cultural compatibility hypothesis, which states that when classroom instruction is designed to be *compatible*

with the students' natal culture, improvements in students' academic learning can be expected (Deyhle, 1983; Jordan, 1985; Jordan & Tharp, 1979; Vogt, Jordan, & Tharp, 1987). Thus, the intent of this intervention is to match the classroom environment and teaching practices with the students' natal or home culture in order to minimize conflicts and maximize achievement for students with disabilities from culturally diverse backgrounds.

The intervention study will utilize a single-group case design. Before instruction begins, an informal math test based on fractions and a student satisfaction survey will be administered to all of the students. Then instruction will be presented daily, for a 50-minute time period, over eight weeks by the classroom teacher (who will be trained and observed by the researcher on a weekly basis) for a total of 30 lessons over six phases. The length of each phase will be randomly selected and will last between 7 and 10 days. The math curriculum is based on the district-mandated standards and textbooks for each grade level. During the baseline phase, students will receive traditional instruction. Curriculum-based measurement probes will be administered at the end of each lesson. During the intervention phases, students will receive research-based math instruction that integrates one of the African cultural themes (a baseline phase will follow each intervention phase). One week after the last instruction phase, all of the students will be given the same informal math test and student satisfaction survey again. Means analysis will be conducted on the lessons' probes from each of the phases. Descriptive and inferential statistics (e.g., t test) will be applied to the pretest/posttest data collected from all the students to determine whether application of the intervention was related to significant differences between the pre- and posttest scores.

(6) Potential Risk to Subjects

There are minimal risks to the subjects in the study such as fatigue and frustration when learning new fraction concepts. The students will be allowed to take breaks as needed. The BCTEP approach will be implemented during regular class time so as to not take away precious instructional hours. Furthermore, during classroom observations, the researcher will make a significant effort not to distract students from their learning.

(7) Minimization of Potential Risk

All personal information regarding the students involved in the study will remain confidential throughout and following the study. This includes not disclosing the names of the teachers, students, school, and parents. Since most of the data collection will occur as a natural part of the daily instruction and assessment, the students will not feel like they are being bombarded with tests and questions.

(8) Potential Benefit to Subjects

The BCTEP represents an instructional math curriculum that builds on previous research for culturally and linguistically diverse students with and without disabilities. The instruction will focus on three major African cultural themes: *communalism, movement,* and *orality.* If the results are successful, these themes could be utilized and integrated with research-based math instruction for students with disabilities. Following integrated instruction within the three cultural themes, students will be expected to achieve the following outcomes: increased math performance on informal math assessments and increased student satisfaction.

(9) Costs to Subjects

There are no financial costs to the participating students. All of the supplies needed for instruction will be provided to the students by the researcher. All of the BCTEP instruction will be delivered during normal instruction time during the school day.

(10) Reimbursement/Compensation to Subjects

Student participants will not be reimbursed or compensated for participating in this study. The classroom teacher who participates will be given a small honorarium for her time (e.g., during informal meetings) and help with collecting consent forms.

(11) Confidentiality of Records

All data from the study will be kept confidential and the subjects' identities will not be revealed before, during, or after the study. The students' names will be removed from the pre- and posttest data, and they will be assigned numbers to ensure confidentiality. Data will be kept by the researcher in a locked file away from the school site. Computerized data will be inputted into a password-protected laptop computer that will also be removed from the school site. Only the researcher and her assistant will have access to the data.

_____   _____

Signature of Applicant   Date

Appendix B

Sample Cover Letter

Dear Sir or Madam:

[introduction] My name is (insert your name) and I am a(n) (insert your role) in the Department of (insert your department/school) at (insert name of college/university).

[purpose] I am writing to you to request your consent for your child to participate in a research study that I am doing to investigate the effectiveness of an intervention called Bridging Cultural Themes in Educational Practices (BCTEP) on students' math performance.

[description of study] This intervention integrates the African American cultural themes of communalism, movement, and orality with standards-based mathematics instruction for students with disabilities. For example, students will work in interdependent groups (i.e., communalism) to solve math problems together. Movement will be integrated during the math instruction through dance, rhythm, and music. Orality will provide the opportunity for students to participate in the mathematics instruction through various forms of spoken language (e.g., call and response). The intent of this intervention is to match the classroom environment and teaching practices with the students' home culture in order to minimize conflicts and maximize achievement for students with disabilities from culturally diverse backgrounds.

[procedures] If you allow your child to participate, your child's classroom teacher, (insert name of teacher), will teach a math curriculum on fractions for eight weeks (50 minutes per day) using standards-based math materials by integrating the African American cultural themes. Before and after the study, your child will take math tests and a satisfaction survey to measure the effects of the intervention. A mini-math test will also be given after every lesson.

[confidentiality] Rest assured that I will take steps to maintain confidentiality of your child's records by keeping all data materials, including teacher reports and academic records, in a locked filing cabinet at my home. All records will remain confidential and your child's participation or nonparticipation will in no way negatively affect the quality of education your child receives, or the quality of services you receive as a parent of a child attending the researcher's school.

[cost/benefit] There will be no cost to your child for participating. At your own request, I will provide you with a copy of the completed study at no cost. There will be no payment available to you for your child's participation; however, it is my feeling that your child will benefit greatly from the math instruction and teachers will also be informed of effective math instruction.

[informed consent] Participation in research is voluntary. You are free to decline your child's participation in this study, or withdraw from it at any point. (insert name), Principal of (insert name of school), is aware of this study, but she is not requiring that your child participate in this research and your decision as to whether or not to participate will have no influence on the quality of education your child will receive at (insert name of school), nor will your child's participation or nonparticipation influence future interactions between him/herself and school personnel.

[contact information] Thank you for your consent and assistance with this study. If you have any questions please feel free to contact me by phone at (insert phone number) or by e-mail at (insert e-mail address) or by regular mail at (insert mailing address).

Sincerely,

(insert your name) Yvonne N. Bui, PhD
(insert your title) Associate Professor

Appendix C

Sample Informed Consent Form

PARENT INFORMED CONSENT FORM
(INSERT NAME OF COLLEGE/UNIVERSITY)
CONSENT TO BE A RESEARCH SUBJECT

Purpose and Background

(Insert name, role, school/college, university) is doing a study to investigate the effectiveness of Bridging Cultural Themes in Educational Practices (BCTEP), an intervention that integrates the African American cultural themes of communalism, movement, and orality with standards-based mathematics instruction for students with disabilities.

My child is being asked to participate because he/she is a student in the special education classroom in which the teacher has voluntarily agreed to participate in the study.

Procedures

If I allow my child to be a participant in this study, the following may happen:

1. The classroom teacher will teach my child math strategies daily (50 minutes) for eight weeks using standards-based math materials that integrate African American cultural themes.

2. (Insert name) will have access to my child's relevant documents/ educational records (which will remain confidential).

3. My child will complete a math test before and after the study is completed.

4. My child will complete a satisfaction survey about math before and after the study is completed.

5. My child will complete a mini-math test after each lesson is completed.

Risks and/or Discomforts

1. It is possible that some of the questions on the satisfaction survey may make my child feel uncomfortable, but he/she is free to decline to answer any questions or to stop participation at any time.

2. Participation in research may mean a loss of confidentiality. Study records will be kept as confidential as is possible. No individual identities will be used in any reports or publications resulting from the study. Study information will be coded and kept in locked files away from the school site at all times. Only study personnel will have access to the files.

Benefits

There will be no direct benefit to me for letting my child participate in this study. However, it is likely that my child will improve his math performance and increase his satisfaction with school and math. Other benefits include minimizing the probability of cultural misunderstandings and therefore maximizing achievement for students from culturally diverse backgrounds who have special needs.

Costs/Financial Considerations

There will be no financial costs to me or to my child as a result of taking part in this study.

Payment/Reimbursement

There will be no payment for my child's participation in this study. However, my child will receive school supply materials at no cost to the school or me.

Questions

I have talked to (insert your name and chairperson) about this study and have had my questions answered. If I have further questions about the study, I may call him/her at (insert phone number) or e-mail him/her at (insert e-mail address)

If I have any questions or comments about my child's participation in this study, I should first talk with the researchers. If for some reason I do not wish to do this, I may contact the Institutional Review Board for the Protection of Human Subjects (IRBPHS), which is concerned with protection of volunteers in research projects. I may reach the IRBPHS office by calling (insert phone number), by e-mailing (insert e-mail address), or by writing to the IRBPHS at (insert school address).

Consent

I have been given a copy of the "Research Subject's Bill of Rights" and I have been given a copy of this consent form to keep.

PARTICIPATION IN RESEARCH IS VOLUNTARY. I am free to decline to be in this study, or to withdraw my child from it at any point. My decision as to whether or not to participate in this study will have no influence on my or my child's present or future status as a student or employee at (insert name of college/university).

My signature below indicates that I agree to have my child participate in this study.

_____   _____
Student's Name   Student's Teacher

_____   _____
Signature of Parent/Guardian   Date of Signature

(PLEASE KEEP ONE COPY OF THE CONSENT FORM FOR YOUR RECORDS)

Appendix D

Dr. Bui's Writing Tips
and Rules from A to Z

A:

- Active vs. passive voice: Use the *active voice* so that your sentences are more concise:
  - ○ "The dog bit the boy." (active)
  - ○ "The boy was bitten by the dog." (passive)
- Affect vs. effect:
  - ○ Affect is the *verb* form: "The students' reading scores were affected by the instruction."
  - ○ Effect is the *noun* form: "There was a positive effect on the students' reading scores."
- Also: Do not start a sentence with "also"—use other transitions such as "in addition," "further," and so on.
- Always use APA format in the text and in the reference section.

B:

- Back it up: When you make a definitive statement such as, "Students with disabilities perform lower on standardized tests," you need to back this up with a citation.
- Buffers: Do not write paragraphs where every sentence ends with a citation. This makes the writing extremely choppy. You need to include buffer statements in between the citations where you are connecting the information or expanding/commenting on it in some way.

C:

- Citations in text use APA format.
- Colons: Only use them sparingly and when you're making a long list. Then number the items.
  - o "The intervention included the following components: (1) blah, (2) blah blah, (3) blah blah blah, and (4) final blahs."
- Commas: Do not go crazy with your use of commas.
  - o Use them with lists: "preferences, attitudes, and behavior."
  - o Use them in between compound sentences: "The students increased their scores, and the teachers improved their instructional methods."
  - o Use them after dependent clauses: "When the students were grouped by disability, there was a difference in their scores."

D:

- Data are always plural. Say, "Data are" or "data were."
- Don't (do not) use contractions in the thesis at all—spell them all out.

E:

- Edit, edit, edit. Read your writing aloud to make sure it makes sense. Then have someone else read it before you turn it in to your chairperson.
- Et al.: This can only be used if you have listed all the authors the first time or if there are six or more authors (see APA). If you are going to use it, then it should be (Bui et al., 2007).

F:

- Fragments: Sentence fragments are incomplete sentences, such as "While they were taking the test," or "Because they had a disability."
- Fluency: Use transitions and segues so your writing is not choppy (see buffers).

G:

- Graphs (all figures) follow APA format.

H:

- Headings: Use three level headings for major sections of the thesis. Use four level headings if you want to organize using the three parallel ladders strategy.

I:

- "It" is a pronoun—do not start your sentence with "It."

J:

- Jargon: Terms that are uncommon should be briefly defined in the text. Longer definitions belong in the definition of terms section in Chapter One.

K:

- Keep paragraph structure intact. Start the paragraph with a good topic sentence and then make sure all the sentences within the paragraph fit the topic sentence.

L:

- Label all the acronyms the first time they appear: "students with learning disabilities (LD)"—after that, you can use the acronym alone, "students with LD."

M:

- Match the subject with the appropriate pronoun: "The *student's* score and *his* or *her* attitude." "The *students'* scores and *their* attitudes."
- Multiple works: When you have multiple works, group them together in alphabetical order—"Students of color are overrepresented in special education (Bobbett, 2004; Bui, 2008; Edwards, 2005; Hawk & Lee, 2001)."

N:

- Numbers should always be spelled out when they start a sentence. Spell out numbers under ten and figures to express numbers 10 and above.

O:

- Organizational structure: Be sure to structure your chapters using the three parallel ladders strategy.
- Outline: Before you write, you should create an outline of the topic sentence for each paragraph. Then you can see if your paper has funneled correctly in the Introduction and if you have the three related areas in the *Statement of the Problem* and the *Background and Need*.

P:

- Pace yourself: Set a writing goal for yourself every day whether it is a time goal or a completion goal. Do not wait two weeks before the thesis deadline. This is not something you can "wing" at the last minute.
- Paraphrase; do not plagiarize.

- Possessives:
  - o For singular, the apostrophe goes before the "s"—"The teacher's class had eight students."
  - o For plural, the apostrophe goes after the "s"—"The teachers' classes had a total of 50 students."

Q:

- Quotes: Use quotes sparingly and if you do, you need to cite the exact page number from the source.

R:

- References: Look to see how APA formats citations in the text and in the reference list.
- Rhetorical questions: Do not ask rhetorical questions in the text.
- Run-on sentences: Break "long" sentences into shorter ones. This does not mean you should only write simple sentences. However, if your "sentence" is longer than four lines, it is probably a run-on.

S:

- Save: Press the "save" button every time you finish writing a sentence or paragraph—this will keep you from having a nervous breakdown when your computer freezes.
- Segues and transitions: Make sure to segue between paragraphs. Headers are not transitions.
- Semicolons: Semicolons are used to separate independent clauses: "The students' behavior was atrocious; the teacher sent them to the principal's office." If you are not certain of whether or not to use a semicolon, use a period instead.
- Soften your language: Unless you have evidence to back it up (with a citation), you should soften your statement so it is not so definitive.
  - o "Students' low motivation causes them to have poor self-esteem."—strong statement, needs a citation.
  - o "Students' low motivation may negatively affect their self-esteem."—softer, does not need a citation.

T:

- Tense: 95% of the thesis will be in the past tense since most of the research has already been conducted.
- Their/there: *Their* is used to show possession—"Their behaviors were inappropriate." This is different from *there*, which indicates location—"The books are over there."

U:

- Use "people first" language:
  - o "Students receiving special education services"
  - o "Students with disabilities"
  - o "Students with special needs"
  - o "Students with autism"

- Utilize formal, technical language and terms. Do not use informal language, slang, vernacular, or "preach" to the reader (no standing on a soapbox).

V:

- Value judgments: Do not use words that express worth or value. For example:
  "There were *only* eight students in the study."
  "The students *finally* improved on their tests."
  "The mean gains from pre- to posttest were *pitiful*."

- Versions: Always date and properly label the versions of your writing—this will keep you from revising an old draft.

W:

- Write, write, and rewrite.
- Writing center: If you need writing help, get it!

X:

- Xerox copies: Have some form of copy of your writing—either in hard copy or electronic. E-mail drafts to yourself or save it on a jump drive or external hard drive. Computers crash all the time—you do not have to.

Y:

- You: "You" do not belong in the thesis—neither do we, our, I, us—always keep the writing in the third person.

Z:

- Zzzzzzzz . . . get sleep. Writing is easier when you are rested. Take frequent (but short) breaks to rest your eyes—blink a lot when you are at the computer (do not strain your eyes). Write difficult sections when you are most alert. If you are hitting a mental writing block, do a less demanding task such as typing up your references.

Appendix E

Sample Chapter One Introduction

Adapted from Williams, A. (2006). *Motivation, metacognition, and self-determination among students with learning disabilities.* Unpublished master's thesis, University of San Francisco, California.

[broad problem: national level]

The quality of public education in the United States is often judged by student academic performance. One of the four pillars of the No Child Left Behind Act of 2001 (NCLB) is stronger accountability for academic results (United States Department of Education, 2003). In looking at national academic performance data, there appears to be ample room for improvement. For example, the Program for International Student Assessment (PISA) reported in 2003 that 15-year-olds in the United States performed below their peers in 29 industrialized countries in the academic area of mathematics (PISA, 2003). Only 24% of 12th-grade students nationwide performed at or above the *proficient* level in writing, and average reading scale scores were lower among 12th graders in 2002 than in 1992. Given the consequences of not meeting academic standards as outlined in the NCLB, states are eager to improve students' academic outcomes.

[implications/manifestations of national problem]

Poor academic performance may lead to student discouragement and disenchantment with the public education system, which may contribute to student drop-out rates. Nationally, 5% of students enrolled in high school in 1999 left school before October 2000 as reported by National Center for Education Statistics (NCES) studies. NCES also reported that in October 2000, approximately 3.8 million people between the ages of 16 and 24 were not enrolled in high school or had not completed a high school program (NCES, 2005a).

Given the level of noncompletion of high school programs, poor postsecondary outcomes at the national and state level may be expected. According to NCES, one of the goals of public education is to provide young people with the academic skills necessary for success in a postsecondary learning environment. Students who do not complete a secondary program do not receive this academic training and will most likely be unsuccessful in a postsecondary school setting or not attempt enrollment in a college or university at all (NCES, 2005a). The Organization for Economic Cooperation and Development calculated the first-time entry rate in postsecondary education for students in the United States to be at 42% in 2003. This was a shamefully low percentage compared to Australia, Finland, Iceland, New Zealand, Norway, Poland, and Sweden, which had first-time entry rates of 60% or more (NCES, 2005b).

Disinterest in education among adolescents in the United States is an issue that has very serious consequences, including increased risk for poor academic performance, school drop-out, poor postsecondary outcomes, and criminal activity (Caraway, Tucker, Reinke, & Hall, 2003). According to Caraway et al., one third of high school seniors in 1999 felt that what they were learning in school was not important to their future. Between 1980 and 1999, the percentage of high school seniors who felt like what they were being taught in school was *meaningful and important* declined by 29%. A study reported that peer support and encouragement of antisocial behavior has been steadily increasing since 1976 (Boesel, 2001). These negative attitudes toward school relate to poor academic achievement and postsecondary outcomes.

An alternative to attending a postsecondary program after graduating or dropping out of high school would be obtaining gainful employment; however, statistics with regards to employment opportunities for youth without high school diplomas do not appear to be very encouraging. For example, in 2003, 44% of people between 16 and 24 who dropped out of high school before receiving a diploma were not enrolled in a postsecondary program or employed. Education level was cited as an important factor in youth unemployment rates (NCES, 2005a).

In addition to poor employment prospects, young people who do not complete a high school program and/or do not continue their education in a postsecondary environment are more likely to be involved in criminal activity. Approximately 75% of state prison inmates did not complete high school, and approximately 47% of drug offenders do not have a high school diploma or a GED (Harlow, 2003). Additionally, high school dropouts are 3.5 times more likely than high school graduates to be arrested in their lifetimes (Alliance for Excellent Education, 2003). These figures seem to support the importance of academic achievement and enrollment in high school and postsecondary programs for young people. Clearly, school personnel should sustain drop-out prevention programs and encouragement of postsecondary education. If the present trends continue, a growth in the number of incarcerated and jobless youth can be expected. These national statistics are causing growing concern among educators, politicians, parents, and students across the country.

[one-step funnel: problem on state level]

States, such as California, are not immune to these growing national trends, and education data for California were found to be similar to national data. For example, in 2003 only 22% of eighth-grade students in California performed at or above the *proficient* level in math and reading on the National Assessment of Educational Progress (NAEP) assessment. For the 2003–2004 Academic Performance Index (API) cycle, fewer than half of the high schools in California met their API growth target as reported by the California Department of Education (2004).

[implications/manifestations of state problems]

In California, the drop-out statistics were also consistent with those of the rest of the country. A 2003 study conducted by the Pacific Research Institute (PRI) showed that over 30% of California's students did not complete a high school program within four years (PRI, 2005). This study also noted that due to tracking challenges, this figure might actually be higher than 30%. State postsecondary enrollment figures are equally discouraging. A study conducted by the Los Angeles Unified School District (LAUSD) found that fewer than 50% of graduating high school students in California attended college in 1998 (PRI, 2005).

[one-step funnel: specific sample group]

Students with disabilities were reported to be at an even greater risk for poor academic achievement, noncompletion of high school programs, and involvement in criminal activity than their average-achieving peers. The NCES reported in 2000 that 8% of students enrolled in public elementary and secondary schools were classified as having a learning disability (LD), emotional or behavioral disorder (EBD), or mental retardation (MR) (NCES, 2000). This means that 3.8 million young people fall into the disability categories mentioned above. Students with disabilities lag behind their peers in the areas of employment, wages, postsecondary education, and residential independence. Fewer than 20% of students with disabilities enter postsecondary education, only 55% are competitively employed, and fewer than 30% are living independently (NCES, 2005b). Moreover, students with disabilities who found employment within the first two years after leaving high school were earning poverty-level wages (Blackorby & Wagner, 1996). As a consequence, adults with disabilities are less successful than their average-achieving peers in finding and sustaining employment, maintaining an acceptable standard of living, and developing independence than persons without disabilities (Field, Sarver, & Shaw, 2003).

A lack of interest in school may play a role in the negative outcomes of students with LD. Students with LD and low achievers are more likely to exhibit negative attitudes and less motivation with regard to their education than higher-achieving peers (McCoach, 2000). The challenges of encouraging positive attitudes toward school and fostering student educational involvement may be more important than ever in improving outcomes for young people.

[one-step funnel: specific research problem/study]

For students with LD to realize academic success and positive post-secondary outcomes in today's educational climate, developing self-direction may become an essential part of a special education program. A successful special education program promotes positive attitudes towards education by providing students with disabilities the skills and opportunities to have a lead decision-making role in their education and adult life. Students with disabilities require instruction on the tools that lead to this self-advocacy and self-empowerment (Grigal, Neubert, Moon, & Graham, 2003). According to a 2004 report by the Northwest Regional Education Laboratory (NREL), one of the top priorities of teachers and administrators is to assist students in becoming responsible for their own learning and academic performance. High school students with LD may be able to realize academic, behavioral, and social benefits if taught a method of self-directed learning.

Appendix F

Sample Chapter One
Statement of the Problem

Adapted from Williams, A. (2006). *Motivation, metacognition, and self-determination among students with learning disabilities.* Unpublished master's thesis, University of San Francisco, California.

The challenges present in encouraging high school students with learning disabilities (LD) to become self-directed learners are related to three important components of a self-directed educational program: [three areas] motivation and self-efficacy, metacognition skills, and self-determination. High school students with LD lack motivation and self-efficacy, struggle with metacognition, and are often not exposed to opportunities for developing self-determination (Deci & Chandler, 1986; Shimabukuro, Prater, Jenkins, & Edelen-Smith, 1999). A motivated student would take a genuine interest not only in subject matter, but also in identifying the best strategies to accomplish learning about the subject matter. This skill is referred to as metacognition. Simply stated, metacognition refers to thinking about thinking. This includes a student's ability to self-regulate and self-evaluate his or her learning processes and adjust his or her learning behavior when necessary. The last challenge in promoting self-directed learning involves supporting and encouraging aspects of the self-determination theory in classroom curricula. In the field of education, the theory of self-determination involves a student actively engaging in making decisions regarding his or her education with a full sense of choice (Ryan & Deci, 2000). Self-determination requires a student to know and value him- or herself, plan, act, and experience outcomes, and learn.

Motivation and self-efficacy. [**problems in area #1**] Motivation and self-efficacy are important facets to encouraging student educational involvement because a lack of these attributes contributes to poor academic performance and postsecondary outcomes. Motivation and self-efficacy appear to be closely related in that motivation refers to a student's interest in a subject matter or task, while self-efficacy describes a student's judgment about his or her abilities concerning a specific subject or task (NREL, 2004). A student with adequate levels of motivation and self-efficacy approaches his or her education with the attitude of "I want to succeed and I can succeed." Motivated students may be said to be actively interested in what they are learning and the tasks involved in the learning process. A student may be intrinsically or extrinsically motivated to attempt or accomplish specific tasks. The effectiveness of intrinsic versus extrinsic motivation is debatable (Cameron, 2001; Deci, Ryan, & Koestner, 2001), but researchers agree that motivation plays an important role in a student's success (Linnenbrink & Pintrich, 2002; Ryan & Deci, 2000).

Motivation is a key element of a successful learning environment for students with LD. However, motivating students with LD can be difficult. Generally, the educational research community has accepted that students with LD have low levels of motivation (Adelman, Lauber, Nelson, & Smith, 1989; Wilson & David, 1994). Motivation has been said to diminish when a student is faced with repeated failure. Students with LD have had more experiences with failure than their peers without disabilities and therefore, experience lower levels of motivation (Deci & Chandler, 1986).

Students with LD also had a lower sense of self-efficacy than their peers without disabilities. Attributing academic success or failure to external factors was found to be a common practice among students with LD. This lack of self-efficacy among students with LD contributed to the amount of difficulty they experienced in academic settings (Dev, 1996).

Metacognition. [**problems in area #2**] In addition to wanting to accomplish a task (motivation) and feeling as if they have the ability to accomplish a task (self-efficacy), students with LD may also benefit from knowing the best way for them to go about accomplishing a task (metacognition). Students with LD have difficulty with metacognition skills, including self-evaluation and self-regulation (Klassen, 2002). Accurately evaluating their own academic skills presents challenges to students with LD (Stone & May, 2002). This inaccurate self-evaluation may lead to difficulties for students with LD in organizing and planning assignments because the student will have trouble determining the course of action best suited to his or her abilities. Students with LD are challenged by analyzing task requirements, choosing and applying appropriate strategies to complete tasks, and evaluating and adjusting performance because they have a tendency to place more of their focus on lower-order processes than on the evaluative aspects of metacognitive skills

(Butler, 1998). Another aspect of metacognition is making adjustments to learning. There is a connection between adjustment, learning, and achievement in that people learn by adjusting and people adjust in order to learn (Martin, Mithaug, & Cox, 2003).

Developing an understanding of a student's own cognitive processes may be a particularly difficult aspect of metacognition for a student with LD due to difficulties he or she experiences with self-regulation (Price, 2002). Self-regulation involves the student being able to understand the requirements of a task or goal and to monitor progress and deadlines. When a task is attempted but not accomplished, the student must be able to self-regulate, or make academic, behavioral, or social adjustments to meet his or her goal (Martin et al., 2003). Students with LD, including students diagnosed with attention deficit or hyperactivity disorders, found behavioral self-regulation especially difficult due to the nature of these disorders (Shimabukuro et al., 1999). Students with LD typically have difficulties in making adjustments and transitioning, which may present another metacognitive challenge to the student (Shimabukuro et al., 1999). An understanding of one's cognitive strengths and weaknesses seems crucial for students with LD to make effective choices and decisions about their learning.

Self-determination. [**problems in area #3**] Combining motivation, self-efficacy, and metacognition skills with the development of self-determination among students with LD may improve these students' outcomes. Students that embodied the skills of self-determination had a higher rate of success both academically and in making transitions to adult life (Bremer, Kachgal, & Schoeller, 2003). The Individuals with Disabilities Education Act (IDEA) of 1997 promoted student self-determination in intent and spirit by mandating that students be involved in the Individual Education Program (IEP) and transition planning (Grigal et al., 2003). Unfortunately, rather than supporting and encouraging development of self-determination, many educational environments rely on short-term solutions such as overreliance on accommodations or overuse of course waivers. This results in high drop-out rates and low postsecondary education rates among students with disabilities (Field et al., 2003).

Research indicated that students with disabilities had greater difficulty developing a sense of self-determination than their typically achieving peers (Wehmeyer, Palmer, Agran, Mithaug, & Martin, 2000). One reason for this was that the stigma attached to having a learning disability encouraged many students to deny that their disabilities existed. This denial led to nondisclosure, which limited resources available to students with LD. This lack of self-awareness also diminished the students' belief in themselves, which undermined the development of self-determination (Hoffman, 2003).

Other barriers to developing a sense of self-determination for students with LD were the attributes of learned helplessness and self-deprecation

(Bos & Vaughn, 2002) and negative or unrealistic self-concepts exhibited by these students (Price, 2002). These distortions of self may inhibit a student's ability to make effective choices and decisions, which will have a negative effect on developing self-determination. Unfortunately, students with LD have greater difficulty developing a sense of self-determination than their typically achieving peers (Hoffman, 2003).

[section summary] As noted, students with learning disabilities have lower levels of motivation and self-efficacy, metacognition skills, and self-determination than their nondisabled peers. These shortfalls negatively impact their academic performance and may cause them to drop out of school altogether. In order to improve students' with disabilities chances for successful life outcomes, educators need to implement research-based strategies that will enhance their motivation and self-efficacy, metacognition skills, and self-determination.

Appendix G

Sample Research Syntheses

Adapted from Kendall, D. (2006). *The power of communication: A special day class teacher and her students' perceptions on effective communication, lesson efficacy, and teacher-student relationships within a cross-cultural framework.* Unpublished master's thesis, University of San Francisco, California.

Ideally, it can be argued that all teachers enter their classroom with their own ideas for how their students should conduct themselves behaviorally. Furthermore, each educator's personality, cultural identity, race, and manner, which play a large role in conveying these expectations, are diverse. Previous research (Sherwin & Schmidt, 2003) has indicated a need for educators and service providers to be aware of the cultures they serve, in order to prevent miscommunications. A study by Dennis and Giangreco (1996) investigated similar notions by exploring aspects of cultural sensitivity in standard family interviewing practices that guide, develop, and implement students' individualized education programs (IEPs). The researchers emphasized their perspectives as professionals and as members of minority groups in the United States. The purpose of this qualitative study was to listen carefully to interview responses, consult current research in the area of cultural sensitivity, and construct more culturally sensitive family interviewing practices.

The researchers in this study utilized criterion sampling in order to select the 14 participants. The three criteria that needed to be met in order to be a participant in the study were: (1) being a member of a minority group in the United States, (2) being knowledgeable about cultural issues related to their own heritage, and (3) being knowledgeable about current common practices in educating students with severe disabilities in the United States. Participants were identified as members of the following minority groups in the United States: African American, Latino, Chinese American, Japanese American, Native American, Asian Indian, Native Hawaiian, and Native Alaskan.

The data collection process included providing each of the 14 participants with a copy of the study's protocol and asking them to read and respond to the document. The document, *Choosing Options and Accommodations for Children: A Guide to Planning Inclusive Education* (COACH), was developed in an earlier study, and expanded on the previous research by asking family members about the importance of specific current and future life outcomes (e.g., health, safety, social relationships), as well as their priorities for learning outcomes. After reading the protocol, the participants were asked to write a report and critically assess COACH from a cross-cultural perspective. Interviews were formed based on the reports, and subsequent semi-structured, recorded telephone interviews were administered.

The research was driven by three questions: (1) "What does cultural sensitivity mean in family interviewing," (2) "How do professionals approach their work in culturally sensitive ways," and (3) "How can family interviews be conducted in more culturally sensitive ways?" These variables in the form of participant interview responses were transcribed and entered into *Ethnograph* (a computerized software program) for data analysis.

The results of this study revealed that with regard to the definition of cultural sensitivity in family interviewing, the participants conveyed the need for professionals to understand each particular student's family environment, in order to more accurately interpret the family's future life and learning goals. With regards to professionals approaching their work and conducting family interviews in more culturally sensitive ways, participants stated that professionals needed to form positive attitudes, greater sensitivity, and respect for other schools of thought, even if they were contrary to the values they currently identify with. This is an important implication for educators who teach students from diverse backgrounds. The aforementioned work approaches and open-mindedness may prove successful for the educator who will meet with the parents of students from various cultures. Knowledge of the students and families one serves, as well as genuine sensitivity to their cultural norms, can function to alleviate misunderstandings and may help to clarify communicative intent in the classroom as well as in IEP meetings.

Although the research discussed many salient and pertinent issues in the areas of cultural sensitivity, a threat to the internal validity of the study was a lack of clarity of the variables measured, and subsequently, a lack of clarity of the results. Threats to the external validity include vague descriptions of the setting and duration of the investigation of the issue. Thus, the generalizability of these findings to other groups may be limited.

Adapted from Iniguez, D. (2007). *Providing primary language support for English language learners with learning disabilities through affirming intervention models.* Unpublished master's thesis, University of San Francisco, California.

A study based on professional development was implemented to help support teachers of culturally and linguistically diverse students. Project CRISP (Culturally Responsive Instruction for Special Populations) was established to assess teachers' perspectives about multicultural education, its place in the school curriculum, and how it can affect the number of referrals for special education services (Voltz, Brazil, & Scott, 2003). Awareness of multicultural education can prepare teachers of culturally and linguistically diverse students to avoid overrepresentation and reduce referrals for special education services. This project was aimed at lowering the overrepresentation of students of color in special education and providing a meaningful theoretical framework of multicultural education for educators.

The participants were 33 teachers from large urban school districts. The ethnic background of the participants was 45% African American and 55% European American. The teachers volunteered for the study and were also paid a modest stipend. The criteria for the participants included having only elementary and middle school teachers and a collaboration of at least two teachers from the same school. In addition, the school groups had to have at least one special educator. As a result, 60.6% were general educators with an average of 9.6 years of experience, and 39.4% were special educators with an average of 11.9 years of experience. The majority of the participants were elementary educators at 85% and 15% were middle school educators.

The participants engaged in professional development activities based on a multicultural education framework. Project CRISP was created to help teachers understand the importance of "culturally responsive pedagogy" (Voltz et al., 2003, p. 64). In addition, the influence of culture on learning styles and behavior was also integrated into the project. The foundation of the project was based on Bank's model of multicultural education (2001), which has five main components: (1) content integration, (2) knowledge construction process, (3) prejudice reduction, (4) empowering school culture, and (5) equity pedagogy.

The professional development was divided into several stages. The initial part of the project was conducted as a seminar that lasted three days. The seminar was organized to begin with Bank's (2001) model of multicultural education. The other activities included were hands-on activities, developing plans with same-school participants, discussions, and demonstrations. One of the final activities included goal setting for the participants. All the participants had to name at least one goal that would continue and extend the participants' learning in the areas discussed during the seminar. From the goals, teachers wrote their own ongoing professional development plan. All schools worked in collaborative teams and worked about 26 hours to accomplish their defined goals. The participants' professional development plans included action research projects, curriculum development projects, and reading groups.

A variety of measurement tools were administered to assess the effects of Project CRISP. First, the participants were administered a questionnaire as a pre- and postassessment based on a five-point Likert-type scale that included responses from (1) strongly disagree to (5) strongly agree. The post-questionnaire had two extra questions that were relevant to the effects of the project on the participants' teaching methodology that was administered 15 weeks after participants attended the seminar. In addition, all participants were interviewed over the phone as a pre- and postassessment of overall familiarity and understanding of multicultural education and the process they used to refer students for special education services. The interviews averaged about 20 minutes each. The final measurement tool used by Project CRISP was a pre- and postlesson plan analysis that required participants to deconstruct a given lesson plan by creating a culturally appropriate one.

There were several methods of data analysis for the different measures. The data for the questionnaire were analyzed by using a paired t test to determine whether the differences in pre to post mean ratings were statistically significant. The interviews were transcribed and coded to look for frequent themes cited in the interviews by the participants. To add to the validity of the project, a trained graduate assistant concurrently coded the transcripts and the interrater reliability was found to be 78.8%. For the lesson plan analysis, the ideas were classified in the areas of content, methodology, materials, and assessments. Again, an interrater reliability was used and had a rate of 82.9%. The amount of change between the prelesson plan analysis and the postlesson plan analysis was rated on a one-to-four scale. The total mean ratings were comparatively analyzed with a paired t test.

Results from the questionnaire indicated that most teachers thought Project CRISP was effective in helping them become better teachers. The results of the pre-questionnaires showed that most general educators felt comfortable and able to work with culturally and linguistically diverse families and were also familiar with the culture of their students. Yet, a distinction was found in three areas: meeting the needs of their culturally and linguistically diverse students, identifying the differences between a learning disability and learning differences, and how to teach and implement a curriculum from a multicultural standpoint. The three areas that were identified as a need were rated significantly higher (.05 level) on the pre-questionnaire results. Most participants revealed that their teacher training program was inadequate in preparing them to work with a culturally and linguistically diverse student population. The post-questionnaire showed that teachers continued to feel comfortable teaching a diverse student population.

The results of the interviews were grouped in the following categories by the authors of the study: referral practices, prereferral interventions, behavior management, and teacher perceptions on the effects of Project CRISP. The questions about referral practices during the pre-interview showed that 65% of general educators had referred students for special education services because of academic difficulties in math and/or reading. The post-interview showed similar rates, at 60%, of teachers referring students for special education services. Yet, at the post-interview, about 25% of the participants noted the need to address a variety of factors, such as home environment and communication with other educators in the referral process. The pre-interview about pre-referral interventions highlighted three areas that were commonly used as a response: accommodations (35%), parent collaboration (35%), and professional collaboration (25%). The post-interview noted a new category adapting the methodology for the needs of diverse students. About 54% of special educators among the participants were found to be involved with pre-referral interventions. The pre- and post-interview results about behavior management found minimal differences; 53% of general educators and 45% of special educators believed students' cultural backgrounds can affect their behavior. The teacher perception results of Project CRISP were noted as making a difference in teaching methodology by 45% of general educators and 69% of special educators.

The lesson plan analysis noted the most changes in the area of content and methodology. The variation of the mean for general educators was 2.00 during the pre-lesson analysis and 2.44 on the post-analysis of the lesson. The variation of the mean for special educators was 1.83 during the pre-lesson analysis and 2.25 during the post-analysis of the lesson. There were no statistically significant changes between the pre- and post-ratings.

The authors of the study indicated that teachers believed they lacked the methodology and cultural understanding to adequately teach culturally diverse students before the intervention. A difference was also found in the level of confidence by special educators to work with culturally diverse students in comparison with general educators. The study also highlighted how Project CRISP was able to influence teacher reflections of classroom practices with culturally diverse students. Participants in the study also added depth to their prior knowledge.

The implications of these results indicate a need for educators to receive more training to teach a culturally diverse student population in order to reduce the amount of referrals for special education services. This can be obtained by providing a positive school environment and workshops for educators on how to teach to different students' cultural learning styles. This current study addresses this need by providing reading instruction in the students' primary language. The authors also suggested that special educators should participate in professional development programs focused on working with culturally diverse students.

The study had several limitations as noted by the researcher. First, the length of the professional development was a weakness because the seminar only lasted three days, in comparison with courses at the university level, which last for several months. More time could have been valuable for the participants. Another possible major limitation of the study was that participants volunteered for the study, and there was a small sample size. The project's sample group might have been composed of participants who wanted to learn about multicultural education theories. Other teachers may not have been present at the study because of their personal biases. Future studies need to be conducted with larger sample sizes with a diverse group of educators.

Glossary

abstracting: Abstracting is a method of organizing information about an article that includes a brief summary and selected critical information about the study.

accessibility: Accessibility refers to the ability to gain access or entry to the research site and participants.

advance organizer: An advance organizer is an outline for the literature review and informs the reader of what will be addressed in the chapter.

American Psychological Association (APA) style: APA style is the writing and editorial form used by the American Psychological Association to publish books and manuscripts. This style form is commonly used in various social science disciplines such as education, psychology, sociology, business, economics, nursing, and social work.

and: The "and" Boolean operator combines two or more terms so that each record contains all of the terms.

answerable research question: An answerable research question is one where the researcher is able to collect data or information (using a measurement instrument) to answer the question related to the problem.

Belmont Report: The Belmont Report is a summary of the basic ethical principles and guidelines for conducting research with human subjects.

beneficence: Beneficence is the second principle in the Belmont Report and refers to two general rules: "(1) do not harm; and (2) maximize possible benefits, and minimize possible harms."

Boolean operators: Boolean operators are used in electronic databases and other search engines to define the relationships between words or groups of words.

chairperson: The chairperson is the faculty member who is assigned or selected by the graduate student to advise him or her throughout the master's thesis process.

chunking method: The chunking method refers to breaking up large tasks into smaller, more manageable chunks such as writing one section of a chapter rather than the entire chapter.

column head: In an APA table, the column head identifies the items listed under one column.

column spanner: In an APA table, a column spanner is a broad heading that covers two or more columns.

Common Rule: The Common Rule is a federal policy for the protection of human subjects followed by most of the federal departments and agencies that sponsor research with human subjects.

confidentiality: Confidentiality refers to protecting the participants' identity and records.

convenience sample: In a convenience sample, the researcher selects the individuals who are available and accessible at the time.

cost-benefit analysis: In a cost-benefit analysis, researchers must weigh the potential benefits against the anticipated risks and decide whether the benefits are so great that they justify putting subjects at a certain level of risk or the risks are so high that the benefits are not worth the potential harm to subjects.

data coding: Data coding is a data analysis process used in qualitative research to categorize and label the major themes.

data triangulation: Data triangulation is one type of triangulation procedure where multiple methods of data collection are used to study one phenomenon.

deception: Deception occurs when the researcher omits information about the study or gives false information.

deductive reasoning: A logic/reasoning approach that moves from the general to the specific.

degrees of freedom: For the independent-samples t test, the degrees of freedom is calculated by adding the sample sizes of the two groups together minus two ($n1 + n2 - 2$). For the paired-samples t test, the degrees of freedom is calculated by the sample size minus one ($n - 1$).

dependent variable: The dependent variable is the variable that is observed to see if there is a change (e.g., effect) in response to the independent variable. The researcher cannot manipulate the dependent variable.

descriptive statistics: Descriptive statistics are the basic level of statistical analysis for a data set from a sample group. Typically, reported statistics include the mean, median, mode, variance, and standard deviation.

descriptors: Descriptors are used in electronic databases to give every record a subject indexing term (i.e., controlled vocabulary or subject headings).

dictionary definition: A dictionary definition is a definition that is offered in a dictionary to define ambiguous terms related to the study or research question.

dissertation: A dissertation is typically the culminating requirement for a doctoral degree.

Digital Object Identifier (DOI): The DOI is a unique code of letters and numbers that provides a link to a journal article's location on the Internet.

edited book: An edited book is a book where the individual chapters are written by different authors, and there are one or multiple editors who edit the entire book.

editorial style: The editorial style is a set of rules or guidelines that writers must adhere to for publishing manuscripts, books, and so on.

electronic database: An electronic database is an electronic collection of information (e.g., books, journal articles, reference materials) where an individual can research and retrieve resources. Electronic databases can be interdisciplinary or organized around a particular subject area or field.

empirically based: Empirically based research findings are those that are based on data that is produced by experiment or observation rather than opinion or theory.

example definition: An example definition is a definition that uses examples to define ambiguous terms related to the study or research question.

expanders feature: The expanders feature is the opposite of the limiters feature and broadens an electronic search by allowing the user to combine or add key terms.

external validity: External validity (outside the study) refers to whether the results of the study are applicable or can be generalized to other settings and groups.

feasibility: Feasibility refers to how realistic it will be to access data or participants and the time needed to complete the study.

full-text (see PDF): Full-text is when the entire resource is available either in a printable web page format or a PDF format.

funnel writing strategy: The funnel writing strategy is analogous to a funnel where your first paragraph about the problem is broad and every subsequent paragraph narrows the topic toward a specific problem.

general notes: In an APA table, general notes appear at the bottom of the table and explain information relating to the entire table such as abbreviations or symbols.

generalizability: Generalizability refers to the extent to which the results about a sample group from a study are applicable to the larger population.

guided research: Guided research is setting specific parameters (e.g., date, author, subject) around your search in order to narrow the pool of resources and results.

hanging indent: A hanging indent is used in the reference list. A hanging indent refers to when the first line of a reference is flushed all the way to the left margin and the rest of the lines are indented one-half inch.

heading (see also levels of heading): A heading is the name of a section or subsection used to organize the paper. A heading at the same level has equal importance. The headings are formatted depending on how many levels of headings there are in the manuscript or thesis.

heading capitalization: Heading capitalization is when all the major words are capitalized like in the title of a movie.

hypothesis: In quantitative studies, a hypothesis involves making assumptions or predictions based on probability distributions or likelihoods of events.

independent-samples t test: The independent-samples t test is used to determine whether the difference in means on the dependent variable between two independent groups is a real difference or one that is due to chance.

independent variable: The independent variable is the variable that is deliberately manipulated (e.g., cause) by the researcher to produce a change in the dependent variable.

inductive reasoning: A logic/reasoning approach that moves from the specific to the general.

inferential statistics: Inferential statistics are the higher level of statistical analysis where inferences are made from a sample to a population. Inferential statistics may also include hypothesis testing and set probability levels to test for statistically significant differences between groups or treatments.

Institutional Review Board (IRB) application: A typical IRB application consists of the research plan, a cover letter to the participants, an informed consent letter, all the measurement instruments that will be used in the study, and your chairperson's signature (it will be his or her responsibility to ensure that you conduct the research in an ethical manner).

Institutional Review Board (IRB) research plan: The IRB research plan describes the need for the study and the research design and may include the following sections: (1) background and rationale, (2) sample, (3) recruitment, (4) consent process, (5) procedures, (6) potential risk to subjects, (7) minimization of potential risk, (8) potential benefits, (9) costs to subjects, (10) reimbursement/compensation to subjects, and (11) confidentiality of records.

Institutional Review Board for the Protection of Human Subjects (IRBPHS): At institutions of higher education, the Institutional Review Board for the Protection of Human Subjects is a group that has been formally designated to review and monitor research applications involving human subjects.

interlibrary loan: Interlibrary loan is a service provided by libraries whereby a user of one library can borrow books, acquire photocopies of articles in journals, and so on that are owned by another library (sometimes there is a fee involved).

internal validity: Internal validity (within the study) refers to whether the changes in the dependent variable were due to the independent variable or some other variable.

justice: Justice is the third principle in the Belmont Report and refers to fairness and equity in the selection of participants and distribution of benefits.

Kefauver-Harris Drug Amendments: The Kefauver-Harris Drug Amendments increased the regulatory powers of the Food and Drug Administration so that drug manufacturers had to prove that their drug was safe and effective before marketing and selling it to the public. The act also required that subjects from medical studies give their informed consent.

key terms: Key terms are typically two to three words or short phrases that are fundamental to the research topic, problem, or questions and are used to refine the search process.

levels of heading (see also heading): The levels of heading refer to the organizational structure or hierarchy of the sections in the manuscript or thesis. Five is the maximum number of levels of heading in a manuscript or thesis.

limiters feature: The limiters feature narrows an electronic search by allowing the user to set specific limits, so the search results will only contain research with the chosen specific criteria.

literature matrix: A literature matrix is an organizational tool such as a table, chart, or flow chart to display the relationship or common attributes among multiples studies.

literature synthesis: A literature synthesis (also referred to as a research synthesis) is a type of article in which the results of several related studies are compared and summarized.

Master of Arts (MA): The Master of Arts degree is typically awarded in the disciplines of arts, sciences, social sciences (e.g., education, psychology), and humanities (e.g., history, philosophy, religion).

Master of Science (MS): The Master of Science degree is typically awarded to students in technical fields such as engineering, nursing, mathematics, and health care management but can also be in the social sciences.

master's degree: A master's degree is a postbaccalaureate degree conferred by a college or university upon candidates who complete one to two years of graduate study.

master's degree program: A master's degree program is a graduate-level, postbaccalaureate program in a specific field or discipline that typically involves a culminating activity, project, or thesis.

master's thesis: A master's thesis is an empirically based research study that is an original piece of work by the graduate student.

mean: The mean is the arithmetic average and calculated by the sum of the scores divided by the number of scores in the distribution.

measure of central tendency: The measure of central tendency is the "typical" or "average" score in a distribution.

measure of variability: A measure of variability is a statistic that indicates how close or spread apart (i.e., dispersed) the scores are in a distribution.

measurement instruments: Measurement instruments are data collection tools (e.g., surveys, observations, tests) that are used to measure changes in dependent variables or variables of interest.

median: The median is the middle score in a distribution or the score that divides the distribution in half (50% above and 50% below).

meta-analysis: A meta-analysis research study is one in which the results of several related studies are analyzed and reported with statistical measures (e.g., effect sizes).

mode: The mode is the most common or most frequently occurring score in a distribution.

multidisciplinary database: A multidisciplinary database is an electronic database that covers different subjects rather than just one specific field or discipline.

National Commission for the Protection of Human Subjects of Biomedical and Behavioral Research: The National Commission for the Protection of Human Subjects of Biomedical and Behavioral Research was the first national public group whose responsibility it was to identify a set of basic ethical principles and guidelines for conducting biomedical and behavioral research involving human subjects.

National Research Act of 1974 (Public Law 93-348): The National Research Act created the National Commission for the Protection of Human Subjects of Biomedical and Behavioral Research.

nonnumerical data: Studies that use qualitative approaches collect nonnumerical data to answer their research question(s). Nonnumerical data are narrative data (i.e., words).

non-refereed: A non-refereed article is one that did not go through an external review process before being published.

nonresearchable question: A nonresearchable question is a type of question where the researcher cannot collect measurable data to answer the question or the "answers" are based on philosophical, spiritual, or religious beliefs.

not: The "not" Boolean operator searches terms so that records with certain terms are excluded from the results.

null hypothesis: The null hypothesis, H_0, represents the "chance" theory, meaning any observed differences are due to chance, and the treatment has no significant effect on the dependent variable.

numerical data: Studies that use quantitative approaches collect numerical data to answer their research question(s). Numerical data are mathematical (i.e., numbers) data.

Nuremberg Code: The Nuremberg Code is a set of standards of ethical medical behavior that all physicians should adhere to when involving human subjects in medical experiments.

operational definition: An operational definition is a definition that describes attributes or characteristics of the term that need to be present in order to measure it.

or: The "or" Boolean operator searches terms so that at least one of the terms is present in the record.

paired-samples *t* test (also referred to as nonindependent samples and dependent samples): The paired-samples *t* test is used to determine whether the difference in means on the dependent variable between two sets of related scores is a real difference or one that is due to chance.

paraphrase: Paraphrasing is maintaining the gist or essence of the original work (with appropriate citations) but writing it in your own words.

PDF: The PDF format is full-text electronic "picture" of a document and resembles how a research article actually looks in the journal.

periodical: A periodical refers to items that are published on a regular basis such as articles in journals, magazines, newsletters, or newspapers.

personal communication: A personal communication is a source of information in the form of a letter, e-mail, interview, phone conversation, and so on. Personal communications are cited in the text but not listed in the reference list.

plagiarize: Plagiarizing refers to using another person's ideas or words without giving them proper credit.

primary sources: Primary sources are the actual or the original results of studies reported by the researcher(s) (i.e., firsthand information)

probability notes: In an APA table, probability notes appear after the specific notes and indicate whether results were statistically significant (meaning that the null hypothesis was rejected).

purposeful redundancy: Purposeful redundancy refers to intentionally reiterating main points about the research problem and study throughout the thesis.

purposive sample: In a purposive sample, the researcher selects individuals who are considered representative because they meet certain criteria for the study.

qualitative research: A qualitative research method delves into a particular situation in order to better understand a phenomenon within its natural context and the perspectives of the participants involved.

quantitative research: A quantitative research method includes but is not limited to research using descriptive, correlation, prediction, and control (cause-effect) methods.

random assignment: In random assignment, each participant in the sample has an equal and independent chance of being selected for the treatment group.

random sample: In a random sample, every individual in the population has an equal and independent chance of being selected.

range: The range is the difference between the largest and smallest scores in a distribution.

refereed: A refereed (also referred to as peer-reviewed) article has been submitted for external review by a panel of reviewers before being published.

reference materials: Reference materials are collections of information such as encyclopedias, handbooks, indexes, and dictionaries.

relevancy ranked: The "relevancy ranked" option shows the search term first and then lists subject headings (i.e., descriptors) that are related to the search term displayed in order of relevance.

reliability: Reliability refers to the extent to which an instrument *consistently* measures what it was intended to measure.

replicability: Replicability refers to the ability to replicate (i.e., copy) the study in order to verify and interpret the results or adapt and expand the study.

research question: A research question is related to the problem in a study and is the question that the researcher attempts to answer. The research question guides the type of data that will be collected and/or how the data should be collected.

Research Subject Bill of Rights: The Research Subject Bill of Rights is a list of rights that is guaranteed for every participant in a study.

resources: Resources are tangibles such as materials and finances necessary to conduct a study but also include nontangibles such as personal health and energy.

respect for persons: Respect for persons is the first principle in the Belmont Report and includes "two ethical convictions: first that individuals should be treated as autonomous agents, and second, that persons with diminished autonomy are entitled to protection."

sample group: The sample group is the group of participants in a study. They are the group that the researcher collects data from or about.

sampling: Sampling refers to the process of selecting participants for a study from a population.

search engine: A search engine is a computer system where information is stored and organized for easy retrieval. The most common search engines search for information on the World Wide Web through the Internet.

secondary sources: Secondary sources describe or summarize the work of others (i.e., secondhand information).

seminal article: A seminal article is an article that was significant to the topic (e.g., classic) or created a change in the field.

sentence capitalization: Sentence capitalization is when only the first word of the title and proper nouns are capitalized like in a regular sentence.

specific notes: In an APA table, specific notes appear after the general notes and explain information pertaining to an individual column, row, or item.

standard deviation: The standard deviation indicates how much the scores vary from the mean in a distribution.

stub: In an APA table, the stubs are the row headings, which are the major independent variables related to the stub head.

stub column: In an APA table, the first column on the left side of the table is called the stub column.

stub head: In an APA table, the stub column's heading is called the stub head.

term begins with: The "term begins with" option searches and lists the subject headings (i.e., descriptors) in alphabetical order.

term contains: The "term contains" option shows the search term first followed by an alphabetized list of subject headings (i.e., descriptors) that contain or include it.

terminal degree: A terminal degree is the generally accepted highest academic degree in a field of study.

thesaurus: The thesaurus contains alphabetized descriptors that are used in the electronic database and can be browsed online or from a printed copy.

thick description: A thick description is an explanation that includes both the behavior and the context in which the behavior was displayed.

three parallel ladders strategy: The three parallel ladders strategy is an organizational writing strategy. The three ladders represent sections of your thesis chapters that are aligned by topic or order (e.g., *Statement of the Problem, Background and Need,* and so on).

time: Time refers to the researcher's time that is available to devote to the study as well as the duration (length) and frequency (how often how often the researcher will interact with participants) of the study.

timeline: A timeline is a schedule that is created by the researcher that outlines all the necessary steps and phases to complete the study within the allocated time.

truncation symbol: The truncation symbol is represented by an asterisk (*) and when used at the end of a term, it allows the user to expand the search term to include all forms of the root word.

t **test:** A *t* test is a statistical test that is used to determine whether the observed difference between two mean scores represent a true difference or is due to chance.

Type I error: A Type I error is rejecting the null hypothesis when it is true.

validity: Validity refers to the extent to which the instrument measures what it was intended to measure. Validity can also refer to the quality of findings in a qualitative study.

voluntary informed consent: Voluntary informed consent is when a person has the capacity to give consent and receives sufficient and accurate information about the study (e.g., purpose, methods, risks, benefits) to make an informed decision to participate.

vulnerable populations: Vulnerable populations are children, pregnant women, prisoners, or others who may need additional protection from harm, depending on the risks involved.

wildcard symbol: The wildcard symbol is represented by a question mark (?) and can be used to find the correct spelling or alternative spellings of a word (each question mark placed in the word represents a single character).

References

About graduate education in the U.S. (n.d.). Retrieved September 9, 2007, from the U.S. Department of State, Bureau of Educational and Cultural Affairs Web site: http://educationusa.state.gov/graduate/about/degrees.htm

American Psychological Association. (2001). *Publication manual of the American Psychological Association* (5th ed.). Washington, DC: Author.

Becker, L. B., Vlad, T., Huh, J., & Prine, J. (2001). Annual enrollment report: Number of students studying journalism and mass communication at all-time high [Electronic version]. *Journalism & Mass Communication Educator, 56*(3), 28–60.

Bell, N. (1991). Gestalt imagery: A critical factor in language comprehension. *Annals of Dyslexia, 41,* 246–260.

Blaum, P. (2004, March 10). 'R.E.A.L.' offers multicultural approaches to substance-abuse prevention among middle-schoolers [Press release]. *EurekAlert!*. Retrieved January 11, 2008, from http://www.eurekalert.org/pub_releases/2004-03/ps-om 031004.php

Borgatta, E. F., & Montgomery, R. (Eds.). (2001). *Encyclopedia of sociology* (2nd ed., 5 vols.). New York: Macmillan Reference USA. Retrieved December 18, 2007, from University of San Francisco Gleeson Library Web site: http://www.usfca.edu/library/research/socref.html

Creswell, J. W. (2003). *Research design: Qualitative, quantitative, and mixed methods approaches* (2nd ed.). Thousand Oaks, CA: Sage.

Creswell, J. W. (2007). *Qualitative inquiry and research design* (2nd ed.). Thousand Oaks, CA: Sage.

Creswell, J. W. (2008). *Educational research: Planning, conducting, and evaluating quantitative and qualitative research* (3rd ed.). Boston: Pearson Allyn & Bacon.

Criminological transition in Russia. (n.d.). Retrieved January 11, 2008, from Indiana University Web site: http://newsinfo.iu.edu/news/page/normal/3876.html

Drew, C. J., Hardman, M. L., & Hosp, J. L. (2008). *Designing and conducting research in education.* Thousand Oaks, CA: Sage.

Ethical principles: The Belmont report. (n.d.). Retrieved January 5, 2008, from Duke University, Office of Research Support Web site: http://www.ors.duke.edu/irb/regpolicy/ethical.html

Ferretti, R. P., MacArthur, C. D., & Okolo, C. M. (2001). Teaching for historical understanding in inclusive classrooms. *Learning Disability Quarterly, 24,* 59–71.

Fraenkel, J. R., & Wallen, N. E. (2006). *How to design and evaluate research in education* (6th ed.). New York: McGraw-Hill.

Galvan, J. L. (2006). *Writing literature reviews: A guide for students of the social and behavioral sciences* (3rd ed.). Glendale, CA: Pyrczak.

Gay, L. R., Mills, G. E., & Airasian, P. (2006). *Educational research: Competencies for analysis and applications* (8th ed.). Upper Saddle River, NJ: Merrill Prentice Hall.

Gillberg, C. (1991). Clinical and neurobiological aspects of Asperger syndrome in six family studies. In U. Frith (Ed.), *Autism and Asperger syndrome* (pp. 122–146). Cambridge, MA: Cambridge University Press.

Glazer, J. (1988). *The master's degree.* Retrieved October 10, 2007, from http://www.ericdigests.org/pre-9210/degree.htm

Goldstein, A. P., & McGinnis, E. (1997). *Skillstreaming the adolescent: New strategies and perspectives for teaching prosocial skills.* Champaign, IL: Research Press.

Gomes, C. (2008). *The effects of graphic novels on reading comprehension and motivation for students with Asperger's syndrome.* Unpublished master's thesis, University of San Francisco, California.

Good, R. H., & Kaminski, R. A. (Eds.). (2002). *Dynamic indicators of basic early literacy skills* (6th ed.). Eugene, OR: Institute for the Development of Educational Achievement.

Henderson, L. (2007). *The relationship between expressive language and social skills.* Unpublished master's thesis, University of San Francisco, California.

Hess, L. (2008). *The effects of peer-mediated instruction on the inferential reading comprehension and social skills of elementary school students with emotional disturbance.* Unpublished master's thesis, University of San Francisco, California.

History of research ethics. (n.d.). Retrieved January 5, 2008, from University of Nevada Las Vegas Office for the Protection of Research Subjects Web site: http://research.unlv.edu/OPRS/history-ethics.htm

Ho, A. (2006). *The effects of the prior knowledge expository text experiential learning (PEEL) intervention on historical content knowledge of secondary students with learning disabilities.* Unpublished master's thesis, University of San Francisco, California.

Iniguez, D. (2007). *A reading intervention study for English language learners with learning disabilities.* Unpublished master's thesis, University of San Francisco, California.

Institutional Review Board for the Protection of Human Subjects manual. (2001). Retrieved January 5, 2008, from University of San Francisco Web site: http://www.usfca.edu/humansubjects/

Irey, R. (2008). *The effects of fluency instruction on comprehension for third grade English learners with learning disabilities.* Unpublished master's thesis, University of San Francisco, California.

Jerry Rice. (n.d.). Retrieved July 14, 2008, from http://www.nfl.com/players /jerryrice/profile?id=RIC128880&campaign=Google_NFLPlayer_JerryRice

Johnson, P. (2003). Immigration. In Ponzetti, J. J. (Ed.) *International encyclopedia of marriage and family* (2nd ed., Vol. 2, pp. 859–864). New York: Macmillan Reference USA. Retrieved December 18, 2007, from Gale Virtual Reference Library via Gale at http://0-go.galegroup.com.ignacio.usfca.edu/ps/start.do ?p=GVRL&u=usfca_gleeson

Kemmis, S., & Wilkinson, M. (1998). Participatory action research and the study of practice. In B. Atweh, S. Kemmis, & P. Weeks (Eds.), *Action research in practice: Partnerships for social justice in education* (pp. 21–36). New York: Routledge.

Kendall, D. (2006). *The power of communication: A special day class teacher and her students' perceptions of effective communication, lesson efficacy, and teacher-student relationships within a cross-cultural framework.* Unpublished master's thesis, University of San Francisco, California.

Kornhauser, M. (2006). *Fostering protective factors to promote resiliency in secondary students with learning disabilities.* Unpublished master's thesis, University of San Francisco, California.

Lane, D. (2003, July 7). *Measures of variability.* Retrieved July 14, 2008, from the Connexions Web site: http://cnx.org/content/m10947/2.3/

McLeod Assessment of Reading Comprehension. (1999). Novato, CA: Arena Press.

McMillan, J. H. (2008). *Educational research: Fundamentals for the consumer* (5th ed.). Boston: Pearson Allyn & Bacon.

Mertler, C. A., & Charles, C. M. (2008). *Introduction to educational research* (6th ed.). Boston: Pearson Allyn & Bacon.

Mireles, S. (2004). *Student preferences and self-esteem with regards to the resource specialist program.* Unpublished master's thesis, University of San Francisco, California.

Neighborhood. (n.d.). In *Merriam-Webster online dictionary.* Retrieved September 14, 2007, from http://www.merriam-webster.com/

Niolin, R. (2001). *Families and substance abuse.* Retrieved January 11, 2008, from http://www.psychpage.com/family/library/familysubstanceabuse.htm

Nixon, B. (2004). *Improving reading comprehension of sixth grade students with learning disabilities using drama techniques in reading instruction.* Unpublished master's thesis, University of San Francisco, California.

The Nuremberg Trials: The Doctors trial. (n.d.). Retrieved May 23, 2008, from http://www.law.umkc.edu/faculty/projects/ftrials/nuremberg/NurembergDoctor Trial.html

O'Donovan, C. (1997, June–July). Which master's matters? A real world look at the MBA versus MA . . . and even the ABC designation. *Communication World.* Retrieved November 21, 2007, from http://findarticles.com/p/articles/mi_m4422 /is_n6_v14 /ai_19717342

Onwuegbuzie, A. J. (2002, Spring). Why can't we all get along? Towards a framework for unifying research paradigms. *Education.* Retrieved June 10, 2008, from http://findarticles.com/p/articles/mi_qa3673/is_/ai_n28923153

Orcher, L. T. (2005). *Conducting research: Social and behavioral science methods.* Glendale, CA: Pyrczak.

Ponterotto, J. G., & Grieger, I. (2007). Effectively communicating qualitative research. *The Counseling Psychologist, 35*(3), 404–430.

Rau, S. (2006). *The effects of increased student choice opportunities on off-task behaviors of students with learning disabilities.* Unpublished master's thesis, University of San Francisco, California.

Raygor, A. L. (n.d.). *Procedure for writing a term paper.* Retrieved September 9, 2007, from Virginia Tech, Cook Counseling Center Web site: http://www .ucc.vt.edu/stdysk/termpapr.html

Recommended search engines. (n.d.). Retrieved November 10, 2007, from the University of California, Berkeley, Teaching Library Internet Workshops Web site: http://www.lib.berkeley.edu/TeachingLib/Guides/Internet/SearchEngines.html

Reporting statistics in APA style. (n.d.). Retrieved July 20, 2008, from http://www .ilstu.edu/~mshesso/apa_stats_format.html

Shavelson, R. J. (1996). *Statistical reasoning for the behavioral sciences* (3rd ed.). Boston: Allyn & Bacon.

Spader, C. (2008). *Cheering on patients. DC/Baltimore nurses use motivational interviewing to encourage change.* Retrieved June 3, 2008, from http://include.nurse.com/apps/pbcs.dll/article?AID=/20080602/NATIONAL02/306020021/0/frontpage

Stephens, D. (2006). *Referral of Spanish-speaking English language learners for special education services.* Unpublished master's thesis, University of San Francisco, California.

U.S. Department of Health and Human Services. (1979). *The Belmont report.* Retrieved January 5, 2008, from http://www.hhs.gov/ohrp/humansubjects/guidance/belmont.htm

U.S. Department of Health and Human Services. (1991). *The common rule* [Electronic version]. Retrieved January 5, 2008, from http://www.hhs.gov/ohrp/references/comrulp4.pdf

U.S. Department of Health and Human Services. (2004, March 17). Prevention program curbs drug abuse among middle-school youth. *NewsScan, 29.* Retrieved January 11, 2008, from National Institutes of Health, National Institute on Drug Abuse Web site: http://www.drugabuse.gov/newsroom/04/NS-03.html

U.S. Department of Health and Human Services. (2005a). *Milestones in U.S. food and drug law history.* Retrieved January 5, 2008, from the U.S. Food and Drug Administration Web site: http://www.fda.gov/opacom/backgrounders/miles.html

U.S. Department of Health and Human Services. (2005b). *Thalidomide: Important patient information.* Retrieved January 5, 2008, from the U.S. Food and Drug Administration, Center for Drug Evaluation and Research Web site: http://www.fda.gov/cder/news/thalidomide.htm

U.S. Department of Health and Human Services. (n.d.). *U.S. public health service syphilis study at Tuskegee.* Retrieved January 5, 2008, from Centers for Disease Control and Prevention Web site: http://www.cdc.gov/tuskegee/timeline.htm

U.S. Department of Justice. (2005). *Co-offending and patterns of juvenile crime.* Retrieved February 25, 2008, from the Office of Justice Programs, National Institute of Justice Web site: http://www.ojp.usdoj.gov/nij/pubs-sum/210360.htm

Wehmeyer, M. L., & Kelchner, K. (1995). *The Arc's Self-determination Scale.* Arlington, TX: The Arc of the United States.

What is plagiarism. (n.d.). Retrieved January 5, 2008, from Plagiarism.Org, Learning Center Web site: http://www.plagiarism.org/learning_center/what_is_plagiarism.html

Williams, A. (2006). *Motivation, metacognition, and self-determination among students with learning disabilities.* Unpublished master's thesis, University of San Francisco, California.

Woodcock, R., McGrew, K., & Mather, N. (2000). *Woodcock Johnson III Tests of Achievement.* Rolling Meadows, IL: Riverside.

You can eat an elephant. (n.d.) Retrieved September 14, 2007, from http://www.funnyjunk.com/pages/elephant.htm

Author Index

Adams St. Pierre, E., 207
Akin-Little, A., 19
Alter, S., 43
American Educational Research
    Association, 207
American Psychological Association
    (APA), 15, 95-98, 119, 210, 245
Angrosino, M. V., 189
Airasian p. 8, 9, 12, 115, 142

Babbie, E., 158
Becker, L. B., 4
Bell, N., 194
Blaum, 109
Borgatta, E. F., 49, 51
Bosch, J., 158

Carson, R. L., 138
Charles, C. M., 68
Cormier, R., 97
Creswell, J. W., 14, 50, 68, 70, 71,
    110, 119, 143, 151, 158, 181, 185

Dennis, A. R., 43
Denzin, N., 181, 185, 189, 207
Drew, C. J., 82

Elliot, R., 189
Ercikan, K., 19

Fenton, P., 136
Ferretti, R. P., 126
Fischer, C. T., 189
Fletcher, K. M., 19
Folkman, S., 95

Fontana, A., 189
Fraenkel, J. R., 34, 46, 49, 68, 83
Frey, J. H., 189

Galvan, J. L., 69, 136
Gay, L. R., 8, 9, 12, 115, 142
Geertz, C., 181
Gelfand, H., 245
Gibran, K., 192
Gillberg, C., 193
Glazer, J., 2
Goldstein, A. P., 145
Gomes, C., 150, 154,
    193–194, 201
Good, R. H., 148, 150
Granello, D. H., 76
Grieger, I., 181, 190
Guttmacher Institute, 207

Hardman, M. L., 82
Henderson, L., 169
Hess, L., 196, 199, 202
Ho, A., 125
Hosp, J. L., 82
Huh, J., 4

Iniguez, D., 170, 272
Irey, R., 142, 148, 150, 169, 202

Johnson, P., 52
Johnson, S., 46

Kaminski, R. A., 148, 150
Kelchner, K., 232
Kemmis, S., 14

Kendall, D., 141, 143, 144, 149, 151, 184, 197, 203, 270
Kopala, M., 189
Kornhauser, M., 145

Labaree, D. F., 19
Lane, D., 168
Law, M., 158
Lee, H. B., 19
Letts, L., 158
Lincoln, A., 2
Lincoln, Y. S., 189, 207
Little, L., 190
Little, S. G., 19
Lomand, T. C., 76

MacArthur, C. D., 126
Mather, N., 146
Maugham, W. S., 210
McCotter, S. S., 158
McGinnis, E., 145
McGrew, K, 146
McLeod, 150
McMillan, J. H., 47, 70
Mertler, C. A., 68
Mills, 8, 9, 12, 115, 142
Mireles, S., 182
Montgomery, R., 49, 51
Morrow, S. L., 19, 190

Niolin, 109
Nixon, B., 151–153

O'Donovan, C., 4
Okolo, C. M., 126
Onwuegbuzie, A. J., 185
Orcher, L. T., 82

Patenaude, A. L., 19
Pollock, N., 158
Ponterotto, J. G., 181, 190
Prine, J., 4

Rau, S., 170, 200
Raygor, A. L., 7
Rennie, D. L., 189
Richardson, L., 207
Roer-Strier, D., 190
Roth, W. M., 19
Ryle, G., 181

Sales, B. D., 95
Sands, R. G., 190
Shavelson, R. J., 164, 171
Smith-Tyler, J., 95
Spader, C., 145
Stephens, D., 154
Sternberg, E., 19
Steudel, H. J., 19
Stewart, D., 158
Suzuki, L. A., 189
Szuchman, L. T., 119, 245

Thomas, C., 44

University of Wisconsin-Madison Writing Center, 245
U.S. Department of Health and Human Services (USDHHS), 80, 81, 82, 84, 92, 109
U.S. Department of Justice, 25

Vlad, T., 4

Walker, C. J., 245
Wallen, N. E., 34, 46, 49, 68, 83
Wehmeyer, M. L., 232
Westmorland, M., 158
Wilkinson, M., 14
Williams, A., 141, 179, 262, 266
Wiesel, E., 78
Woodcock, R., 146

Yauch, C. A., 19

Subject Index

ABI/Inform, 53, 54
Abstracting, 71
Abstract page, 239
Academic OneFile, 53
Accessibility, 31
Acknowledgments page, 239
Acronyms, 259
Active voice, 257
Advance organizer, 10, 124, 201
Advanced Scholar Search, 25–26
Affect, 257
Ambiguous terms, 33–34
America: History and Life, 54
American Educational Research
    Association (AERA), 84
American Psychological Association
    (APA), 15, 210
  ethical standards, 84
  See also APA style
"And" Boolean operator, 58
Answerable research question, 33–34
APA style, 15, 208–212
  citations in text, 216–220
  electronic source references,
    223–228
  figures, 233–235, 258
  levels of heading, 212–215
  PDF format, 53
  preparation and organization, 211
  publication manual, 15, 210,
    211–212
  reference list, 220–228
  reporting results, 180
  tables, 228–233
  Web sites, 69, 218–219

Appendix formatting, 235–237
Appendix list, 240
Applied research, 8
Arithmetic mean, 164, 166
Asterisk (*), 59
Author citations, 216–220
Average, 164

Background and Need section, 9, 10,
  107–109
Backing up work, 156, 260
Belmont Report, 81–84
Beneficence, 82
Benefit to subjects, 88, 251, 253, 255
Binding and copying, 240–241
Book references and book chapters,
  222–223
Boolean operators, 57–58
Breaks, 261
Buffers, 36, 257
Business and Company Resource
  Center, 54

Capitalization, 219, 221
Captions, 234
Central tendency measures, 164–166
Chairperson, 5–6
  signature on thesis, 237
"Chapter One." *See* Introduction
"Chapter Two." *See* Review of the
  Literature
"Chapter Three." *See* Methods
"Chapter Four." *See* Results
"Chapter Five." *See* Discussion
Checklist, final, 242

Chicago style, 15
Chunking method, 39, 122
CINAHL Plus With Full Text, 54
Citations, 216–220
    direct quotes, 216–217, 260
    group as author, 219
    multiple authors, 217–218
    multiple works, 218
    one author, 216–217
    personal communications, 219
    reference list, 220–228
    secondary sources, 219–220
    Web sites, 69, 218–219
    writing tips and rules, 257–258
Closing paragraph, 204
Coding, 128, 181
Colons, 258
Column head, 232
Column spanner, 232
Common rule, 84–85
Communication Abstracts, 54
Communication and Mass Media
    Complete, 54
Conclusions section, 12, 129–130,
    200–203
Confidentiality, 89, 251, 253
Consent. See Informed consent
Control group, 114, 176
Convenience sample, 143
Copying and binding, 240–241, 261
Cost-benefit analysis, 83
Costs to subjects, 88, 251, 253, 255
Cover letter, informed consent,
    252–253
Cover pages, 236
CQ Researcher, 54
Critical issues in the field, 24

Data, plural, 258
Data analysis, 11, 161–162
    in Methods, 153–155
    research synthesis, 128
    See also Results ("Chapter Four");
        Statistical analysis
Data coding, 128, 181
Data collection, 13
Data Collection section, 150–153
Data triangulation, 185
Deception, 81

Deductive reasoning, 13
Defining terms, 34, 259
Definitions section, 113–114
Degrees of freedom, 175, 178
Demographic data, 143
Dependent variable, 12–13
Description statement, 111–112
Descriptive statistics, 11, 164–171.
    See also Statistical analysis
Descriptors, 53
Dictionary definition, 34
Digital Object Identifier (DOI), 225
Direct quotes, 216
Discussion ("Chapter Five"), 12,
    191–192
    Conclusion section, 200–203
    Discussion section, 194–197
    Introduction section, 193–194
    Limitations section, 197–199
    preparation and organization, 192
    Recommendations for Future
        Research section, 199–200
    sections, 193
    three parallel ladders strategy,
        194–195
Dissertation, 7–8
Dissertation Abstracts International
    database, 53
Doctoral dissertation, 7–8

Edited books, 222–223
Editorial style, 15, 210, 212. See also
    APA style
Education Full Text, 54
Electronic database search, 26–28,
    52–68
    advanced search, 55, 58–61,
        64–66, 75
    basic search, 55–56
    Boolean operators, 57–58
    descriptors, 53
    examples, 54
    expanders feature, 57
    file formats, 53
    key terms, 55–56
    limiters feature, 56–57
    multidisciplinary databases, 53
    special symbols, 59–60
    thesaurus, 58, 61–68

Electronic source references, 223–228
Empirically based research, 6
ERIC, 28, 53, 54, 55, 61
Et al., 258
Ethical Considerations section, 115
Ethical issues, 77–79
  Belmont Report, 81–84
  beneficence, 82
  confidentiality, 89
  cost-benefit analysis, 83
  federal policy, 84–85
  Institutional Review Board
    application, 85–89
  justice principle, 83–84
  Nuremberg code, 79–80
  plagiarism, 90–91
  professional standards, 84
  researcher behavior, 90
  Research Subject Bill of Rights, 89
  research topic selection, 28–29
  thalidomide, 80
  Tuskegee syphilis study, 80–81
  vulnerable populations, 82
  See also Informed consent;
    Institutional Review Board
Ethnic NewsWatch, 54
Example definition, 34
External validity, 115

Feasibility, 29–30
Federal policy, 84–85
Figures, 233–235, 258
  captions and labels, 234
  graphs, 235
  list of, 240
  placement, 234
  size and font, 234
  text discussion, 233–234
Final tips and checklist, 242
Formatting. *See* APA style
Fragments, 258
"Front pages," 237–240
Full-text format, 53
Funnel writing strategy, 99–103

Generalizability, 115, 144, 171
General notes, 232
Glossary, 276–286
Google Scholar, 25

Government reports, 25
Graphs, 169, 235, 258
Guided research, 25

Hanging indent, 221
Heading capitalization, 219
Headings, 106, 212–215,
  231–232, 258
Historical Abstracts, 54
"How to eat an elephant," 39–40
Human subjects. *See* Ethical issues;
  Informed consent; Institutional
  Review Board
Hypothesis, 13
Hypothetical questions, 35

Independent-samples *t* test, 172–176
Independent variable, 12
Inferential statistics, 11, 171–180.
  See also Statistical analysis
Informed consent, 89
  Belmont Report, 81–82
  Institutional Review Board
    application, 87
  Kefauver-Harris Drug
    Amendments, 80
  Nuremberg code, 80
  sample consent form, 254–256
  sample cover letter, 252–253
  subject consent process, 249
IngentaConnect, 69
Institutional Review Board (IRB), 84–85
  application process, 85–89
  forms and records, 211
  research plan, 86–89
  sample application, 247–251
Institutional Review Board for the
  Protection of Human Subjects
  (IRBPHS), 29
Interlibrary loan, 68
Internal validity, 114
Internet search engines, 25–26, 68–69.
  See also Electronic database
  search
Interpreter services, 89
Interrater reliability, 150
Intervention and *Materials* sections
  (Methods), 11, 144–146
Introduction ("Chapter One"), 9–10

Background and Need section,
    107–109
Definitions section, 113–114
Ethical Considerations section, 115
Introduction section, 99–103,
    262–265
Limitations section, 114–115
Purpose of the Study section,
    109–112
Research Questions section, 112–113
sample sections, 262–269
sections, 98–99
Significance to the Field section, 113
Statement of the Problem section,
    103–107, 266–269
Introduction chapter ("Chapter One"),
    97–98
IRBPHS. *See* Institutional Review
    Board for the Protection of
    Human Subjects
"It," 258

Jargon, 259
Job market, 4
Journals, 222, 225
Justice principle, 83–84

Kefauver-Harris Drug Amendments, 81
Key terms, 50–52, 55–56

Labels, 234
Language translation, 89
Legal Periodicals Full Text, 54
LegalTrac, 54
Levels of heading, 212–215, 258
Librarians' Internet Index, 69
Limitations section, 12, 47, 114–115,
    130–131, 197–199
Limiters feature, 56–57
"List of Appendixes," 240
"List of Figures," 240
"List of Tables," 240
Literature matrix, 71
Literature Resource Center, 54
Literature search, 24–28, 45–46
    abstracting, 71
    benefits of conducting, 46–48
    electronic databases, 26–28, 52–68

interlibrary loan, 68
key terms, 50–52, 55–56
organizational system, 70–72
primary sources, 48
refereed articles, 70
reference materials, 48–49
search engines, 25–26
secondary sources, 48–50
selecting key terms, 50–52
types of articles, 69–70
See also Electronic database search;
    Review of the Literature
Literature synthesis, 69

Master of Arts (MA) degree, 2
Master of Science (MS) degree, 2
Master's degree, 2–5
program, 5, 16, 23, 32
Master's thesis, 6
    backing up work, 156, 260
    chairperson and committee member
        signatures, 237
    committee, 5
    components of, 8–12
    doctoral dissertation versus, 7–8
    final tips and checklist, 242
    redundancy in, 123–124
    selecting chairperson , 5–6, 18–18
    term paper versus, 7
    writing tips and rules, 257–261
    See also specific components
Master's thesis, topic selection. *See*
    Research topic selection
Materials section, 11, 144–146
Mean, 164, 166
Measurement instruments, 13
    developing answerable research
        questions, 33
    observation checklist example, 149
    reporting results and data analysis,
        163–180
    research synthesis, 128
    section in Methods, 11, 146–150
    standardized measure example, 148
    validity and reliability, 149–150
Measures of central tendency,
    164–166
Measures of variability, 167–169

Median, 165
Meta-analysis, 69
Methods ("Chapter Three"), 11, 137–138
   Data Analysis section, 153–155
   "draft" or "proposal" of, 138–139
   Intervention and *Materials* sections, 144–146
   Introduction section, 140–141
   measurement instruments, 11, 146–150
   preparation and organization, 138–139
   Procedures section, 150–153
   research questions, 141
   Sample/Participants section, 142–144
   sections, 139–140
   Setting section, 142
   three parallel ladders strategy, 146
Mode, 165
Modern Language Association (MLA) International Biography, 54
Modern Language Association (MLA) style, 15, 210

National and government reports, 25
National Commission for the Protection of Human Subjects of Biomedical and Behavioral Research, 81
National Research Act of 1974, 81
Nonnumerical data, 13
Nonresearchable questions, 34–35
Normal distribution, 168
"Not" Boolean operator, 58
Notes in tables, 232–233
Null hypothesis, 173
Numbers, spelling out, 259
Numerical data, 12
Nuremberg code, 79–80
Nursing and Health Professions Premier Collection, 54

Observation checklist, 149
Online document references, 226–227
Online journals, 225
Operational definition, 34

"Or" Boolean operator, 58–59
Organizational structure, 259
Outline, 259

Paired-samples *t* test, 176
Paragraph structure, 259
Paraphrasing, 91, 106, 216, 259
Participants section (Methods), 11, 142–144
Past tense, 260
PDF format, 53, 68
Peer-reviewed articles, 70
"People first" language, 261
Periodicals, 222
Personal communications, 219
Personal significance, 23–24
Philosophical questions, 34–35
Photocopies, 261
Plagiarism, 90–91, 216, 259
Possessives, 260
Primary sources, 48
Probability level (alpha), 173
Probability notes, 233
Procedures section, 11, 150–153
ProQuest, 53
PsycARTICLES, 54
Psychology and Behavioral Sciences Collection, 54
PsycINFO, 28, 53, 54
PubMed, 54
Purposeful redundancy, 124, 140, 193
Purpose of the Study section, 9, 109–112
   description, 111–112
   purpose statement, 110
   rationale statement, 110–111
Purposive sample, 143

Qualitative research, 9, 13–14
   coding, 128, 181
   data analysis, 153–154
   data collection procedures, 151
   inductive reasoning, 14
   major themes and patterns, 180
   research questions, 183–185
   research synthesis, 128
   thick description, 181
   validity of findings, 185

Quantitative research, 9, 12–13
  data analysis, 154, 163–180
  data collection procedures, 151
  deductive reasoning, 13
  research synthesis, 128
Question mark (?), 59–60
Quotes, 260

Random assignment, 143
Random sample, 142–143
Range, 167
Rationale statement, 110–111
Recommendations for Future Research
    section, 12, 47–48, 199–200
Redundancy, 123–124, 140, 193
Refereed articles, 70
Reference list, 220–228, 260
  books, 222–223
  electronic sources, 223–228
  order and format, 220–228
  periodicals, 222
Reference materials, 48–49
Reimbursement/compensation to
    subjects, 88, 251, 255
"Relevancy ranked" option, 63–64
Reliability, 149–150
Replicability, 138
Representative sample, 172
Research question, 9, 22, 33
  defining terms, 34
  developing answerable questions,
    33–35
  examples, 141
  feasibility issues, 30
  Introduction ("Chapter One"),
    112–113
  nonresearchable types of questions,
    34–35
  organizing research findings,
    183–185
  See also Research topic selection
Research Questions section, 9
Research Subject Bill of Rights, 89
Research synthesis, 69, 125–131
  conclusions/implications, 129–130
  data analysis, 128
  intervention/issue, 126–127
  introduction, 126

limitations/weaknesses, 130–131
  procedures, 127
  purpose statement, 126
  results, 129
  sample, 270–275
  sections, 9–12, 36, 39, 86, 98
  setting/sample, 126
  variables/measurement
    instruments, 128
Research topic selection, 21–22
  accessibility, 31
  developing answerable questions,
    33–35
  ethical considerations, 28–29
  factors to consider, 22–24
  feasibility, 29–30
  resources, 32
  searching existing research, 24–28
  time, 32
  topic narrowing and refocusing, 29
Reserving time, 38–39
Resources, 32
Respect for persons, 81
Rest, 261
Results ("Chapter Four"), 11,
    160–162
  descriptive statistics, 164–171
  graphical representation, 169
  inferential statistics, 171–180
  preparation and organization, 162
  qualitative data, 180–185
  quantitative data, 163–180
  research questions, 183–185
  sections, 162
  three parallel ladders strategy, 163
  validity of findings, 185
  See also Statistical analysis
"Results" section, research
    synthesis, 129
Review of the Literature ("Chapter
    Two"), 10, 120–122
  advance organizer, 10, 124
  body of the review, 124–131
  Chapter Summary section, 131–132
  Introduction section, 123–124
  preparation and organization, 121
  research synthesis, 125–131
  section summary, 131

seminal articles, 123
three parallel ladders strategy, 122
See also Literature search; Research
   synthesis
Rhetorical questions, 34–35, 260
Risk to subjects, 88, 250, 255
Run-on sentences, 260

Sample group, 30
   Institutional Review Board
      application, 86–87, 248–249
Sample/Participants section,
   142–144
Sample size, 30, 115
Sampling, 142–143
Saving work, 156, 260
Schedule timeline, 35–38
Search engines, 25–26, 68–69. *See also*
   Electronic database search
Searching the literature. *See* Literature
   search
Secondary sources, 48–50, 219–220
Section headings, 212–215
"Section summary" section, 131
Segues, 102, 131, 260
Selecting research topic. *See* Research
   topic selection
Semicolons, 260
Seminal articles, 123
Sentence capitalization, 221
Sentence fragments, 258
Setting section, 11, 142
Signature page, 237
Significance to the Field section, 113
Sleep, 261
Social Science Citation Index, 53
Sociological Abstracts, 53, 54
Specific notes, 233
SPSS applications
   independent-samples *t* test, 174
   paired-samples *t* test, 177
Standard deviation, 167–168
Statement of the Problem section, 9,
   10, 103–107, 266–269
Statistical analysis, 11
   central tendency measures, 164–166
   descriptive statistics, 11, 164–171
   graphical representation, 169

independent-samples *t* test, 172–176
inferential statistics, 11, 171–180
null hypothesis, 173
paired-samples *t* test, 176–179
representative sample, 172
tests of significance, 172–180
variability measures, 167–169
Stub column, 231
Stub head, 231
Stubs, 231–232
Style, 14–15, 97–98. *See also* APA style
Subject recruitment procedures, 87
Summary section, literature review,
   131–132
Synthesis of literature, 69

Table of contents, 211, 239–240
Tables, 228–233
   headings and body, 231–232
   list of, 240
   notes in, 232–233
   placement and spacing, 230
   text discussion, 230
   three "C" rules, 229
   titles, 230
Tense, 260
"Term begins with" option, 62–63
"Term contains" option, 63
Terminal degree, 3
Term paper, 7
Terms and definitions, 34, 113–114,
   259, 276–286
Tests of significance, 172–180
Thalidomide, 80
The Internet Public Library, 69
"Their" versus "there," 260
Thesaurus, 58, 61–68
Three parallel ladders strategy,
   104–109, 122, 146, 163,
   194–195
Time constraints, 32
Timeline, 35–38
Time management, 38–39
Title page, 237
Topic selection. *See* Research topic
   selection
Topic sentence, 102
Transitions (segues), 102, 131, 260

Translation, 89
Triangulation, 185
Truncation symbol (*), 59
t tests, 172–180
  independent-samples, 172–176
  paired-samples, 176–179
Tuskegee syphilis study, 80–81
Type I error, 173

University of Chicago style, 210
URL, 218–219, 224, 225, 226

Validity, 114–115, 149–150, 185
Value judgments, 261
Variability measures, 167–169
Variables, 12–13, 128
Velobind strips, 240–241
Versions, 261

Voluntary informed consent, 80. *See also* Informed consent
Vulnerable populations, 82

Web link resources, 19–20, 44, 76, 95, 119, 136, 159, 190, 207, 246
Web sites, 69
  APA style, 69
  citations, 69, 218–219
  reference list formatting, 227–228
Wildcard symbol (?), 59–60
Wilson OmniFile, 53
Worldwide Political Science Abstracts, 54
Writing style, 97–98
Writing tips and rules, 257–261

"You," 261

Supporting researchers for more than 40 years

Research methods have always been at the core of SAGE's publishing program. Founder Sara Miller McCune published SAGE's first methods book, *Public Policy Evaluation*, in 1970. Soon after, she launched the *Quantitative Applications in the Social Sciences* series—affectionately known as the "little green books."

Always at the forefront of developing and supporting new approaches in methods, SAGE published early groundbreaking texts and journals in the fields of qualitative methods and evaluation.

Today, more than 40 years and two million little green books later, SAGE continues to push the boundaries with a growing list of more than 1,200 research methods books, journals, and reference works across the social, behavioral, and health sciences. Its imprints—Pine Forge Press, home of innovative textbooks in sociology, and Corwin, publisher of PreK–12 resources for teachers and administrators—broaden SAGE's range of offerings in methods. SAGE further extended its impact in 2008 when it acquired CQ Press and its best-selling and highly respected political science research methods list.

From qualitative, quantitative, and mixed methods to evaluation, SAGE is the essential resource for academics and practitioners looking for the latest methods by leading scholars.

For more information, visit **www.sagepub.com**.